J. M Stone

Eleanor Leslie: A Memoir

J. M Stone
Eleanor Leslie: A Memoir
ISBN/EAN: 9783743462748
Manufactured in Europe, USA, Canada, Australia, Japa
Cover: Foto ©ninafisch / pixelio.de

Manufactured and distributed by brebook publishing software (www.brebook.com)

J. M Stone

Eleanor Leslie: A Memoir

ELEANOR LESLIE

A Memoir

BY

J. M. STONE

Author of "FAITHFUL UNTO DEATH," ETC.

LONDON AND LEAMINGTON:
ART AND BOOK COMPANY
1898

CONTENTS.

Chapter		Page
I.—Introductory.—An English Family a Hundred Years ago		1
II.—Springtime		9
III.—Early Married Life. Journal in Scotland		23
IV.—Joys and Sorrows		47
V.—Dissenting Influences		56
VI.—High Church Influences		69
VII.—The Parting of the Ways		90
VIII.—Reunion		104
IX.—Vocations		128
X.—The Catholic Revival in Scotland		150
XI.—Four Years in Rome		174
XII.—Greetings and Farewells		222
XIII.—Autumn		252
XIV.—At St. Margaret's		274
XV.—Work Finished		306

List of Illustrations.

Eleanor Leslie at the age of Twenty-Three	*Frontispiece*
Archibald Leslie	18
The Tolbooth, Elgin	28
Invergarry Castle	33
Urquhart Castle	35
The Sound of Mull	36
"The Cobbler," Loch Low	45
Putney and Fulham Churches in 1826	71
John Falconer Atlee	76
Part of St. Margaret's Convent, Edinburgh	275
In the Grounds of the Old House on West Hill, Wandsworth	282
Mrs. Leslie at the age of Eighty-Six	299

ELEANOR LESLIE.

CHAPTER I.

INTRODUCTORY.—AN ENGLISH FAMILY A HUNDRED YEARS AGO.

PERHAPS in these days of multiplied biographies little apology is needed for writing the life of one who, in an unassuming womanly manner, and as much by her large warm heart and clear judgment as by her marked individuality, exercised no small influence on all around her. This influence, at first limited to her family and immediate surroundings, was afterwards apparent in the lives of many whose names were well known in the social and religious world about the middle of the present century.

As every character is more or less built up out of early associations, and is not entirely independent of its antecedents, it may be well to glance at the history of Mrs. Leslie's parents in the years preceding her birth and during her childhood.

She was the eldest daughter of Mr. John Falconer Atlee, the son of a country gentleman, from whom he should have inherited a considerable family property, named Fordhook, near Acton in Middlesex.* But when still quite a young man, he discovered that his father had gambled away his estate and had fled, leaving him to support his mother and a younger brother. His handsome appearance, and a certain stateliness of manner were indications of a noble and elevated mind. Uncrushed by this heavy blow to his prospects, he at once took upon himself his father's obligations, and sought and obtained employment as clerk in a distillery at Bristol. He must soon have made his mark and have impressed his employers with confidence in his abilities, for when

* According to an article which appeared in the *Philadelphia Inquirer* in 1895, an ancestor of Mr. Falconer Atlee's, a certain William Atlee, of Fordhook, left England in the reign of George II. as private secretary to Lord Howe. His father had sent him out of the way to prevent his marriage with a Miss Jane Alcock, a niece of William Pitt, afterwards Lord Chatham. The young lady was maid of honour to Queen Caroline, and both the King and the Queen wished her to marry a member of the royal family. But she followed Mr. William Atlee to Barbadoes in 1731, where she was united to him on her arrival. The couple afterwards settled at Philadelphia, which became the cradle of the American branch of the Atlee family. William Atlee joined Washington's forces, raised a regiment called "Atlee's brigade," and after the war acquired a property to which he gave the name of Fordhook. A word may be added as to the origin of the name Atlee, written by some of the American representatives of the family in two words—At Lee. Richard I. is said to have given the name to an illegitimate child of his, whose mother was a lady of his Court. When the child was born, a messenger came to inform the King, and asked what its name was to be. "Where was it born?" asked the King. "At Lee in Kent," was the answer. "Then let him be called At Lee," was the royal pleasure.

still very young, and occupying a subordinate position, Pitt having drawn up a Bill which distillers feared would injure them, Mr. Falconer Atlee was appointed one of a deputation sent from Bristol to interview the Prime Minister on their behalf. After the interview, these gentlemen spent the day on the Thames. As they passed Wandsworth, they were struck with the remains of some sort of factory, which appeared to have been a failure, and was in ruins. They landed, examined the place, agreed that it would do very well for a distillery, and in imagination started one there. Later on Mr. Atlee got some men of capital to advance money, built a distillery on the site of the ruined factory, and eventually bought out the shareholders. Through this distillery he, in course of time, realized a large fortune.

In spite, however, of his practical character and strong business capacity, his mind was somewhat curiously impressionable and sensitive. Being one day in a boat with several companions, he was all at once without any apparent reason, seized with an imperative desire to be put on shore. The others remonstrated, but on his insisting, agreed to land him, but at a place where, to reach the shore, he must wade through a quantity of deep mud. He got out of the boat, waded through the mud and returned home. All his companions were drowned, and he would have shared their fate but for his unaccountable impulse.

At another time he was dreaming, in the middle of the night, that a piece of wood had got into a pipe in his distillery and had stopped it up. In the midst of his dream he was awakened by the arrival of a messenger. Something had gone wrong with the machinery. He hurried off to the distillery, pointed to the place in the pipe which he had seen in his dream, and ordered it to be cut there. Those about him demurred, but he held to his point, the pipe was cut in the place indicated and there was a piece of wood which had caused the mischief.

The ambition of his life was to save enough money to buy back the property which his father had lost, and if his son had been like-minded he would doubtless have succeeded. The place had a great fascination for him. One day, as he was walking near Acton, a gentleman in a gig pulled up and asked if he would like a drive. He accepted the offer and got up. Presently they passed Fordhook, and Mr. Atlee said, "My grandfather used to drive out of those gates four-in-hand."

"What!" exclaimed the other, "are you one of the Atlees of Fordhook?" He answered that he was, and the man replied, "Then, sir, I am not ashamed to own that my grandfather was coachman to your grandfather."

About the year 1796, Mr. Falconer Atlee married a Mrs. Palmer, a widow, and the daughter of that Mr. Tomkinson who had the merit of discovering Turner's genius. Turner was the son of a barber, and Mr. Tomkinson placed him as pupil with the best artist of the day. The lad soon surpassed his master and became our greatest landscape painter. The son of his friend and patron was a well-known authority on art.

Mrs. Palmer had been left badly off, and had accepted the position of governess in the Talbot Bridges family of Godnestone,* by all the members of which she was greatly beloved and esteemed. When she married Mr. Atlee, her former pupils, for whom she had the greatest affection, were often tobe seen at her house. Her tenderness for children was very marked, and in after years, Mrs. Leslie would speak of her mother as having had it in a far greater degree than herself, a statement, however, which her family did not allow to pass unchallenged.

Mrs. Falconer Atlee's charm of manner, resulting from a sweet and amiable disposition, and from a very sincere and gentle piety, was felt by all who came in contact with her. She

* In Kent.

had a great admiration for her husband, and appreciated his grand qualities. They shared the same tastes as well as the same religious opinions, which were for the most part those of the evangelical school then in vogue. In one point, however, she formed an independent judgment, and was known not to admire those preachers who made "so much of St. Paul, and so little of our Lord." Her reverence for the office of a clergyman would perhaps be thought exaggerated in these days. It led her to give him precedence over every one else, and although one or two successive vicars of their parish were anything but agreeable men, when invited to dine at her house they were always placed at her right hand, whatever the rank of the other guests might be. Her pity for the poor induced her to give to every beggar.

The home life of this typical English family was a particularly happy one. The Atlees enjoyed great wealth, and the ease and abundance which wealth brings. The days still were when servants were proud to identify themselves with their employers, and in this instance all were as a matter of course devoted to master, mistress, and children. The household was conducted on lines of patriarchal simplicity, with something of patriarchal impressiveness. Every Sunday the head gardener with his wife, who attended to the lodge gates, would proceed solemnly to the servants' hall to dinner, a portentous nosegay figuring in his button-hole. They would pass the dining-room windows towards the end of luncheon, and Mrs. Falconer Atlee would sometimes be standing there with her children to see them pass, the worthy couple evidently delighted to be noticed, but as evidently considering it an unpardonable breach of etiquette to look up. But tempers were sometimes bad even in those contented days, and the gardener's wife was reputed to be something of a shrew. One day Lord Arthur Gordon Lennox rode up to the lodge gate with a present for the children under his arm, and rang the bell. She took him for a groom, and rated him soundly for not going to the back door, a kind of mistake which was curiously of less frequent occurrence in the past than in the present democratic age, which tends to make individuals of all classes at least *look* alike.

Among his many varied gifts Mr. Falconer Atlee possessed that of music in a very remarkable degree, a talent which his eldest daughter inherited from him and which greatly added to the charm of home life and social intercourse. There was at Wandsworth a colony of Quakers, among whom the Atlees numbered some acquaintances. Theoretically, the Quakers hold, or, at any rate, at that time held, music to be an utterly worldly and good-for-nothing pastime. But the fascination of Mr. Atlee's playing was irresistible, and he was once invited to bring his violin to an evening gathering of Friends. The entertainment was at its height, when suddenly a loud ring at the door-bell seemed to awaken their dormant consciences, the violin was hastily pushed under a sofa, and the Quakers assumed a demure air as they sat waiting for the result of the peal that had startled them. Presently an old gentleman entered, cast a severe, searching look round the room, and, addressing the master of the house, said sternly:

"Friend, methought I heard sounds of vain sport as I approached thine house!"

A chorus of reassurances arose from all present, but the violin remained hidden till the old man had taken his departure, a circumstance which adds a humorous element to the commonly received notion of Quaker truthfulness.

CHAPTER II.

SPRINGTIME.

Mr. Falconer Atlee's eldest child, Eleanor, was born on December 3, 1800. Her first years were passed at Wandsworth, then a pretty country place not too near London, and entirely different from the populous suburb it has since become. She must have been a singularly happy child, reared as she was under the eye of the tenderest and most sensible of mothers. The first incident recorded of her childhood is that her nurse used to take her out into the garden very early in the morning, and after spreading a clean cloth on the grass still wet with dew, would wash her face with it in order to give her a fresh, rosy colour. Perhaps her life-long habit of early rising dated from this time. Her young life was certainly not vexed with premature study, for her mother's theory was that until a child is seven years old, it needs chiefly to be taught but three things—to say its prayers reverently, to speak the truth always, and to obey at the first word. When the time came for other less important things, the greatest care was taken that the instruction should be the best of its kind. The day had not yet come when the world was ringing with the battle cry "education," but in some ways people were better educated than now. Learning fewer things, they learned them well.

Prout taught her drawing, a pupil of Beethoven's music. As for French, she learned it of a distinguished *émigré*, le Général de Missy, who even after his return to France continued to take an interest in his former pupil, keeping up a correspondence with her, and carefully pointing out any mistakes in her French letters to him. Three younger sisters subsequently shared her studies and the attention of two successive governesses, until Eleanor fell ill of a fever, so severe and prolonged that when she recovered it was found that she had forgotten all that she had previously learned, and must even be taught to read over again. In after years, no one would have supposed that her education had been thus completely wiped out as far as it had gone, so accomplished, well read, and highly cultured did she appear. But besides her natural gifts of mind and intelligence enhanced by education, she had inherited her mother's charm of manner, and had been taught to have that thoughtful consideration for others which made her so irresistibly attractive throughout her life. Not perhaps strikingly handsome, she was nevertheless very prepossessing in appearance, with sweet English blue eyes, and soft fair hair, rather *petite* than otherwise, but graceful. Her bright and gentle words and ways won all hearts.

The many interesting people whom the Atlees gathered about them in the picturesque old house at Wandsworth were Eleanor's friends of many years to come. Among them were the Wilberforces, the Langdales (who suffered so much in the Lord George Gordon riots), the Brackenburys, the Talbot Bridges, the Owens, Rückers, and many others. She had a special gift for friendship, knew how to value it, and probably never lost a friend through want of attention or of tact on her part.

As an illustration of her fidelity to the affections of her girlhood may be mentioned her delight at meeting Lady Hardynge (*née* Brackenbury) at the age of seventy-eight, after an interval of nearly sixty years. But her tenderest sympathies were reserved in those early days for her immediate family circle, and her three sisters and only brother claimed a large share in the joys and sorrows of her whole life.

Of this beloved brother, Falconer, something must be said here. With all his talents, and they were many, perhaps his greatest aptitude in those days was for getting into scrapes. He was confided to the care—or neglect—of one clergyman after another, to be educated, and was invariably sent home as unmanageable. But the religious spirit of the family sometimes came out in him, and in an amusing way. On one memorable occasion, when he came home as usual in disgrace, being rather seriously disturbed about the matter, he got some bread and wine, read over them the words of the Communion Service in the Church of England Prayer Book, gave himself Communion, and in a diary which he kept at that time, wrote that he felt much better. When old enough he was sent to Winchester, where he was a contemporary of the future Lord Beaconsfield and of Earl Cowley. In after years, when the latter was British Ambassador in Paris, the three passed a merry evening in recalling the event which had caused young Atlee's career at Winchester to end abruptly. It was during what has since been known as "the great rebellion." Some encroachment had been made by the masters on the boys' rights, granted to them by royal charter,* and a sort of barring-out ensued. The little boys, among

---

* The boys' grievance was that a master who was not a Wickhamite had been appointed.

whom was young Falconer Atlee, were not allowed to take part in the insubordination, but when all the authorities, in full academic costume, went to hold a parley with the barrers-out at a certain window, the small insurgents, determined to have their share of the fun, turned the college fire-engine upon them. When the Principal began to address the malcontents he was deluged with water, and a good many panes of glass were broken. Some of the boys went home without waiting for the consequences; but the affair was mentioned in Parliament, and subsequently the Winchester boys celebrated the triumph of British fair-play. The friendship between Lord Cowley, then the Hon. Henry Richard Wellesley, and young Falconer, dated from this time and continued throughout their lives. When the veteran statesman became Ambassador in Paris, he at once made his old friend's son his private secretary.

Falconer was something of a dandy, in the days when dandyism, as distinct from the style of the present young man of fashion, was in vogue, and an anecdote concerning his dress carries us back to a far simpler world. When he was about fifteen, swallow-tail coats came into fashion, and he had one. But his mother was distressed about it—there was something ridiculous to her mind in a coat having such extremely long, narrow points, and secretly, at night, she cut off about an inch of it. The boy was naturally indignant, and at first his father sided with him, with a grave: "Goodie," to his wife, "you should not have done that," adding: "Now, my boy, put on the coat, and let me see how it looks." And then, with charming diplomacy: "Well, I declare, it does look better!" Upon which the young dandy was pacified.

Another instance of the way in which Mr. Atlee managed his family is interesting from its cleverness.

He was a regular Church and King man, devoted to the Established religion, and abhorring anything like dissent, which was at that time beginning to make progress in the country. His wife and daughters having heard of a certain dissenting minister who had the reputation of being very eloquent, were anxious to hear him preach. Mr. Atlee, without forbidding them to go to his chapel, made it clear that he did not much like their going. However, he said nothing, but when they had started, he went there himself, returned before them, and when they came back, questioned them about the sermon. They began to give an account of it, he interrupting them occasionally by suggesting: "Then I suppose he said this, or that?" letting them know that he thought the sermon stale stuff, and so put them out of conceit of the preacher.

In course of time, Falconer went to Cambridge, and whatever else he did to distinguish himself, he introduced boating there.

There was one point of resemblance at least between him and his father. Both were extremely generous, but in different ways. Mr. Atlee never refused a beggar, his son never gave to one, but would lavish large sums on any one in whom he was interested. Sometimes, of course, he was a victim of impositions. One day, at Cambridge, there was a knock at his room door, and in came a delicate-looking young man, who declared himself to be in very bad circumstances, and by his own fault. He was, he said, too weak to do hard work, but he copied rare poems and other things, a bundle of which he had with him. Falconer told him to leave those he had with him, and to call another day. By degrees he became interested in the young man, and gave him money and clothes. During the long vacation, he saw him in Hyde Park, very smartly dressed, and congratulated him on his improved fortunes. To his amazement, the man declared that he had not the honour of his acquaintance. Falconer was furious, but saw nothing more of his former protégé till well on in the next term, when at last the well-known knock was heard. After inviting his visitor to enter, he sprang to the door, locked it and began to give a sound thrashing to the poor wretch, who shrieked and bellowed to such a pitch that soon there was a hammering without. Falconer opened the door, feeling sure that it was the Dean, but it turned out to be a friend of his, named Hammond.

"What on earth are you about?" cried Hammond.

"Why," said Falconer, "this blackguard White has done me out of £40 and a lot of clothes, and then cut me in the Park."

"That's not White," replied Hammond, "his name is Black."

"He told me it was White."

"He told me it was Black," assured Hammond, and added: "He has been *doing* me too. I'll help you."

So the two pummelled the wretched fellow till he was glad enough to slink away, and say nothing about the thrashing he had received.

On leaving Cambridge, young Falconer Atlee made what was then called the "grand tour," in company with an infidel tutor, who undermined whatever foundation of faith he had received from his parents. The man had been thought admirable in every way, and the greatest confidence was placed in him by the Atlees. However, on the very first evening of their travels, seeing a Bible among his pupil's baggage, he contemptuously asked the young man whether he believed in that book. On receiving a reply in the affirmative, he begged for the loan of it, and sat up all night, drawing lines under passages which he thought bad. Falconer was taken aback, and at his tutor's suggestion began to read Voltaire and other infidel authors. In time, it became a sort of craze with him to argue against revealed religion, and as he was very clever, he of course got the better of those who entered into the fray of words, less well equipped than himself. When he returned home from his travels, his father insisted on his working in the distillery, a vocation not at all according to the young man's taste or inclination. Nevertheless he made up his mind to the inevitable, and for some time did very efficient work, introducing a steam-engine, one of the first instances of steam power being applied to machinery.

After some years, he married a very charming woman, his father making him the handsome allowance of £3,000 a year, in the hope that he would save money, and eventually realize his own darling project of buying back Fordhook. But as has been already said, Falconer did not share his father's ambition. He preferred to retire from the business, and live on a much smaller income abroad, ultimately settling in Paris; and the property was let slip for ever.

But to return to Eleanor. She had received one advantageous offer of marriage after another and had refused them all, to the despair of her younger sisters, who complained pathetically that no one would think of proposing to them until she was out of the question. There was no doubt that she was blocking the way, and, always ready to sacrifice herself for others, she promised her sisters that she would accept the next suitable offer. Perhaps, too, she had some vague notion as to the direction from which it would come, although there were at least two eligible aspirants to her hand at that time. It came from a gentleman whose acquaintance she had made through his cousin, the Hon. James Sinclair, connected by marriage with intimate friends of the Atlee family. Eleanor used to distinguish him from her other admirers by speaking of him as "the man with the pretty eyes." He was a certain Mr. Archibald Leslie. When her father desired to have some information with regard to his position and worldly prospects, he described himself as the son of a Scottish

Archibald Leslie
From a miniature by Robertson

minister in Morayshire, in business in London. On making further inquiries, Mr. Falconer Atlee found that Mr. Leslie had represented his position in the least advantageous light possible ; that his father, a very remarkable man, belonging to a good old family, was, like Lockhart's father, one of a now almost extinct class of laird-ministers in the Highlands, living on his own estate, and had married the sister of the Earl of Caithness, a sister of his own being married to Lord Duffus. It was further discovered that Mr. Leslie had come to London with the double purpose of making a fortune and of prosecuting his father's claim to the Lindores title. He was born in 1789, and was therefore eleven years older than Miss Falconer Atlee, another item of suitability in the match. The second of three sons, and one of a numerous family, he had lost his mother while he was still very young, and Lady Caithness having a tender affection for the motherless boy, a great part of his childhood had been spent at Barrogill Castle, his uncle's place in Caithness-shire. At other times he had paid long visits to his grandfather, the old laird of Balnageith, and had frequented the one school at Forres for all classes of boys. Here the foundation of his studies was laid, the only companion of his own position being William Gordon Cumming of Altyre, with whom he formed a lasting friendship. The education received at this school, which appears to have been good as far as it went, was probably supplemented by his father, for he afterwards went to Aberdeen College, where he remained till 1808, a step for which he would scarcely have been prepared by the village schoolmaster of those days. He then went to live with a Unitarian clergyman, the Rev. Dr. Lyndsay, who had a large school at Blackheath, and seems to have made the best of his opportunities, for he became a very good classical scholar, and for those times spoke French well. But he was always diffident about his acquirements, and when an over-confident friend proposed that they two should make a tour in France, he objected that he couldn't speak the language.

"Oh, I'll parley for you," assured his friend glibly, and they got on very well with English till they arrived at an hotel in Calais. They were washing before dinner, and were thoroughly wet before they perceived that there were no towels in the room, whereupon the friend who could speak French rang the bell, and this attempt at conversation ensued:

Garçon: " Monsieur?"
Englishman: " Towels."
Garçon: " Monsieur?"
Englishman (impatiently): " Towels!"

Garçon: "Monsieur?"

Englishman: "D—— your eyes, give me something to wipe my face with!"

When young Leslie could speak for laughing, he said, "Essuie-mains," and their wants were at once supplied. It was generally in this way that the one who did not speak French came to the rescue of his friend who thought he did.

There was a singular fascination about him, and a natural refinement, together with a readiness to do a kindness or pay attention to any one who seemed neglected, which perhaps even more than the "pretty eyes" attracted Miss Falconer Atlee. But a miniature taken about the time of his marriage shows him to have been extremely handsome, with an indescribable air of bright distinction. His high spirits, good looks and agreeable conversation made him a welcome guest everywhere, and fitted him more for a dilettante life than for the plodding business one to which he had pledged himself. If he could but have followed his natural bent, how different might his lot have been! But for a time the sky was cloudless, and when on July 8, 1823, these two exceptionally gifted beings were united, it would seem as though more than most mortals they might look forward to an existence "happy ever after."

Eleanor's three sisters now came in for their share of attention, Mary, the eldest of the three, being married to Major Maxwell four months later.

CHAPTER III.

EARLY MARRIED LIFE.   JOURNAL IN SCOTLAND.

For the first two years after their marriage, with the exception of a short visit to Scotland, in which Mrs. Leslie was introduced to her new relations, the young couple resided in Charlotte Square, Bloomsbury, then a very central part of London. Little seems to have been wanting to their happiness and comfort; but unclouded happiness is for the most part uneventful, and until 1825 the family records are extremely meagre in details. Sharing the same tastes, and notably, that of music, they would take every opportunity of hearing the best of its kind, and since at that time the Mass music at the church of the Bavarian embassy in Warwick Street was much talked of, they would often assist at High Mass there. Dogma counted for little in the Church of England in those days; people went to whichever place of worship seemed to promise a good sermon, and at Warwick Street the Rev. Dr. Archer preached somewhat in the Addison manner, which was much admired. Mr. and Mrs. Leslie would therefore go to hear him on account of his excellent style and delivery, without adverting to the difference of his teaching from that to which they had always been accustomed, and it does not appear that what they heard on these occasions had any influence on their religious feelings or convictions, or that it in any way shocked or surprised them. Mr. Leslie also accompanied his wife to the Church of England services, although he much preferred the Presbyterian form of worship, and never felt at home in the English Church, and was unable to the last to find his places in the Prayer Book. He probably shared his father's way of thinking, the good old minister being often heard to say that he could understand the Presbyterian or the Catholic Church, but that he could not understand the Church of England. On Mrs. Leslie's first visit to his manse, soon after her marriage, when she dutifully attended the services of his kirk, he seemed to think it was his duty Sunday after Sunday to give her "a bellum against the Episcopalians." Many years afterwards his son expressed his horror when for the first time he saw a clergyman of the Church of England preach in a surplice, denouncing it as an innovation and "a rag of Popery."

Mr. Leslie's wit and singular grace of manner, together with his wife's accomplishments—her musical talent was exceptionally fine—attracted round them a large circle of friends. Hospitality of the most generous, open-hearted kind was his favourite hobby. He prided himself on his wines and on his glass, cut to his own designs, while the innate refinement of mind which reveals itself in a man's dress, was especially remarked in the exquisite quality and style of his linen, a much more noticeable item, in the days of ruffles and general elaboration than now. It was even whispered about society that the fineness and originality of Mr. Leslie's shirts had so attracted the Duke of Devonshire that the maker had borrowed one of them to show him. The rest of his attire was a kind of declaration of political principles. Being a Whig, he wore the Fox uniform, blue coat, brass buttons and buff waistcoat, colours perpetuated to this day in the Whig organ of that party, the *Edinburgh Review*.

Here and there we have glimpses of gaieties, a dinner at Mr. Leslie's before the Caledonian ball, for instance, at which the ladies were in fancy dress, and Mr. Leslie himself, handsomer than ever, in kilt and plaid, carrying all before him with a grand and noble simplicity all his own.

In April, 1824, his eldest child, a daughter, was born, and named after her mother. Then, gradually the joyous note dies down. Enterprising and sanguine, he soon grew weary of counting-house routine, for which he was in every way unsuited, and tried to push his fortunes independently. In this he failed signally; his health suffered under the pressure of harassing business difficulties, and gloomy forebodings only too well grounded. The crisis came a few months after his child's birth, and it is characteristic of the generous and more than honourable, if also improvident nature of the man, that he promised (although legally absolved) to indemnify all those who had suffered by his failure. This obligation, gratuitously undertaken, weighed him down throughout the greater part of his life, although there were occasional intervals of prosperity, or at least of freedom from carking care. It now became necessary to exercise the greatest economy; the home in Charlotte Square was broken up, and a visit to Scotland undertaken, in the hope that it would have a beneficial effect upon Mr. Leslie's health and spirits.

It is to these circumstances that we owe the interesting journal which his wife wrote for her mother's entertainment during her travels in Scotland, which was a comparative *terra incognita* to English people at the beginning of this century. For with the exception of Dr. Johnson's *Tour in the Hebrides* and one or two smaller books, little had been written about the manners and customs of a country as far away as Russia is in these days, and incomparably less well known.

Moreover, *autres temps autres mœurs*, and readers of to-day, knowing their Scotland as they know every corner of Europe, may be interested to see it through the eyes of an English lady who described it in 1825, when travelling meant something more than occupying a corner of a comfortable railway carriage with a *Murray* or *Bædeker*, and the certainty of ease and convenience at the journey's end.

In the summer of 1825 [writes Mrs. Leslie] we visited Scotland, in the hope that his native air and relaxation from business might restore Leslie to health. We journeyed to Edinburgh with Major and Mrs. Sinclair, and after passing ten days there with Lady Caithness* and her son, proceeded to Mount Coffer.†

A fortnight of kindness and attention from Major Dunbar and Jessie, though it alleviated, did not cure, Archie, and we then travelled on to Elgin. In consequence of the Manse of St. Andrew's having been burnt the previous February, the worthy minister ‡ had taken up his abode in one of his ancestor's dwellings in the town. This was entered by a low, arched way, paved, and leading to a small garden for vegetables, ornamented by a sun-dial, with angels carved round it, standing in the centre. On the right side, under the arched

---

* Mr. Leslie's aunt by her marriage with the 12th Earl of Caithness, his mother's brother.

† In Banffshire, a property belonging to Lord Fife, and rented by Major Dunbar, Mr. Leslie's brother-in-law.

‡ The Rev. William Leslie, of Balnageith, Mr. Leslie's father.

way, was the door of the house, which opened upon a flight of narrow, steep stone steps, winding round one small pillar as their centre, and leading, on the first landing, to two tolerable sitting-rooms, and on the second, to several bedrooms. In these homely and primitive apartments, notwithstanding their lack of furniture, we might have been comfortable, had Leslie's aching head permitted him to be so. But, alas! he suffered constantly and acutely, and the exertions of his sister Mary met with no better success than those of Jessie. Occasionally I went out to sketch. The scenery about Elgin is neither bold nor romantic, but it is very pretty, and quite within the compass of a somewhat untaught and unskilful pencil. In the evening, too, I usually walked with the dear old minister. He was very kind to me. He seemed to court these little rambles, and urged me to talk, and this I did the rather

> To win a part from off the weight
> I saw increasing on his father's heart,

than from any desire to chatter; for I was in low spirits, and the poor old man was depressed about his son, and thought of the five blooming children he had survived. One evening he was more cheerful, and mentioned his right to the title of Lindores. He explained how he claimed kindred with the Earls of Fife and Lord Byron; and as we returned home through the town, he made me cross the street to observe his coat of arms, initials, and a very old date, chiselled and still very fresh, on the stone turret of Isaac Forsyth's library. He also bade me take notice, ere I re-entered the house, of the sun-dial in the garden, and told me how many centuries it had been in his family; and that there was one older still—he believed the second or third introduced into Scotland – at Balnageith.

On July 27 Archie took me and his sister Mary to Black Hills. The laird had arrived there from Demerara a few days before, and good, warm-hearted Nelly Cumming deemed herself the happiest of human beings in thus being again near her brother. Her eyes seem to glisten with gladness as they rested on his withered and sun-burnt cheeks; and beneath his raillery at her homely and aged appearance I fancied some affectionate admiration might be detected.

THE TOLBOOTH, ELGIN.
(From Mrs. Leslie's Sketchbook.)

[To face page 28.

We stopped at Linkwood,* to say farewell on our road home. Ellen begged me to stay for tea, and Peter Brown pressed Archie to take a drop for "Auld lang syne." A little misunderstanding had occurred from an ill-natured report circulated about Archie's affairs very prejudicial to his character. This Mr. Brown had listened to, too readily, and, without enquiry, acted upon. On the morning of this day, he had been convinced of his error, of the whole being a fabrication, and he was desirous to evince his regret at his past want of hospitality by being doubly warm on the present occasion. We were willing to be reconciled, and this joy prevented our reaching Elgin until some time past sunset, for which I thought the minister's looks reproached us, as he carefully handed us out of the carriage, saying to each: "Dinna be rash."

He asked no questions about the cause of our detention, but laid his hand upon the book he had been reading. Ere he raised it, however, he looked at me, and said:

"Ye'll no be for a walk, I guess, the nicht?"

I told him I was quite ready, which pleased him, and having locked up his book (one of his customs), he said he would take me to St. Mary's Well. This is a spring of very pure water, close to the Lossie, along the banks of which we walked. The night was perfectly clear and the air warm without being sultry, and the fields we crossed were far enough removed from the town to be tranquil.

I told the worthy man what had detained us at Linkwood, not by way of making peace, for that in his kind breast had never been broken, but to give him the satisfaction of knowing that an ill-natured story had been explained away and its falsehood detected.

"It has always," he replied, "surpassed the powers of my imagination to conceive the pleasure some idle, malicious folk tak' in inventing wicked tales o' their neebors. Forbye the ill-will they get from man for sic a deed, they draw upon themselves the wrath of Almighty God. I canna recollect," continued he, coming to a full stop in our walk, "ever having told a lie in my life. At all events, if I have —— " he paused

* The house of a brother-in-law, Peter Brown, brother of General Sir George Brown. He married Ellen, sister of Archibald Leslie.

again and was silent for some seconds, then placed the forefinger of the right hand upon the thumb of the left, "it canna have been mair than ae wee ane, at the outside."

I looked at his benevolent countenance as he spoke, and it expressed all the singleness of his heart; and I felt that he was an enviable being who at the age of seventy-seven could with equal truth make such a declaration.

The following morning we left Elgin. Mary Leslie accompanied us, and the minister had gone forward on his way, but stopping to say a few words to everyone he met, we soon overtook him, and we were the first to reach Forres. This ancient place, immortalized by Shakespeare, interested me merely from its vicinity to Balnageith, where we all went after taking lunch at the inn. Balnageith disappointed me, I confess. My ideas of it had been formed from the representations of Charlotte;* and these were drawn from the recollections of a happy childhood, which had coloured places and events and persons with a brightness and beauty not their own, which impressions, never having been disturbed by subsequent association, remained gilded with sunshine in her memory. Instead of the large, comfortable farmhouse then, I found a very moderate-sized, dilapidated dwelling, with two sitting-rooms, one a kitchen on the ground floor, and two sleeping-rooms accessible by a rude stair—almost a ladder— on the upper storey, just suited to the needs and station of Sandie Souter and his wife, Kate Robinson, the tenants. There was a pig-sty at the back of the house and a large pigeon-house by the side. The old sundial was before the door, but almost concealed amidst the barley that was growing round it. The belt of fir-wood I had heard Archie mention with some degree of pride looked melancholy from the bare and withered state of the trees and the want of variety in the foliage. The once flourishing kitchen garden was overgrown with weeds, the walks could scarcely be traced, and the fruit-trees and shrubs were dead or barren. However, I do believe the place has great capabilities; the soil is good, and there are many spots upon it commanding picturesque views. A stream of clear water runs through it, and the river Findhorn bounds it on one side, in which there is

* Her sister-in-law, married to Arthur Geddes.

excellent fishing. It is peculiarly well situated too in regard to neighbourhood, there being at least six superior families within three or four miles, independent of others residing in Forres.

All this passed in my mind as the worthy minister led me round Souter's territory, without making any remark, until we came to the middle of a large field, situated between the barns, stables, offices, &c. (which were really excellent), and the river.

"Here," he said, "where I stand is the place where the house should be biggit. And it is here you and Archibald must big one when ye come to live here. But why should I say this? Ye'll never bide here——" He turned round.

"And why not?" I asked.

"Because ye have baith lived too long in the sunshine and luxuries of the South, to relish this bleak, lonesome countrie."

I was sorry to hear him say this, and to see him look sad as he pondered over his declaration; but I did not reply, since I feared in assuring him his conviction was wrong, that I should be ungracious in referring to a time when he would be no more the Laird of Balnageith.

Between the bridge and Nairn, where we slept, tradition shows the spot where the witches accosted Macbeth.

July 29.—We left Nairn early in the morning, and on arriving at Port George a signal was hoisted that soon induced the ferry-boat to put out for us from the opposite side. It was but a few minutes crossing the Forth, and while the carriage was being placed in it, the poor minister stood on the beach holding the bridle of his pony.

"Ye'll no forget to write me soon?" he said.

"Surely, sir," exclaimed Archie, "you are going over with us?"

"'Deed, I am just ganging back again to the Manse."

"Well," persisted Archie, "this is one of the maddest pranks I ever knew; just to see us embark you have come all this way; and now to think of trotting back again when you are almost within sight of Braelangwell! I am certain Captain Sinclair will be very much offended with you."

"Weel, weel, I canna help that. I said I would be at Balnageith the night, an' Miss Sinclair * gie me but ane shirt wi' me in my pouch. An' sae, ye'll just present my respectful compliments to Captain Sinclair and his leddy, an' say I maun be hame for my Sunday duties. And maybe I'll mak' oot a visit to them some ither time."

"Ah!" said Archie, "you'll join us there next week?"

"Na, I did na say *that*. Is there onything," he said, turning to me, "that I can send ye, forbye the hive o' honey and Secker's sermons?"

I told him nothing

"Weel, ye'll write often, if it be only a wordie, to say how his head is. An' I'll no despair yet. He has gude pure bluid in his body, and a naturally strong constitution. All may be right yet, as he has youth on his side, gin he'll tak' the proper precautions."

In my turn, I enquired if there was anything we could send him with a cushion of brawn Archie had promised him, and I named Bellamy's Bible.

"I am no *verra* anxious," he answered, "sin my mind has been lang eneugh made up to the meaning of most passages necessary to our salvation. But if ye like it, an' there be room in the box, ye may sen' it, an' maybe I wad tak' a glint at what your frien' has to say to the two Misses Lot and the foxes' tails."

Archie here announced everything to be ready, and the poor old gentleman holding my arm led me to the side of the boat, and assisted me to get in, saying, "Dinna be rash," and afterwards, "God be wi' ye." Archie and his sister quickly followed his example, and a quarter of an hour carried us to the Ross-shire side. The minister tarried full five minutes steadfastly watching our progress, and then turned slowly, mounted his pony and trotted home.

I have nothing agreeable to associate with Braelangwell besides the kindness of our host and hostess, and having experienced that elsewhere, under happier auspices, it was not enough to make the place interesting to me when there, nor dear to my memory when I am never likely to revisit it. The

---

* A relative of the minister's wife. She kept house for him.

INVERGARRY CASTLE.
(From Mrs. Leslie's Sketchbook.)

(To face page 33.)

laird of Culduthil and his brother, Captain Fraser, dined there on August 2; and our plan of returning by the Highland Road and Glasgow discussed. Culduthil strongly urged us in preference to take the steamboat from Inverness, by which means we should see the fine scenery of the Western coast, and reach Glasgow with less fatigue. Archie was pleased with the suggestion and agreed to it.

Duncan Davidson, the laird of Tulloch, and his wife, the second daughter of Lord Macdonald, arrived on the 4th. Her marriage was still so recent that she might be considered a bride; and he had not yet exchanged the *empressement* of the lover for the more sober manner of the husband. Mrs. Davidson's appearance strongly resembled that of the Princess Charlotte. The King was so struck with it at her presentation that, after saluting her, he turned to one of the lords in waiting, exclaiming, "How like poor Charlotte!" She was good-natured and lively, and not deficient in grace or dignity. Moreover, she was young—I think not twenty—and was exuberant with happiness and health.

On the following Saturday, the 6th, I feared I must have wounded her susceptibilities as much as I shocked my own, by a thoughtless remark which I made about some friends of hers, as we sat working in the drawing-room. For a moment I entirely forgot the connection between them, but immediately afterwards wondered that I could have been so oblivious of another's feelings. Burning blushes suffused my face, and I could well nigh have wept at the thought of the pain I should cause if my unkind speech were repeated. From that moment it was impossible for me to take any reasonable part in the conversation, and when directly addressed, I stammered and hesitated, powerless to think of anything but the harm which I had perhaps done. I must allow Mrs. Davidson behaved very kindly by not appearing to notice my confusion and by pursuing the subject to Mrs. Sinclair; but I left the room almost immediately for my own, and stayed there until dinner, ruminating over the misery of idle words. Mrs. Sinclair most good naturedly tried to comfort me ere I went downstairs, by assuring me of her conviction from Mrs. Davidson's subsequent discourse that she had not noticed the remark to which I have alluded, but I have discovered that this was unfortunately not the case.

The next day we left Braelangwell, and slept for a few hours at Inverness, preparatory to our starting the following morning by the steamboat for Glasgow.

August 8.—We arose very early, bade adieu to Mary Leslie, and were on board the *Comet* steam vessel at four o'clock. The scene was very animated: there was another vessel to start at the same time, and this occasioned a great deal of contention. There were only three ladies besides myself on board the *Comet*; these were dressed in deep mourning, and appeared under some heavy affliction, so that they did not speak to the other passengers. There might have been about thirty men (some of them gentlemen), and a great many poor Highland women going for the harvest to Glasgow. I did not discover the names of all my fellow sailors, but there are a few I remember, who interested and amused me extremely. Two brothers named Becket were well informed, well-mannered men; and were very polite and attentive to me, which I considered the more from Archie being oftentimes too ill to raise his head from a sofa or whatever he could find to recline upon. There was a young man from Oxford, a walking gentleman, who had been trudging through Scotland, and seemed full of enthusiasm at its romantic beauties. Then there was a most uncouth-looking creature, tall, stout and ill-made. His features were peculiarly vulgar in their cast, and his dress was an attempt at fashion and military cut, which, with a look and strut, aping the great man, made him a very conspicuous object. His coarse hands were decked out with rings, and a ponderous watch chain swinging backwards and forwards caused a variety of seals to jingle, and occasionally turned up one on which was a huge coronet. This, of course, produced some speculation as to who he was, and our curiosity was still more raised by his dog, a rough, wretched looking little animal, round

URQUHART CASTLE.
(From Mrs. Leslie's Sketchbook.)

whose neck was a collar with a Gaelic inscription: "Behave well, for you are a great man's dog." This strange being had christened himself FitzStrathern, and wished to pass himself off as a scion of royalty in the relationship of one of the illegitimate progeny of the Duke of Clarence. We subsequently discovered from an Orkney laird that he was the son of Mr. Petrie, the jailor at Kirkwall. A round, smooth-faced, self-satisfied cockney in white corduroy breeches and well polished top-boots tormented every one with questions, until he could no longer obtain an answer, and it was a relief to our ears and sentimental sensations, which had been continually shocked by his vulgar ignorance or astonishment.

The weather was peculiarly fine. The scenery on either side of Loch Ness, though slightly varied, is always grand and rich. The ruins of Urquhart Castle (of which I made a slight sketch) are extensive, and prove the building once to have been of considerable strength. At Fort Augustus the vessel had to pass through several locks, and this detained us nearly two hours. The houses belonging to the fort are neat, but the place itself is poor and dirty, and wears an aspect of desolation that is very depressing. There was little to interest us during the afternoon. We passed Invergarry with its ruined castle, and the unpretending dwelling of the chieftain of Glengarry by its side, of which I made a drawing. The hills in the background were fine, and one called Ben Shee is the fairy land of the North. The poor Highland women at the request of Mr. Becket sang several of their wild, native airs. He begged me to come close to them, which pleased them; and one, who spoke a little English, explained the subject of the Gaelic verses. Of course it was love—and "true love that never runs smooth." One woman began and sang the air; and then all joined in a sort of chorus at the end of each verse, of which there were more than we liked, since there was much monotony in the melody. We reached the inn at the foot of Ben Nevis by eight o'clock, where we had bespoken a bed; and it was fortunate we had done so, since Archie's aching head needed rest, and there was scanty accommodation of any kind for the numerous and noisy applicants, who seemed to act on the principle that "might makes right." Such passengers as could not get either a sofa or a bed were resolved not to lose a supper; and the calls upon the poor landlady were unmerciful. She was a nice, cleanly, active young woman, and I witnessed her exertion and good-humoured efforts to please, as I had frequent occasion to walk into the kitchen for hot water and things for my poor, dear, suffering husband, which I found I might have rung for in vain.

Tuesday, 9.—We rose at three, as we had a mile to walk to the vessel, which during the night had been passed through the grand chain of locks called Neptune's staircase. The air was chilly, and the dew heavy on the grass; and we were glad to get on board the vessel. All the passengers were soon assembled, and we left Fort William at half-past four. The clouds were then thickly canopied over the head of Ben Nevis, and mists clung to the sides of the hills. But soon they changed their hue of grey—they became warmer and more glowing, and the firmament itself seemed to open as the sun rose over the Mont Blanc of Caledonia. Then, as every object became illuminated, how interesting the scenery appeared! We were gradually nearing the great Atlantic, and the channel every moment became broader. The Sound of Lismore has classic stories. The Pass of Glencoe, the seat of Lochiel, the country of Morven, are names associated with Scottish history and song, never to be forgotten. I made a sketch off Appin, where some small islands gave a beautiful variety to the colouring of the water. We reached Oban at twelve, and had been previously persuaded by the two Mr. Beckets to quit the vessel there, and get into another proceeding to the Western Islands. The exchange was soon made, and we went on in the *Highland Chieftain*. Lord Strathallan was on board. His had been one of the attainted titles. He was a magnificent old man, and we landed him somewhere on the Sound of Mull. The day was unsettled; heavy storms made us uncomfortable, but when they were occasionally tinged by the sun they formed beautiful rainbows, and relieved the cold appearance of the barren rocks. The evening became serene, and we arrived at Tobermory, in Mull, at six. Here there was some difficulty in procuring beds. The inn was too small to accommodate all the passengers, so many were indebted to private individuals for

THE SOUND OF MULL.

(From Mrs Leslie's Sketchbook.)

[To face page 56.

a night's lodging. We were beholden to a Mr. Culbertson, whose hospitality I shall never forget. We had tea, and then proceeded to a ramble. Nothing could be finer, the air was so soft and pure. We ascended a hill, and when we looked down upon the little bay tinged with the amber of the declining sun, and studded with fishing-boats gently rocked on its bosom, and when we turned to the inland scenery, the bright green turf and the lordly cottages, all seemed to bespeak it an abode of peace. We retired to our little bedroom with mixed feelings of thankfulness and hope.

Wednesday, 10.—" Who could guess" our feelings of disappointment, "since upon nights so sweet, such awful morn could rise"?

The pipers aroused us at four o'clock, when the rain poured down and the clouds looked unrelenting. We dressed, however, and Mr. Culbertson prognosticated fair weather. We went to the vessel trying to be cheerful. But, indeed, there is nothing much more depressing than a thorough bad day for an excursion of pleasure. As soon as we had left the bay, and became exposed to the full force of the Atlantic, we were sensible of the raging of the storm. The vessel was fearfully tossed, the captain was unskilled and alarmed, and the crew insubordinate or intoxicated. Off Ardnamurchan my heart was filled with gloomy forebodings and unavailing regrets. The misery of our situation was not to be compared to the horrid possibility of never again beholding my darling little girl. However, on we went; the wind became more favourable, and we were driven under shelter of Staffa at one. Oh, how thankful I felt! We got into a small boat, which rowed directly into the cave and landed us on the rocky pillars. I need not describe the peculiar formation of this island. I can only say its general impression was disappointment; but I think it would have been better seen on a calmer day, when the greatness of the deep did not sink every other object into littleness. We rested there an hour; the sun came out, we rejoined the vessel (which had been injured by running on a rock), and with the wind directly aft reached Iona in a short time. Nothing can be more miserable than its appearance—no trees, barren rocks, wretched hovels and naked children—ruins, venerable for their antiquity, but without any picturesque effect, demanding our interets but exciting little. I was directed to a miserable house called par excellence "The Inn," and we determined to remain in it rather than venture back in our crazy vessel to Tobermory. Several other passengers coincided with us, and fearing a lack of provisions, got bread, meat and tea from the boat. A young Highlander came in with his gun. His countenance was open and his manner frank. He begged me to return with him to his father's in Mull, where he promised us every comfort; but the *little* walk he encouraged us to take was not less than seven miles, and we were too weary to attempt it. In the evening we had some conversation with Maclean, the English schoolmaster, a simple, kind-hearted, pious man. He gave us up his bedroom, arranged it as neatly as he could, and lighted a fire. The Messrs. Becket tried to induce us to accompany them in an open boat to Port Erscoig, which the fishermen promised them to reach by ten o'clock. But, though the evening was clear and serene, and we had actually put our box on board, we drew back, thinking it better to submit to the evils we knew than to risk others that might be worse. So we went to bed, but—not to sleep. An army of fleas roused me effectually, and drove me first to the fire and then to the window, where with feelings of much discomfort and solicitude I watched the coming dawn.

Thursday, 11.—The sun shone brightly, and the cloudless sky gave promise of a fine day. We rambled among the ruins, after a frugal breakfast, and then went to some of the neighbouring heights, hoping to descry a vessel. Dr. Macleod accompanied us, and at nine we saw the smoke of a steam vessel apparently off Staffa, which proved to be one called the *Highlander.* Archie gave Mrs. Maclean five shillings, which she regarded as great riches, and I gave the good schoolmaster a copy of Bishop Wilson's *Sacra Privata* which I had brought with me, and which he had looked at and admired during my walk. At two we left Iona; the sea was perfectly smooth, and the view of the ocean, dotted with rocks and islands, very interesting. We reached Tobermory in the evening, and were received as old friends by Mr. and Mrs. Culbertson. They gave us their best bedroom, excellent tea, bread and preserves; and when I retired to undress, our kind hostess insisted on bathing my feet herself and doing everything that could conduce to my comfort. There was a charm in this hospitality I shall never forget. But I do not believe it singular in Scotland.

Friday, 12.—It rained heavily and blew a brisk gale; and again we suffered much discomfort. The vessel stopped at Oban, at one. I jumped out and ran to the inn and secured the best bedroom I could find, for Archie was ill, and we had resolved to stay there all night. Most of the passengers determined to do the same. Dr. Macleod returned to Inverness, and the sitting-room was shared with us by a Miss Gleghorn, from Glasgow, and a party of young people who were travelling about for their amusement. This Miss Gleghorn was an admirable specimen of a notable, cheerful old maid. When first she came in, from sea-sickness she seemed very miserable, and begged for our bedroom that she might sit in it. However, she found it would make but a sorry drawing-room, so Archie and I were left in peaceable possession and went to lie down. When we got up we found the worthy spinster restored to health and cheerfulness, and her needle and thread scarcely keeping pace with her tongue. We all dined together; and a poor traveller who had taken a seat in a distant corner was glad to be bidden to our table.

Saturday, 13.—After a wretched night, disturbed by the wind and rain beating against our window, we rose not a little discomfited with the appearance of things. But after breakfast, being told there was little chance of improvement in the weather, we determined to proceed across the country in an open cart, the only conveyance to be had. I must say this vehicle was not in idea very congenial to me; but when it was filled with clean hay, and our boxes were disposed for seats, and I was well wrapped up in shawls and cloaks, although it continued to rain, it was less disagreeable than I could have imagined. Our pony trotted briskly along, and our driver, a fine, tall young Highlander, either ran by the side or sat on the shaft. Occasionally we got out to rest ourselves by walking, for from the want of springs the motion was very uneasy.

The scenery in the neighbourhood of Loch Awe is very

fine, and if favoured by fine weather, would have compensated us for all our inconvenience. There was an ample proportion of wood, and the hills looked warmer and richer than on the east coast. The ride had enlivened me, and we found ourselves at the Inn at Taynult sooner than I had expected. This was a solitary house; a rapid burn much swollen by the rain ran close to the door, and steep hills rose around it. The driver went into the house to get a chair for me to dismount. I saw the pony looking round, and started to catch the reins; but the next moment felt myself being lifted up out of the road, and beheld Archie standing near me with the blood trickling from his forehead. We were neither of us hurt materially by this fall, and I believe less frightened than the good innkeeper and one of his lodgers who witnessed the upset. One of the gentlemen staying in the house was a surgeon, and he strongly urged our lying down for some time, and trying to get rest, which we did in a miserable room.

We rose, however, refreshed with our sleep, and then, at the request of Mr. Gordon, went to his apartment. This gentleman had believed I was killed, and was dreadfully alarmed at witnessing my fall. He seemed scarcely able to express his joy at my escape, nor to know how to make me comfortable enough. The rain still came down in torrents, and his young friend, a Mr. Peters, was late in returning from his fishing in the loch. But at last he appeared, with a very fine salmon and some smaller fish. We agreed to dine together; and a pretty, smart-looking girl put an excellent dinner on the table, but I was not hungry enough to do justice to it. Not so the gentlemen, who praised and partook of everything, and talked cheerfully until late, over port wine and whisky-punch. At ten, Mr. Gordon and Mr. Peters retired, and we took possession of the bed in the corner of their room. Much as I valued this kindness, I could not do justice to it, for sleep seemed far from my eyelids, and the roar of the burn (now a perfect torrent) sounded hoarsely and gloomily on my ears.

Sunday, 14.—Again the weather was lowering, and prevented an excursion to Bonawe and the Lorn smelting furnace, a most romantic spot, having the river Awe on one side, Loch Etive in front, and behind the magestic Ben Cruachan. Our companions were discouraged, and agreed to go on with us to Inverary. They hired another cart, and we all set out together, choosing the road by Port Sonachan as being ten miles shorter than that by Dalmally. The ascents in this wild region were sometimes very steep, and one, by the side of a tremendous mountain torrent, that tumbled with fearful impetuosity through a ravine, overhung with a beautiful variety of foliage, had so unsafe an aspect that I got out to walk. However, Mr. Gordon reassured me after a time, and I proceeded with him in his cart. He talked much and feelingly of Prince Charlie, and repeated with enthusiasm Lord Byron's well-known lines:

Away ye gay landscapes, &c.

At length we passed the manor of Kilchrenan, and soon after stopped at a poor house close to the loch. The waters of the lake were much troubled, and as the men refused to put out the long boat for us, we had nearly resolved to stay where we were. We went into the house to warm ourselves. It was tolerably cleanly; but the family were in great distress, especially one poor young woman, who cried bitterly. Her brother had been detected smuggling, and on being seized by the gaugers had made so fierce a resistance that she feared he would be visited with the extremest punishment that the law could inflict. It was vain to try and console her. The little boat was ready and I still hesitated, but kind-hearted Mr. Peters told me he could and would row, and would engage to carry us over safely. So then I stepped in with him, Archie and Mr. Gordon, the surgeon we had seen the previous day, and a companion of his. The wind blew a hurricane, the waves were high and dashed into the boat. There were no proper grooves for the oars, which consequently slipped every moment; but Mr. Peter's strength seemed sufficient to pull our crazy bark in whatever direction he pleased, and, after being buffeted and wet through, he landed us safely at Port Sonachan. How wrong it is to be prejudiced by appearance! This young man was an ungainly-looking person, tall and stout, but ill put together, with rather large and coarse features, merely expressive of quiet good-humour. But of what service he was to us who had no claim upon him! Mr. Gordon had been well-looking, and his manner was more polished; but he was extremely timid, and therefore less useful. He soon made an excellent peat fire at the little inn, where the pretty young wife promised to cook us *something*. She soon put some eggs and bacon before us, excellent butter, and oat-cakes, and whiskey and water, which for the first time I liked, feeling the benefit of its warm and social qualities after our late exposure to the inclement elements.

We had scarcely finished our meal ere we saw "the muckle boat" crossing the ferry with two gentlemen, a gig and a fine grey horse. Mr. Peters went down to reconnoitre, and, after a short absence, returned with a face glowing with joy.

"That's just my old school-fellow Burns," he said to Mr. Gordon. "We have na met since we were sixteen—and now," he continued, turning to me, "I have been taking the liberty to speak to him about you, and ye'll just gang on in comfort wi' him, and I'll answer for his carrying ye safely; and his friend walks with us; and so that's all settled comfortably."

In vain I remonstrated at the inconvenience to be caused to Mr. Macdonell, and the probability of Mr. Burns not liking the exchange of companions. Mr. Peters would listen to no objection of mine, and ran for the gentlemen to confirm the arrangement. They did it with so much cordiality that I submitted like the good wife who

> Never once saith nay, when he saith yea ;
> "Do this" saith he; "All ready, sir," saith she.

And being "all ready" as well as Mr. Burns and the gig, into it I jumped, assisted by worthy Mr. Peters, patting my shoulder with a truly paternal air, and whispering into my ear: "Do not be afraid; he was a good fellow when he was at school, and he'll guide ye surely enough to Inverary, and long before us."

There was something very droll in this adventure, and as I turned my head to nod farewell to Archie, it overawed me. I was going to cross a wild country with a perfect stranger, introduced to me but a few minutes before by the casual acquaintance of a day, who had recognized each other after a separation of twelve or fourteen years. However, the comparative, or I may say positive, comfort of my situation reconciled me fully to it. There is something indescribably exhilarating to the spirits in passing rapidly through the open air. I experienced this, in spite of the atmosphere being rather heavy, and of an occasional drizzling rain. The horse was the finest and most docile animal I ever beheld; Mr. Burns had but to hold the

EARLY MARRIED LIFE.

reins and leave him to his own discretion; and the road being good, we went at a swift pace.

The country was very barren; but any spots of interest Mr. Burns pointed out, especially one very nervous and narrow point on the edge of a steep bank, overhanging some river or small lake, where Colonel Macdonell (I think he said) had been killed, returning one dark night from Inverary. I was glad when we had passed it. We then emerged on a broad heath, and my companion pulled up near a small lone house within a few yards of the road. He whistled, and a white-headed boy coming out, he desired him to stand by the horse for a few minutes. He was away a quarter of an hour, and when he reseated himself, he said he had been calling on his old nurse, whose son had been taken up for smuggling; and he was on his way to Ayrshire to beg his release, or some commutation of his punishment. We had a great deal of chat. I found Mr. Burns had been originally in the navy, but was now married and settled at Bonawe; he claimed some kindred with his namesake the poet, and spoke disparagingly of the Highlanders, especially of Glengarry. At last we arrived at the Duke of Argyle's enclosures. We stopped at an English-looking cottage, and some children ran out. My companion spoke familiarly to them in Gaelic, and the gate was opened. Oh, what beautiful fields and rich trees! And then such a torrent of water, pouring its way over masses of rock, foaming and dashing through a channel that seemed too narrow to contain its angry waves! A ride of five or seven miles through this enchanting scenery, constantly varying, but always beautiful, brought us to the Inn at Inverary. It was large, and the landlord came to the door to receive us. All looked like comfort and civilization. I felt nearer home, and breathed more freely.

I was shown into a nice parlour by Mr. Mackellar, and I told him we should sleep there, and that I should like to see a bedroom. Upon this, mine host looked rather waggishly at us both, and made no answer but by seating himself. Mr. Burns explained instantly:

"This lady's husband and some of his friends will be here directly." Thus all was correct again, and Mr. Mackellar only seemed desirous to make me eat and drink, which I had neither appetite nor complaisance enough to do. However, I ordered dinner, and Archie and Co. arrived before seven o'clock. Mr. Gordon was all impatience to cross Loch Fyne ere dark, that he might reach Glenfinnart that night; and he would not leave Mr. Peters behind; so after a parting cup of "mountain dew" they set off. Mr. Burns and Mr. Macdonell partook of our dinner, and bade us adieu at ten o'clock to proceed on their benevolent mission into Ayrshire.

Monday, 15.—We awoke to a fine day, and after breakfast went to see Inverary Castle. It is a modern building and rather disappointed me, as I had expected something more antique and magnificent. It is, however, one of the most comfortable houses I ever was in. There is everything for use, little for show. The drawing-room furniture is elegant white satin, beautifully embroidered with figures, flowers and landscapes. This is French work.

On our return to the inn we found the Glasgow "Neddy" we had bespoken ready for us, and we set off along the banks of Loch Fyne. It was a pretty ride, but the heat was oppressive, and our poor Rozinante with difficulty proceeded at a slow pace, which tried our patience sadly and excited in us some fears about his reaching Cairndon. However, there we arrived at last, indefatigable Miss Cleghorn and her party jogging up in their carts at the same time. We immediately bespoke a cart of a much better description than our former vehicle, and after an excellent dinner got into it. We were to go through the barren pass of Glencoe, and for the first six miles, it was one continued ascent. On the summit is the old stone mentioned by Dr. Johnson, upon which is written: "*Rest and be thankful.*" Our ride thence was downhill for nearly seven miles. Nothing could be more wild; huge hills on either side, with little appearance of verdure—nay, sometimes so wholly destitute of it that nothing but masses of black rock appeared. We stopped at a cottage called Cobbler's Hall to get some water for the horse, and Archie gave the wife a loaf of white bread, which seemed an inestimable treasure to her. Soon after this we reached Loch Long, and stopped at the "Sun" at Arrochar. The shades of evening were coming on

"THE COBBLER," LOCH LOW.
(From Mrs. Leslie's Sketchbook.)

[To face page 45.

fast, and we resolved to rest there, and send off a note to our kind friends at Blairvadoch, and order a chair from Helensburgh for the next morning. Thus were we again disappointed of reaching the desired haven. As soon as the bedroom was ready Archie retired to it, while, by his advice, I sat down at the window and sketched the magnificent scene before me. Loch Long like silver, with a few boats upon it, and the lofty peaks of the Cobbler, black and clearly defined against the blue sky in the background. It was a lovely summer evening, but I was weary and spiritless and anxious for the following day.

Tuesday, 16.—We rose early. The sun still shone upon us. When I entered the sitting-room I found a gentleman and lady who proved to be Maclean of Col and his new wife. She did not look very genteel, being much decked out with Birmingham finery, but both entered agreeably into conversation with me. We waited some time after breakfast, but no chaise arriving, we again had recourse to a cart, in which we had proceeded about two miles when the desired carriage appeared.

We made the exchange and went on more briskly. The views were very fine, but not more striking than many we had seen, and I began to think the drive a weary length when we saw a young man, tall, slight and gentlemanly, walking towards us. This was so novel a sight that I exclaimed: "Oh what a smart gentleman!" when my much-esteemed friend William Tritton opened the door of the chaise. I could scarcely express my surprise and joy. I got out directly, and many other figures came running down the hill—all friends, all kind, all dear to me—Louisa Tritton, Mr. Buchanan. Andrew,* Helen and Jane, Charlotte and Mathilda, whom I then first saw; the beautiful Miss Cumming of Logie, Mrs. Denistoun, Mr. Price, etc. I was dragged up the hill between them, where they had been taking their luncheon on the heath. It was a sweet spot at the head of the Gairloch, and they had chosen it that they might see our approach and rush down upon us. I could not eat, but I took a glass of wine, and then got

* He was later on Sir Andrew Buchanan.

into Mr. Buchanan's carriage. Kind Lady Janet and my dear friend Mrs. Tritton received us at the door at Blairvadoch. Seeing the latter made me think of home, and my heart was so full I could not speak. Tears were a great relief to me. I was immediately taken to a snug little bedroom in the turret, where I read my letters, which gave me good tidings of my child. Then I lay down until the evening. I felt all at once relieved from fatigue and anxiety, and the necessity of exertion, for everyone waited upon me and vied with each other in attention.

CHAPTER IV.

JOYS AND SORROWS.

THERE were naturally various episodes in the Leslies' memorable visit to Scotland in 1825 which did not find a place in the Journal. In the hurry of writing down the chief events of the day, pretty little touches were sometimes forgotten or left out for want of time, but were remembered afterwards with the pleasure akin to that with which we light upon an old song or some faint old-world perfume.

One such incident, which Mrs. Leslie sometimes spoke of in after years, is so characteristic of the generous impulses of the people in out-of-the-way parts of Scotland, unspoilt by the inroads of travellers, as to be worth mentioning. They were one day on a steamboat, nearing a desolate-looking island, and Mrs. Leslie, anxious about securing some degree of comfort for her husband, who was more ill than usual that day, asked the captain where they could get accommodation. He pointed to a small white cottage not far from the shore, but said there would be a rush for it. When they reached it, they saw that they had not been misinformed as to the demands upon its slender resources. The entrance passage was crowded with luggage, and Mrs. Leslie, speaking to the woman of the house, entreated that they might at least have one room, seeing that her husband was so ill. The woman promised to do what she could with the people who had just arrived, as she had not a single room to dispose of, and went away to negotiate. A few minutes later she was seen turning all their boxes and bags out of the house in a fury, and upon being questioned, said that as their owners refused to give up one room to a sick gentleman, she would not have such people in her house.

Mrs. Leslie used to tell of this same voyage a very characteristic anecdote of her husband. In the saloon of the steamer a small boy kept up a continual howl. The passengers' patience was completely exhausted, and to Mr. Leslie, suffering intensely as he was, it was extremely trying. Alternately, the boy's mother and aunt implored him in a helpless way, saying "Johnnie, *do* be a good boy." Johnnie's howl was suspended for a moment, and after saying sturdily "I wont!" he began to bellow louder than before. At last Mr. Leslie got up from his sofa, and went over to Johnnie and said to him firmly, "Johnnie, you shan't be a good boy." "I will!" was the resolute reply, and peace was secured for the rest of the voyage.

The visit to Scotland, which Mrs. Leslie describes in her Journal, ended at Blairvadoch on the Gairloch, a place belonging to Mr. and Lady Janet Buchanan, Mr. Leslie's first cousin. Their stay under this hospitable roof was, as we have seen, a happy conclusion to a journey, interesting in many ways, but full of anxiety to the one, and of suffering more or less continual to the other.

On their return to London, affairs for a time looked brighter, and consequently Mr. Leslie's health improved. There is little to chronicle till the spring of the following year, when a letter written shortly before the birth of their second child, and too beautiful in its tender solicitude to be omitted here, gives a closer insight than we have yet obtained into the deep and earnest piety of Mrs. Leslie's character. The letter is dated June 4, 1826. Reverently one scans the pages, slightly yellowed by age, on which the young wife's hand traced unfalteringly words of solemn and sacred import, while she herself stood on the borders of two worlds, prepared equally to die or to live.

MY DEAREST ARCHIE,—I have often wished to write to you lately on some subjects very near to my heart, and which my own weakness has prevented my speaking upon with that composure that ought to attend their mention. I know I must now ere long be laid in my bed; when I shall rise from it God alone knows. Perhaps never. But supposing my death is not to be so immediate, we are certain that it is not far distant to any one of us, and therefore it behoves us to work while it is called to-day, lest the darkness of night overtake us and our duties remain unfulfilled. Dearest Archie, amidst some trials, I have been permitted to pass many happy days with you. You have ever been affectionate and kind to me, and whether suffering yourself, or seeing me suffer, your patience and good temper have remained unruffled. God is the witness of my gratitude to Him and you for this blessing, which I am certain falls to the lot of very few, and least of all should have fallen to me who am so unworthy of it. Indeed, it has been my greatest happiness since our marriage, and this acknowledgement of it may perhaps be a happiness to you when I am gone. In leaving you I have but one anxiety. Your qualities of heart and temper are so good that I think they would always dispose you to do right; but we need a surer, stronger guide than inclination to lead us to that righteousness that shall lead us to heaven. Yes, dear Archie, for this world and for the next, there is but one thing needful. Religion, and the religion of Jesus Christ only, can direct us, support us, comfort us and preserve us. It alone can give us that peace here which the world cannot take away. It alone can procure us that felicity hereafter which the world cannot intermeddle with. Oh, remember this, dearest Archie, probe its truth, act up to its precepts, and so will you be happy here and hereafter. And should you be left to guide, to educate our darling child without me, oh, train her up in the paths of holiness, and strive to instil into her young heart such firm principles of religion, that they may defend her in temptation, and preserve her from evil.

Never suffer the slightest dereliction from the path of duty to pass as a mistake, or a trifling error. Having seen the misery of this, I am the more earnest it should be avoided. Besides, we are not justified in making use of such palliation by Him who has expressly said He will bring every work into judgment with every secret thing, whether it be good or whether it be evil. Teach her to love, to reverence, to habitually remember her Creator, and then He will never forsake her. Thus far, dearest

Archie, I am anxious about my child's education, and most anxious that you should feel and act towards her and yourself upon the principles I have endeavoured to urge. Such talents as Providence may have bestowed upon her it might be well to cultivate if you can afford it. But I am not ambitious for her to be taught many unnecessary things, as many accomplishments lead to vanity, and vanity alienates the heart from all that is good and useful.

Now, God Almighty bless you, my dear husband, and my darling child. That you may be happy here, and that we may all be united after this life in the unspeakable joys of heaven is the fervent prayer of your most affectionate wife, ELEANOR LESLIE.

All went well, and on June 17 Mrs. Leslie gave birth to a son.

For some years after this event there is little to record save the successive births of two daughters, one in 1831, the other in 1833, and the family circle, now complete, lived in comparative happiness and prosperity, not, however, without occasional indications of troubles in store for the future. In 1830 they had removed from London to Wandsworth, where they inhabited a house not far from Mrs. Leslie's old home, and subsequently spent several months under her father's roof. They then went to Scotland, thinking to take up their abode there permanently, and after a summer spent at the Manse with the worthy minister, proceeded to Bervie, near Forres, the house of Mr. Leslie's sister, where they frequently saw the Gordon-Cummings. There were serious plans for repairing the old house at Balnageith for their accommodation, but Sir William Cumming dissuaded them from such a step, and in the midst of their difficulties about fixing on a suitable home, Mr. Leslie, tired of an idle life, began to turn his thoughts again to business. He rapidly conceived a plan for carrying it on without risk, and even with the hope of considerable advantage; the preliminaries were rapidly sketched, and he returned with his family to Wandsworth, settling them in the modest but pleasant old Jacobean house on East Hill, of which Mrs. Leslie always retained happy memories. In the wandering life which she led for many years afterwards, this was perhaps the nearest approach to settled and undisturbed domestic happiness that it was her lot to experience, and here, in spite of ever present cares and anxieties, she was able to enjoy the society of her beloved parents, and that of the many friends of her youth. Absolutely devoted to her husband, and keenly appreciative of his many noble and winning qualities, she was unable to share his sanguine hopes or to believe in the rosy prospects which his lively imagination always held out before him. But when scheme after scheme resulted in disappointment and the buoyant sunny nature was crushed and prostrate beneath the blow which she had foreseen from the beginning, she was ever ready to support, comfort and encourage.

Thus when, in 1834, full of enthusiasm for some new projects, Mr. Leslie went to Scotland to raise money on Balnageith in order to obtain the necessary resources, his wife, a much better man of business than himself, was convinced that the measure was highly unsatisfactory, and that the end must be ruin.

Fortunately, however, even the clearest-sighted people do not constantly see the end before them; for even to them also come moments in their course, when the green hill immediately in front of them shuts out the arid mountain path beyond. Such moments indeed could not have been rare. Happy in each other, and in their children, who were growing up to be all that the most exacting of parents' hearts could desire, there was at least always a green hill in sight, on which their eyes could rest with pleasure.

One of the most constant visitors at their house was Colonel, later Sir Ord, Honyman, of the Grenadier Guards, the very soul of honour and chivalry. He would come at any time uninvited, to breakfast or dinner; everyone in the house, including the servants, delighted to welcome him. An extremely affectionate father, he would hurry off to Mrs. Leslie when anything of interest or importance befell any of his children, sure of her cordial sympathy.

One Sunday morning before breakfast, he was discovered making for the house with an open letter in his hand. As Mrs. Leslie had not yet left her room, he sent it to her by her little son, with a request that she would read it at once. It was a note from Sir Fitzroy Kelly, with whom his son George was a pupil, expressing his entire satisfaction with the young man's progress. When Mrs. Leslie appeared Colonel Honyman burst out:

"Don't you see? George may be Lord High Chancellor any day he likes!"

"George" did become a barrister of eminence, was made a judge younger than most men, and received more congratulations than most. But at his first assizes it was his duty to condemn seven or eight men to death, a matter which affected him so deeply that it caused a stroke of paralysis from which he died.

Colonel Honyman's solicitude was not limited to his children; he took the most affectionate care of his mother, who was somewhat inclined to indulge in sweets at table, which he thought unwholesome.

"Mother," he said impressively one day, "God made beef and mutton, but the devil made tipsy cake." "Ah, weell, Ord," replied the old Scotch lady, "the deil's made mony a gude thing in his day."

Mr. George Bowen, of Coton Hall, Shropshire, Colonel Honyman's brother-in-law, was also a particular friend of the Leslies; and a visit which they paid to him in 1838 with their eldest daughter was indirectly the cause of a great change in their religious convictions. This change was so remarkable and far-reaching that it must be discussed in a separate chapter.

CHAPTER V.

DISSENTING INFLUENCES.

THE railway to Birmingham was opened in 1838, a matter which greatly facilitated a long-promised visit to Coton Hall, where after spending a pleasant week, Mr. and Mrs. Leslie with their daughter Eleanor returned to Wandsworth. In the train with them was a large, loosely-built man, coarse in appearance, but of considerable mental power. He began to talk of religion with a simplicity and earnestness that caught the attention of all. Mrs. Leslie afterwards said, in speaking of this first meeting with one who was destined for some years to exercise a large influence on the religious life of the family, "I made a remark which I thought very wise, and he showed me how foolish I was."

They discovered before leaving the train that he was a certain Robert Aitken, Dissenting minister in London, and that he preached at Zion Chapel in the Waterloo Road.

On the first Sunday after their return home, Mr. Leslie went in search of it, and afterwards said to his wife, "I am sorry and glad that you were not there. The place is low, and the congregation poor and rough, but Aitken is the only man who ever gave me an idea of what John Knox must have been."

After this, they went regularly to Zion Chapel. The services consisted of some Scripture reading—Mr. Aitken had a wonderful voice, and read magnificently—of hymns and a sermon. It was the first really powerful peaching they had ever heard. One main idea recurred constantly, and, indeed, ran through all : to do everything for God. This involved turning away from the world and worldliness, a distinct act which Mr. Aitken called conversion, and which Mrs. Leslie certainly experienced about this time. Her husband remarked a decided change in her. Formerly she would be greatly disturbed by any convulsion of nature—a thunderstorm would agitate and unnerve her; but now she would be perfectly calm even during a great storm. She never did things in a half-hearted way, and entered thoroughly into Mr. Aitken's scheme of conversion, allowing him to make use of her in the conversion of others, and being quite lifted up above human respect or fear. In after years, she always maintained that she had then turned to God in a way she had never done before.

Mr. Aitken's history is not without interest. After a madcap youth, during which, among other wild diversions, he was addicted to the practice of wrenching off knockers, he had started life seriously as a schoolmaster. A professorship of elocution in Ireland was to be competed for, and feeling that he had natural gifts which might ensure his success, he went to Dublin and presented himself as a candidate. Finding that he would have to wait some time before the examination, and that he would have no money to pay his hotel bills, he hired a hall, put out a programme of pieces for recitation, and scored such a success that the next day all the other competitors for the professorship retired and left the field to him. After this, he became a clergyman in the Church of England, and was presented to a living in one of the northern counties. Here he married a lady of good family, and went to the Isle of Man, where, as he himself said, he went through a sudden conversion, which entirely altered the aims and objects he had hitherto striven for. It seemed to him that God had said to him: "You want to write a gospel for Me. I have written one for you." He rushed out of the house, and began to preach to the people in the streets. He made up his mind that the need for conversion was not properly taught in the Church of England, and decided to leave it. He hired a chapel, where he preached and conducted services in his own way. Later on he fell into great extravagances, and led others into them. On Sunday mornings the services at Zion Chapel were decorous enough, but once Mr. and Mrs. Leslie and Eleanor were present at an evening service, when the most melodramatic scenes took place. Mr. Aitken, having preached a rousing and emotional sermon, several women became agitated about their spiritual condition, and he came to beg Mrs. Leslie to go and speak to them, and complete their conversion. While she was gone an elder came up and asked Miss Leslie whether she were converted. The young lady prudently answered, "Yes, I'm all right," whereupon the elder exclaimed, "Praise God! Bless the Lord! Amen," and ran up to some one else, who not giving an equally satisfactory answer was hustled over to a group of people kneeling on the floor, and undergoing the moral throes of the second birth. Another man had, meanwhile, accosted Mr. Leslie with the usual question. He managed to get rid of him in the graceful manner peculiar to himself, and then, turning to his daughter, asked severely, "How long is your mother going to stay in this damned place?"

The scenes were sometimes startling and repulsive enough, if we may trust the writer of an article in *Blackwood's Magazine* for July, 1838, entitled "My First Circuit," which describes vividly the sighs and groans of the would-be converts, the loud prayers and fervent ejaculations, interspersed with the running comments of those who were helping on the desired *finale*, when the sinner should suddenly find peace in believing. The excitement was at its height when the object of all the contortions and frantic appeals declared him or herself converted, and the handshakings and congratulations began.*

It may appear strange that people of refinement and culture like the Leslies should even for a moment have been attracted by teaching that contained such gross and vulgar elements. But it must be remembered that at that time anything like fervour or religious feeling was so entirely non-existent in the Church of England services, that whoever preached a different gospel was sure of a hearing from those who craved something more than the dry bones of formalism and a ritual devoid of heart and soul. The egregious stories told of the perfunctoriness of

---

* There is also an account of these services in Newman's "Loss and Gain"; and a graphic description of Mr. Aitken's methods in O'Neil Daunt's "Saints and Sinners."

DISSENTING INFLUENCES.

hunting squarsons were scarcely exaggerations of the truth, and already a recoil was in preparation from a state of things so bad that they brought their own remedy. But the dissenters were first in the field, and it was partly owing to their exertions on the side of earnestness in the manner of conducting public worship that the Church of England lump began to be leavened. Moreover, in this particular instance, the personality of Mr. Aitken, with all its drawbacks, was nevertheless imposing. His immense power, his eloquence, and a certain laying of his hands on the soul, as it were, could not fail to impress those who looked beneath the surface and were able to discern a mind superior to its surroundings. His preaching was not always of the emotional kind; he could be practical also, and, above all, he believed that "more things are wrought by prayer than this world dreams of." Preaching one day at Zion Chapel, he said that sometimes God granted unreasonable petitions in anger, and he instanced his own case, when anxiously desiring a certain chapel in the north of England, he prayed for it inordinately. The people in that part were profoundly ignorant, and it seemed to him that he might do great good if he could work among them. He told his hearers that not getting any light as he prayed about the matter, he flung himself down and rolled on the floor like a wayward child. Suddenly he heard a ring, and had scarcely time to compose himself when a lady, quite a stranger, came in, said she understood he wanted to buy the chapel in question, and gave him the money to do so. He bought the chapel, but found that he could do nothing with the people. After this, it would seem that he "always prayed temperate prayers" with regard to his own particular desires.

It is doubtful, when all is said, whether Mrs. Leslie did not exercise as much influence on Mr. Aitken's life as he did on hers. He looked upon her as his best convert, and it cannot be denied that she owed much to him in the deepening and broadening of her spirituality; but, at the same time, she never entirely submitted her judgment to his. He was no Pope to her, and the attraction of his teaching for her lay chiefly in the irresistible necessity which prompted her to pursue every broken spar of truth that came in her way.

It was, on the other hand, largely through her influence that he subsequently rejoined the Church of England, with the intention of filling up the gap which he felt existed in it as regarded his favourite doctrine of conversion. The welcome with which he was received speaks for the estimation in which the prodigal was held, the manner of disposing of him being equally eloquent of the want of importance attached to any little wandering from the fold. Dr. Hook, then Vicar of Leeds, having divided the town into twelve parishes, kept one for himself and appointed Mr. Aitken to one of the others; and we shall presently see the odd fusion of his old Calvinism and new High Churchism finding much the same outlet as before, but calling itself by another name. But long before this Mrs. Leslie had passed on to a loftier view and a firmer hold on that truth which she had always sought. The change, however, like all real progress, was gradual, and meanwhile it would have appeared to most onlookers as if, in the Leslie household, Calvinism had come to stay.

A clergyman, who was a frequent visitor, one day asked one of the children who was playing with a doll whether she did not know God's commandment, "Thou shalt not make to thyself any graven image"! On another occasion the same large-minded divine arrived at the house in a state of depression surpassing his wont. He had encountered a lady who wore a narrow velvet ribbon round her head to control some unmanageable lock of hair. "And I know where she will go to," he remarked, with a gloom only exceeded by his cocksureness.

At this period, the children's story-books having been condemned by the powers that overshadowed this singularly innocent household, tracts were substituted, and dismal tales of the Waldenses, the only apparent recreation being the singing of hymns in the evening. A repulsive publication called *The Weekly Visitor* produced such a morbid effect upon the younger children that one of them got up sobbing one night, terrified with the awful doubt as to whether she were a child of God or no. A servant came to Mrs. Leslie in the drawing-room with the startling announcement that "Miss Charlotte," who had been put to bed some hours before, "was in the kitchen." Alarmed, the anxious mother hurried to the kitchen, and found the child in her night-dress. On being questioned, she said she wanted to speak to her mother, and thought it would frighten her less if she sent someone to tell her. Mrs. Leslie carried the child back to bed, and to her earnest entreaty to be told whether she was indeed a child of God, her mother assured her that having been made one in baptism, and never having done anything to forfeit the grace, she might rest satisfied that she was. "That's all I wanted to know, Mammy," said the child, and was asleep in a moment.

The torments of hell being far oftener treated of in sermons than the joys of heaven, as was also the certainty that the greater number of people were doomed to eternal damnation, it seems marvellous to those who have not undergone the same spiritual treatment that there should have been any room left for the *love* of God in hearts so drilled to *fear*. Yet Mrs. Leslie was not alone in rising above these tremendous difficulties to higher and sweeter things. Much of course depended on the soil on which the gruesome doctrine fell. A friend who shared this phase of religious conviction, working through it, like Mrs. Leslie, to the larger, fuller truth beyond, once said in after years:

"I used to think if I did go to hell that anyhow I could not blaspheme there, for I knew that was the language of hell. God had always been so kind, I could not bear the thought of blaspheming Him. But I imagined that perhaps I and some others might get together and still praise God in a corner in hell."

However, as we have seen, Mr. Aitkens' extravagances of doctrine and method were by no means the whole man. Behind these was a fund of faith and real humility, finding vent in a simple eloquence, which constituted his attraction for minds of a high order. One of his hearers remembers a remarkable sermon in which, having read to his congregation the parable of the Sower, he proceeded to enlarge upon it, and said with a simplicity that took all hearts:

"When I was a little boy going to the Sunday school I recollect saying to myself 'How stupid those disciples must have been, not to have understood the parable of the Sower'; and now that I am a man with more than forty summers over my head, I pray God to make me understand the parable of the Sower."

As the preacher went on, the child on whom these words made so deep an impression that he remembered them distinctly after more than fifty years, said to himself, "I will be a good boy."

Perhaps the gentler touches were the more appreciated on account of the usual sternness of the sermons. Sometimes a prophet of a milder type arose, who laid aside the terrors of the Law for the consolations of the Beatitudes. And when one Sunday morning the low, pleading tones of a stranger broke the expectant silence of Zion Chapel, a new era began for some members of the congregation. The preacher was a Mr. Harris, a man of extensive learning, profound faith and the most tender, loving piety.* His health, which had always been feeble from his youth, prevented his taking a very active part in the ministry, but all who came in contact with him were impressed with his sanctity and with the sweetness of his utter abandonment to the will of God. From the time of his first appearance at Zion Chapel he began to exercise a beneficent influence on Mrs. Leslie's religious life. Her intense desire to arrive at the truth made her ready to respond to every suggestion that seemed to lead upwards, with a docility the more remarkable because she remained unentangled in any of the systems or means through which she passed to the longed-for haven. And the childlike singleness of heart and purpose, conspicuous in all Mr. Harris's dealings with souls, was admirably suited to guide without detaining, while he himself, journeying onward towards the same end, was able to illumine the way, in spite of the different paths they trod.

It was in 1841 that High Church tendencies led Mrs. Leslie and her family a step further on the road to truth. Mr. Harris never belonged to the Church of England,

---

* For an account of his life and character see an article in the *Dublin Review* for 1850, entitled "The Priest's Hidden Life," by Cardinal Wiseman.

but so identical were their motives that the change in no wise affected the friendship that united the whole Leslie family to him. Particularly apposite to this growth and progress are the words of the poet in "In Memoriam:"

> "I hold it truth with him who sings
> To one clear harp in divers tones
> That men may rise on stepping-stones
> Of their dead selves to higher things.

CHAPTER VI.

HIGH CHURCH INFLUENCES.

In advising Mr. Aitken to return to the Church of England, Mrs. Leslie was moved by that principle of order and authority which had always so great an attraction for her. He was unable to control the unruly elements, of which the greater part of his congregation was composed, and difficulties abounded in consequence. Before this change took place he was in great poverty, which, however, he bore with the deepest trust and confidence in divine Providence, as the following incident will show. Having been for some years a widower, he had married a daughter of Captain McDowall Grant of Arndilly, an old friend of Mrs. Leslie's, and for some reason Zion Chapel was given up. They were living in very straitened circumstances at Finchley, and one morning Mrs. Aitken put some bread on the table, saying :

"That is our last loaf, and we have no money."

"Trust in God," replied her husband with his accustomed earnestness, and shortly afterwards the door-bell rang, and a letter was handed in containing a five pound note, with an intimation that another would follow, provided that no steps were taken to discover the sender.

After rejoining the Anglican Church Mr. Aitken was appointed, as we have already seen, to one of the twelve parishes at Leeds. He afterwards got a living in Cornwall, and taught High Church—some said Roman—doctrine on very much the same lines as those he had followed as a dissenter. All the people about him were dissenters, and few attended the services of the Established Church until he came among them. But before long his fame had spread far and wide; people crowded to hear him, and there was scarcely room to stand, even in the churchyard, on Sundays during divine worship.

The miners with their own hands built a hall, where on Saturday evenings they assembled to meet their vicar, who would speak to them about the state of their consciences. If one quailed beneath his glance, Mr. Aitken would order him to go into the next room and prepare for confession. All this was very like the soul-searching in Zion Chapel. As there had been a good deal of advanced spirituality in his dissent, so there was now a good deal of Nonconformist sensationalism in his High Church practices.

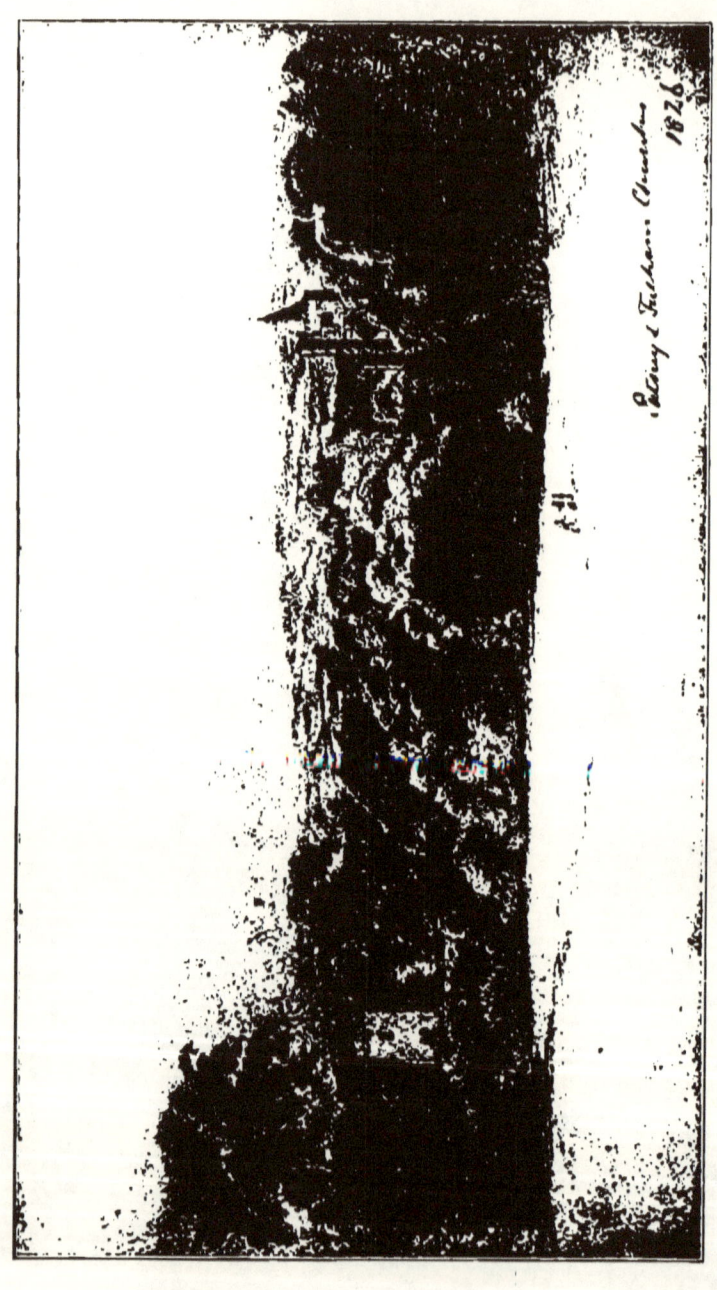

PUTNEY AND FULHAM CHURCHES, IN 1826.
(From Mrs. Leslie's Sketchbook.)

[*To face page 71.*

Moreover, one is surprised to find that it was not when he was a High Churchman, but as a dissenter, when he was preaching sudden conversion and the small number of the elect, that he introduced Mrs. Leslie to the "Imitation of Christ" and Rodriguez's "Christian Perfection."

In the meanwhile High Churchism had invaded Wandsworth. About 1841 a Mr. Shaw, perpetual curate at a chapel of ease in that place, was associated in his work with a Cambridge friend, the Rev. John Joseph Gordon, who had come to live at Wandsworth with his mother, a widow with several younger children. Mr. Gordon had imbibed a considerable amount of High Church doctrine ; he preached regularly and took his share in all the work, but quite voluntarily, not being actually a curate or even licensed by the Bishop. He was much in society, and influenced people perhaps more by his conversation than by his preaching, although his sermons attracted a good deal of attention. He was beloved by all for his very charming qualities of heart and mind. Before becoming a clergyman he had served in the Indian army, but was ordered home on sick leave after two years' service. All his life his thoughts had been turned to piety, and during his illness he had had much time for reflection. The doctors decided that his health would never allow him to live in India, and, having to begin a new career, he determined to take orders in the Established Church. He was entered at Trinity College, Cambridge, in October, 1833. Here he at once got into a religious set. He did not read for honours, although his tastes were literary and intellectual. In 1837 he took his degree and presented himself for ordination. At that time his opinions were decidedly evangelical, but they gradually merged into High Church views, the "Tracts for the Times" and Newman's "Parochial Sermons" mainly influencing him. Mr. Gordon was an ardent admirer of Newman, and one evening a number of people at the Leslie's were discussing the possibility of his going too far and becoming a Catholic. Mr. Gordon defended him with some warmth and ended by saying, "Pusey may go to Rome—Newman, never!"

A friendship sprang up between Mrs. Gordon's children and the young Leslies, who were about the same age, and the new influence made itself agreeably felt among them. It was a novel feature in their religious training to find importance attached to the observance of fasts and festivals, and to be encouraged to go to prayers in the parish church on week-days. Mrs. Leslie was so much grieved at there being no service on Ascension Day that she remonstrated with the vicar, who consented to hold one, and the custom was never dropped. In a letter written in her old age she referred to this fact with evident pleasure. One of her children still remembers that once prayers could not be read, as he and his sister formed the whole congregation.

The juvenile literature disseminated by Mr. Gordon soon replaced the obnoxious *Weekly Visitor*, "The Fairchild Family," etc., and their favourite books were now "Conversations with Cousin Rachel," "Agathos," "The Shadows of the Cross," and above all Keble's hymns, the refined piety of which soon gave them a distaste for the methodistical cant upon which they had been nourished for the last few years.

Mr. Leslie, who, in spite of the exaggerations of Mr. Aitken's methods, always liked the man himself for his rough unworldliness, did not take so kindly to the new lights. His Scotch Presbyterianism was to die a hard death, and he scoffed at the doctrine of sacramental grace preached by Mr. Gordon, while his wife, with her keen perception of truth whenever it was put before her, recognized at once the absolute *necessity* of it.

Another feature of the High Church movement was the more fully developed doctrine of almsgiving. The Rev. Mr. Shaw preached one Sunday a very touching sermon about some distressed family. Sir Ord Honyman and his son George were present, and between them sat George's friend, young Leslie. One of Sir Ord's peculiarities was that he would never carry money about with him, and when the plate was going round he whispered: "Willie, tell George to lend me half-a-crown."

"George, your father says you are to lend him half-a-crown;" whereupon George, handing the money, said with a rueful countenance, "There's a dead loss of half-a-crown."

In the meanwhile Mr. Harris and another intimate friend of the Leslie family, Mr., afterwards Sir George, Bridges, were advancing still more rapidly in the new direction. To one of them, however, the direction was scarcely a new one, for in a strange mysterious way Mr. Harris, from his youth upwards, had recognized and held the doctrines now being taught by the High Church party, although he had never belonged to the Church of England, and had waited with the utmost humility and patience for some outward indication of what he should do, lest any decisive action of his own should be wrong or presumptuous.

In some sort a climax was arrived at when
Mr. Bridges gave Mrs. Leslie a little Catholic
prayerbook for herself, and another, called
"The Young Communicants," for her children.
They were not immediately allowed to read
it, but when they did, with the directness
and uncompromising logic of children, the
younger ones at least drank in and assim-
ilated a large amount of Cathoic doctrine.

In April, 1839, the good minister, whose
beautiful, blameless life, warm heart and
generous sympathies had endeared him to
a large circle of friends, had died,[*] and in
October of the same year Mrs. Leslie suffered
the loss of her beloved mother. This latter
event brought about some changes. The
famous distillery, the cherished idea of Mr.
Falconer Atlee's life, now failed to be anything
but a source of anxiety to him. Either increasing years made the burden too great, or
the changes that had come over the commercial
world were unfavourable to the undertaking.
It was no longer profitable, and Mr. Atlee was
advised to retire from it. He was able to do so
on fairly advantageous terms, and went to live
at Brighton, where it was arranged that each
of his daughters should live with him in turn

[*] Even now (in 1898) the people in Morayshire still talk of the
benevolent old minister who cut down trees round his house, and
kept a light burning on wild nights to invite poor travellers to
come for shelter and food.

and keep house for him. In June, 1842, therefore, Mrs. Leslie went with her children to Brighton, and a memorandum referring to the time spent there in which she speaks of it as "ten months of luxurious ease and comfort, with the most tender and devoted of fathers," is eloquent of the trouble and anxiety undergone before and after.

These were indeed hard times for the whole family. Their son had been got into the Royal Academy at Woolwich, it must be owned, somewhat unfairly. The Whig Master-General of the Ordnance, knowing that he was about to go out of office, pushed in a number of young fellows in an irregular way. The Tory Master-General of the Ordnance coming in, swept a good many out, and among them young Leslie. The blow was the more acutely felt from the fact that the business horizon was less promising than ever. Towards the end of her stay at Brighton Mrs. Leslie had become seriously uneasy on account of the large speculations in which her husband was involved, and her anxieties increased when she found that he, so sanguine in general, was getting alarmed himself. Her place having been taken by her sister Harriet, who had arrived with her husband, the Comte de Pambour, she was free to return to Wandsworth.

The year 1843 was a memorable one in

JOHN FALCONER ATLEE.
(From a Sketch by the Rev. E. W. Leslie, S.J.)

[*To face page 76.*

the annals of financial failures, and Mr. Leslie suffered more seriously than most people. The sudden dissolution of the North American Colonisation Company, and the repudiation of its acts by the directors, among whom was a great Scottish landowner, ruined those who had carried out their orders, and were otherwise involved in the enterprise. So great was the public indignation felt for the shareholders, and against the directors, who had succeeded in completely screening their own interests, that the affair, discussed in a leading article of the *Times* newspaper, was the immediate cause of the passing of the Limited Liability Act. But the severity of the shock to Mr. Leslie, who was made responsible for the whole failure, resulted in serious symptoms of brain pressure, from which he never entirely recovered, and which was greatly owing to the distress of mind he felt at being the innocent cause of losses to other people. His state was such that he was incapable of taking any steps towards settling his affairs, and the whole onus of investigating the extent of the failure and of meeting the creditors devolved on Mrs. Leslie, whose good sense and high principle gained for her the admiration of them all. It was at this crisis that Balnageith was sold. Another misfortune which occurred about this time was, as it were, the last straw in the weight which entirely crushed her husband's courage and the natural buoyancy with which he had borne up for so long against repeated reverses. For many years he had entertained hopes of making good his claim to two very large fortunes, left by one of his uncles in Cuba and by another in Louisiana, and of being thus able to satisfy all his creditors abundantly. But his health never permitted him to go to America, and an agent, whom he sent out in his place, proved unfaithful to the confidence reposed in him, appropriated large sums, and absconded.

In the midst of all these accumulated trials it was thought best that the family should remove to Scotland, where they could live more economically on the small income reserved for their most pressing needs, and where it was hoped that Mr. Leslie's health might improve.

All the painful business of the winding-up of affairs and the arrangements for the sale of their furniture was necessarily done by his wife. Kind and valued friends were not wanting to help and advise at this critical moment, but there was much to be done, the burden of which no friend, however experienced, could lift from her shoulders. When all was in order, one of the trustees said: "Mrs. Leslie is the best man of business I know."

They sailed from London on a Saturday evening in May, 1844. A number of old friends, among whom was Mr. George Honyman, came to see them off and wish them "God speed."

Mrs. Leslie's courage never failed for a moment, though her heart must have been heavy and her mind full of misgivings for the unknown future that lay dark and doubtful before them all. Bending over her children's berths, as they steamed slowly down the Thames, she suggested, in her usual brave clear tones, that the 22nd Psalm would be a good one to say till sleep came.

Late on Monday afternoon the weary travellers arrived in Edinburgh, and went straight to the house of the Dowager Lady Caithness in George Street.

To the three girls, who had spent the last few months in England at their grandfather's bright, sunny house on the Marine Parade, Brighton, the change was not a cheerful one. The house in George Street looked north, and its air of faded grandeur was melancholy. The furniture was heavy and antiquated, and painfully stiff in appearance. The pictures on the walls alone afforded some interest, and the young people at once noted the portraits of their father's uncles the Earl of Caithness, and Lord Duffus, the latter in a kilt. Their grandmother's portrait also came in for a share of their attention; but one of Mary Queen of Scots, painted at the time of her marriage, called forth all their enthusiasm. It was somewhat damping to their youthful spirits to find that the household was entirely composed of old people: their great-aunt, her daughter, Lady Charlotte McGregor, very beautiful and fair, but with hair a silvery white, an old Miss Sinclair, Lady Caithness's companion, a very old housekeeper and an equally venerable coachman—in fact the servants, horses, carriage, even the piano—everything was old. But the welcome they received was so warmly affectionate that the first rather chilling impression soon wore off, and the children were delighted to hear their father called "dearest Archie," and to see both their parents made much of, though it was somewhat of a relief to find that they themselves were to sleep at the house of Mr. Thomas Innes, a friend of their father's. However, after a day or two, Lady Caithness said it was better "to have the bairns under yer ain rooftree," and made arrangements to take them in also. It was, among other peculiarities, a clockless household, but the want of a clock by no means caused a deficit in punctuality—old Lady Caithness saw to that. She had had a blind brother, from whom she had inherited a watch with an embossed dial plate. With this watch in her hand, feeling it but not looking at it, she would walk up and down the house in the most stately manner, when the luncheon or dinner hour or any other formal solemnity was approaching, and emphatically inform all whom it might concern what time it was. She was a charming old lady, tall and still handsome, with a clear silvery voice, and when off her guard spoke with a broad Scotch accent. She was naturally hot-tempered, and moreover of a very delicate conscience. At night-prayers a chapter from the Book of Wisdom was read, and if some expression about a brawling woman occurred, the old lady would clear her throat in an odd way, just as she did when contradicted. The effect was indescribably funny.

On the days following the arrival of their relations from the south, the whole family came to greet them in George Street—Lord and Lady Caithness from Rutland Square, Colonel and Mrs. Sinclair, and Miss Catherine Sinclair the authoress. The younger Lady Caithness was usually called in the family "Lady Fanny," to distinguish her from her mother-in-law. She was a clever woman, admirable in many ways and very highly esteemed. She professed great friendship for Mrs. Leslie and was extremely kind to her children. "Lady Fanny's" eldest son, Lord Berriedale, had a remarkable talent for mechanics, and in his mother's drawing-room was a wonderful toy locomotive which he had made when a child. In a recess was an organ which he had built and which he would sometimes play, with one of his little cousins on his knee trying to take in his explanations about it during the many happy days they spent in the delightful house. Later on Lord Berriedale became a special favourite with the Prince Consort on account of his talents.*

On Sundays the Dowager Lady Caithness drove with her companion in her old-fashioned canary-coloured carriage to the Presbyterian church; but "Lady Fanny" had all the Leslie family with her at St. John's Episcopalian church, where Dean Ramsay and Mr. Berkeley Addison officiated. St. John's was a vision of beauty compared with the churches they had hitherto frequented at Wandsworth and Brighton. The services were carefully performed, the stained glass windows gave a certain warmth and colour to the building, and altogether church-going became more attractive than it had hitherto been.

After all that Mrs. Leslie had undergone during the past months, the cordial welcome from her husband's relations was naturally very cheering, and the sweetness of her daily intercourse with "Lady Fanny," whose High

* After he had become Earl of Caithness, his loyalty and love of mechanics combined prompted him to act as engine driver on the special train that brought the Princess of Wales to London before her marriage.

Churchism at this time resembled her own, was highly prized.

In the autumn other visits were paid before seeking a permanent home and settling down in it for the winter. Mr. Leslie and his eldest daughter went to stay with other members of his family in Banff and Morayshire, and also with the Gordon-Cummings at Altyre, his wife and younger daughters, Mary and Charlotte, going to Midshields on the banks of the Teviot, where Mrs. Leslie's brother, Mr. Falconer Atlee, had taken a place and was staying with his family. Here she found her son, who had been placed with a surveyor at Oxford, his holidays being generally spent at his uncle's. He was extremely fond of sport, and when his grandfather had offered to send him to college, with a view to his becoming a clergyman, he declined on the ground that he should not like to be "a shooting parson."

Midshields was a delightful place for a holiday, and they who were light-hearted young people then, recall with enduring affection the charm of its associations, the views in the neighbourhood, which took in the Minto Crags, the Ruberslaw and the fascinating Eildon Hills, the river with its picturesque windings, the charming walks by its rocky bed, the various expeditions to the ruined abbeys within reach, and the excursions to Branksome Hall. There was no Episcopalian church near, and on Sundays the morning service from the "Book of Common Prayer" was read in the drawing-room. This devotion was chiefly remarkable by the presence of a parrot which, if anyone happened to sneeze would upset the gravity of the congregation by screaming "Fi donc!"

As nothing suitable could be found in Edinburgh, a furnished house was taken at Portobello, and became the home of the Leslie family for the next eighteen months. It was hoped that the sea air would have a beneficial effect upon Mr. Leslie's health, and the society of Colonel and Mrs. Sinclair and of Lady Charlotte McGregor was an attraction to the place. The event proved auspicious in the acquisition of a new friend, the Rev. John Cunningham Robertson, chaplain to the Duke of Buccleuch, who came to live at Portobello until the chapel which was being built by the Duke in Dalkeith Park should be finished.

Mr. Robertson was a clergyman of the Church of England, a singularly devout and learned man, a thorough gentleman of great refinement, and well able to understand Mrs. Leslie's aspirations after all that was true and beautiful. With a keen insight into her character he was able to appreciate both the strength of her mind and the depth of her heart, qualities that made her so valuable and charming a friend. But it cannot be said that Mr. Robertson influenced her, or that he introduced her to any new development of doctrine.

Nevertheless, the devotions which she now practised with her children marked a decided advance on those of the later Wandsworth days. Some one, perhaps Mr. George Bridges, had sent her a manuscript copy of the "Litany of the Holy Ghost," and this prayer she encouraged her children to say at Pentecost. Mr. Robertson gave them the "Life of St. Stephen Harding," "The Birthday," "Amy Herbert," and other books which the children read with avidity. They were greatly surprised when the authoress Miss Sinclair stigmatized the three above mentioned as "the wickedest books that ever were written." These were followed by Herbert's poems and Bishop Cosin's "Devotions."

Although now following a different school, Mrs. Leslie retained as firm a hold as ever on the friendships which had been so much to her in the past. She was always intensely loyal to those whom she had once loved, and, as we have noticed elsewhere, never lost a friend by her own fault. Mr. Aitken had been the first to strike a deep note, to awaken in her a sense of God's claims. He had taught her the necessity of turning to God and of despising the world; and when he had accomplished this work, his mission to her apparently ceased. Beyond this point she was of more use to him than he was to her. Mr. Harris, both on account of his own personal holiness and of the truths he put before her, had great influence not only during the time when she came immediately in contact with him, but to the end of his life. To Mr. Gordon she owed her first notions on the subject of sacramental grace and her release from the bonds of Calvinistic narrowness. Once, when Mr. Robertson was going to London on a visit, Mrs. Leslie asked him to call on the two first of these old friends. Afterwards, in describing his meeting with them, he said that Mr. Aitken had given him an idea of St. Paul, and Mr. Harris of St. John the Evangelist. When Mr. Robertson removed to Dalkeith, the Leslies visited him there, and the children came to look upon him as a sort of spiritual guide and adviser. During one of these visits the two youngest children asked him for an ejaculatory prayer or maxim, and to one of them he replied, "In quietness and in confidence shall be thy strength." To the other he said, "As the hart pants after the fountains of water, so does my soul long after Thee, O God!"

Then he gave them his blessing and traced a cross on their heads.

These visits to Dalkeith resulted in a friendship with Cecil Lady Lothian, which only ended at her death, many years afterwards. Everything was now converging towards the confession of a definite and permanent faith by Mrs. Leslie and by the greater number of those who have already appeared in this memoir in connection with her. At Portobello she became acquainted with a Catholic priest, a Mr. Clapperton. Colonel Sinclair, whose kindness was such that he could not bear to see any one lonely or neglected, and thinking that this gentleman might be both, invited him to dinner and Mr. and Mrs. Leslie to meet him. On this occasion Mrs. Leslie first heard of the existence of a convent in Edinburgh, and not long afterwards the whole family, under Mr. Clapperton's guidance, paid their first visit to St. Margaret's, a convent with which they were afterwards closely connected.

During this time Mrs. Leslie mainly occupied herself with the education of her two younger girls. Eleanor was already grown up and was very little with her parents, often paying long visits to friends and relations, who took her out. She had been brought up partly by her aunt, Mrs. Maxwell, a thoroughly good and conscientious woman, who, however, had little sympathy with her sister's advanced opinions, and it was therefore natural that Eleanor should be somewhat estranged from the rest of her family, and should hold herself aloof from their views and convictions. Later on she lived for long intervals with Lord and Lady Caithness, who had no daughter, and to whom in a manner she supplied the place of one.

The months at Portobello passed away not unpleasantly. There was plenty of variety in the life there, although Mrs. Leslie took care that in their altered circumstances great simplicity should be observed in every detail of their household and dress, which she insisted should be as inexpensive as possible. Occasionally old Lady Caithness sent her carriage for them all, and sometimes the children would be sent alone to visit her. When they went alone, she thought it her duty to read for their edification four chapters from the Book of Proverbs every day, two in the morning and two in the evening. The Sunday evening family prayers would have had the most soporific effect on the children but for the fascination of watching the expression of old Robbie, the coachman, who always made the most horrible faces in his efforts to keep himself awake.

Meanwhile the days at Portobello were drawing to a close. In the spring of 1846 Mr. Leslie and his two youngest daughters paid a visit to Mr. and Lady Janet Buchanan at Blairvadoch on the Gairloch, while Mrs. Leslie went to her brother's in Roxburghshire. The following summer saw them all established in a small apartment in Castle Street, Edinburgh, with the exception of the two eldest children, who were in England. It was an exceedingly hot summer, and one of Mrs. Leslie's daughters had a sunstroke which ended in a dangerous fever through which her mother nursed her. In the autumn they removed to a furnished house in Minto Street, where they spent the most important year of their lives.

CHAPTER VII.

THE PARTING OF THE WAYS.

HITHERTO the pursuit of truth had been accompanied only by consolations. Every new gleam faithfully followed had led to an abundant increase of light and grace, but the time was now rapidly approaching when the logical consequences which cut through marrow and bone must be accepted in the same spirit of faith, and we shall find that Mrs. Leslie did not shrink from them.

Bossuet's "Exposition de la Doctrine de l'Église Catholique," and some letters of Fénelon's to a Protestant gentleman had brought her very near to the Catholic Church, and she had long been familiar with nearly every doctrine that the Church teaches. Her son objecting one day to prayers for the dead, she exclaimed, "Oh, don't talk of that. I never could help praying for the dead since Lady Cumming died."* Perhaps it was the reception into the Church of several of her friends that made her own position clear to her, showing her the necessity of a last definite step before she could be in full

* Wife of Sir William Gordon-Cumming of Altyre.

possession of that truth which she had always loved.

Mr. Harris, who had been unconsciously a Catholic at heart all his life, had at last realised that it was not presumption but duty that urged him to claim his birthright as a member of the one true Church, and his example of entering into actual communion with it was followed about the same time by several others.

A few young men of Catholic tendencies, who were under the impression that a priest had said they were justified in remaining as they were for the present, were living with Mr. Oakeley, of All Saints', Margaret Street, London.* Among them was Mrs. Leslie's friend, Mr. George Bridges, and a Mr. Tickell, who carried their austerities to such extremes that the latter fell ill, and was obliged to go abroad for his health. Their mode of life has been aptly described as "the practice of spirituality without licence." While Mr. Tickell was in Belgium he fell in with some members of the Weld family, who convinced him that his position was an unsafe one, and he accordingly became a Catholic. On his return to London he burst into his friend's room, saying, "Bridges, this is all humbug. I

* Afterwards, as a Catholic, Canon Oakeley, of St. John's, Islington.

have a cab at the door; come and be received into the Church." He was so changed that Mr. Bridges scarcely knew him, and in a few days the friends were again united in one faith. Tickell had won the Eldon scholarship at Oriel College, Oxford, and one day two undergraduates were talking of his conversion. One of them was defending him against the other, who was turning over the leaves of a novel as he spoke, and by a curious coincidence his eyes fell upon this verse:

I see a hand thou canst not see, which beckons me away;
I hear a voice thou canst not hear, which says I must not stay. TICKELL.

Mr. Robertson was also advancing, though more slowly, in the same direction. Miss Henderson, a bitter Protestant friend of "Lady Fanny's," had given to Mrs. Leslie's children a quantity of beads made of berries from the Garden of Gethsemane, and suggested that they should be strung into necklaces. The children showed them to Mr. Robertson, whose eyes filled with tears as he begged them to bestow some on him. When they next saw those which they had given him, he had threaded them in decades, with a little cross attached, forming a rosary. He explained to them the antiquity and origin of counting prayers on beads, and taught them to say the rosary, substituting the *Gloria Patri*

THE PARTING OF THE WAYS. 93

for the *Ave Maria*. In the same way he instructed them in the devotion of the *Angelus*, but not at first with the *Hail Mary*. Then Mr. Bridges gave Mrs. Leslie the little prayer book "Flowers of Piety," containing the Jesus Psalter, the rosary prayers and the ordinary litanies. This book was regarded as a treasure; the children copied out the rosary prayers, and henceforth both Mary and Charlotte said the rosary daily together as well as they knew how, having strung their Gethsemane beads also into decades. From time to time they called at St. Margaret's Convent and obtained the loan of books, among others of "The Travels of an Irish Gentleman in Search of a Religion" and Milner's "End of Controversy." These were carefully read, and notes taken on all the controverted or difficult points.

At length Mrs. Leslie felt that she could delay no longer in taking the decisive step which for some time she had seen was inevitable if she would follow the dictates of her conscience. Letters from Mr. Harris also helped her to see all that was dangerous in her actual position, being, as she was, a Catholic at heart, and yet for want of that one step forward, outside the Church. She asked her husband's permission to be received, well knowing that he would not forbid it; but such was her love of obedience, that she sought to embrace it, as on all other occasions, so in the most important act of her life. Mr. Leslie was much grieved and distressed at her decision, although he respected to the full the purity and sincerity of her motive. Afterwards, in speaking to Mr. Clapperton, the priest at Portobello, he expressed this in touching words, adding that she had long been accustomed to consider the will of God in all things, and that she would often get up in the middle of the night to pray. Still, to her husband the result was a fearful pang, and he felt that her reception into the Church was indeed the separation for God's sake from all whom she so dearly loved. He consulted the Caithnesses and the Honymans. "Lady Fanny's" high and dry Anglicanism came to the front at once, and it was intimated to Mrs. Leslie that if she became a Catholic the friendship that existed between her and her husband's cousins would be severed once and for all, and that their doors would be closed to her for ever. The threat was accompanied by a word of advice to Mr. Leslie. The two younger girls should be sent at once to separate schools, away from their mother's and from mutual influence. Sir Ord Honyman was, on the other hand, a most faithful and loyal friend to Mrs. Leslie, urging that no harsh measures should be taken, and adopting throughout that time of suspense and anxiety a tone as liberal as it was sensible and just. By his influence it was at last arranged that for a time, at least, the two girls were to remain at home, with the understanding that conversation with their mother on religious subjects was to be avoided by all three. Eleanor, whose Protestant education made her extremely hostile and bitter, was fortunately a great deal absent at the time, "Lady Fanny" showing her appreciation of the young girl's attitude by inviting her more and more frequently to Rutland Square.

The day fixed for Mrs. Leslie's abjuration was December 3, the feast of St. Francis Xavier, and her own birthday. She had made her confession to Bishop Gillis the previous evening, and left Minto Street alone and on foot in the early morning of the cold, dark winter's day. The ground was slippery and walking was difficult as she made her way towards St. Margaret's Convent, the outside cheerlessness of things being increased by a sharp mental struggle, which seemed like a last attempt of nature to draw her back when the goal was almost reached. In her agony of mind she prayed that if indeed she were mistaken and about to do anything wrong, God would allow her to fall and break her leg, or be otherwise hindered from carrying out her intention. But the momentary doubt and hesitation yielded to perfect contentment as she knelt before the altar in the convent chapel and was made for ever a child of the Catholic Church. The ceremony was followed by Bishop Gillis saying Mass, at which the new convert received Holy Communion. On her return to Minto Street she was welcomed by Mary and Charlotte with joyful congratulations, and the day which she always regarded as her second birthday, and which to the last year of her life she celebrated with special thanksgivings, was passed by all three in the most fervent dispositions of gratitude and hope; for while Mrs. Leslie rejoiced in having been permitted to attain to the end towards which she had been journeying ever since she first awoke to a sense of the objectiveness of truth and of God's claim to the obedience of every created soul, she and her two children might now look forward to being soon again outwardly united, as they were already one in faith. Nor was it a time to despair of the conversion of the other three beloved members of her family, little likely as it then appeared; and perhaps it was the earnest prayers offered on their behalf on this ever-memorable feast of St. Francis

Xavier that obtained for them, in course of time, the same grace and blessing. Meanwhile, however, there were rough roads to be trodden, and it was no doubt a trial to all when, on the following Sundays, Mrs. Leslie went to Mass and her husband took the children to the Protestant church. They would have preferred the more advanced and less gloomy services at St. John's, but their father liked St. George's, in York Place, a hideous little chapel, served by the Rev. Mr. Suther, afterwards Bishop of Aberdeen. Occasionally they were taken to Trinity Church, a cold, uninviting building on the Dean Bridge, where the services were made as uninteresting as possible. As time went on the feelings and prejudices of their relations made themselves felt. The displeasure of some was expressed with the greatest acrimony and in unmeasured terms. "Lady Fanny" broke off all intercourse with Mrs. Leslie, but old Lady Caithness never ceased to be kind. She loved and was proud of the whole family, and stuck to them when others expressed their disapproval by harsh words or an unbroken silence. As one after the other joined the Catholic Church, all she would say was a surprised "Gude be here!" clearing her throat in the way peculiar to her. Once Mrs. Leslie, with Mary and Charlotte, was staying at her house when "Lady Fanny" came to call. She was sharp and rude in her remarks, and Mrs. Leslie grew faint as she heard herself called "an apostate." The kind old lady took her to her room and applied restoratives, and when she was sufficiently recovered soothed her in the tenderest way, saying: "My dear, we all thought you so perfect and charming we did not see the necessity for any change; but it's no for us to judge, and there should be nae condemnation."

After this the estrangement between the Leslies and Lord and Lady Caithness was complete; but unkind as "Lady Fanny" had been, Mrs. Leslie always fought her battles, as she had hitherto been in the habit of doing. She was not liked by any of the Sinclairs, and there were many opportunities of putting in a good word for her, none of which were missed. Years afterwards, Mrs. Leslie came to breakfast one morning saying, "I have been dreaming all night of 'Lady Fanny,' and thought she was dying and begging my pardon for all her unkindness." They had not heard anything about her for a long time, and did not know that she was ill. It was therefore very startling to find during the day that she had died the night before.

Colonel James Sinclair, brother of Lord Caithness, was one of the most interesting members of the family. He and Mr. Leslie had grown up together, and used to be spoken of in their time as "beautiful dancers," a notable distinction in days when dancing was looked upon as a fine art. He was devoted to Mrs. Leslie, and shortly before she went to Portobello, meeting an old Miss Maclaren, the sister of a Major Maclaren, an old Indian officer, who by much study had been converted from the Presbyterian form of worship to Episcopalianism, said: "Oh, Miss Maclaren, I hope soon to have the pleasure of introducing my cousin Mrs. Leslie to you. Except your brother, she is the most deeply read theologian I ever knew. She has converted hundreds of Jews, to say nothing of Jewesses, and her success with sinners is quite unparalleled." When he next saw Mrs. Leslie he told her of the reputation he had given her, and amusingly entreated her not to let him down. His life had been a stirring one. A war broke out soon after he had entered the army, and his parents, more concerned for his safety than for his career as a soldier, tried to get his commission cancelled. But as soon as he knew what they were about, he went off to the War Office as fast as four horses could take him, and asked to be sent to Canada, the seat of war. His regiment ran from a very hot fire, but young Sinclair, then an ensign, stood firm with his colours, and swore at the men to come back. After this he was for some time with the Scots Greys, and when he left the army he became member for Caithness in Parliament. The same careless, light-hearted temperament which made him so dauntless, and at the same time so attractive, was the cause of his reckless extravagance. He was always hopelessly in debt, and one day Mr. Leslie said to him:

"Jimmy, why don't you call your creditors together and let them see that you have no money to pay them?"

"Oh, my dear fellow," answered his cousin, pathetically, " I couldn't live but for the excitement they keep me in."

As might be expected, Colonel Sinclair was absolutely indifferent to Mrs. Leslie's change of religion, except for the gratification which his sense of humour received from the attitude of her various relations and friends. His love of fun and mischief found vent in the midst of the most unpromising material, and he would make huge signs of the Cross at his mother's table before dinner to cause her to think that he, too, had become a Catholic, and draw forth some of her caustic remarks.

Mrs. Sinclair and her sister, Miss Tritton, had been among Mrs. Leslie's earliest friends.

They were both women of most amiable dispositions, and although they felt her conversion deeply, they did not allow their prejudices to interfere with the warm affection they had always felt for her. It was at their father's house at Wandsworth that Mr. Leslie had first met his future wife, he having been introduced to the Trittons by Colonel Sinclair.

Some time after her reception into the Church, Mrs. Leslie met Miss Maclaren, and held out her hand to greet her as usual. Miss Maclaren drew back, and looked as if at a perfect stranger. "Do you not recognise me? I am Mrs. Leslie." "Oh, yes," answered the old lady; "I know who you are, but you have fallen into darkness since I last saw you." "If that is your opinion," said Mrs. Leslie, "you had better pray to Him who brought light out of darkness, to enlighten me and all others who may need His divine light."

Throughout this trying time Mr. Leslie never swerved from the high-minded and generous position he had taken up towards his wife, treating her with the greatest consideration and confidence. He was obliged at the beginning of the new year to take a short journey on business, and in view of the uncertainty of life, his own in particular, on account of the precarious state of his health, he thought it well to provide for all possible emergencies, and wrote a touching letter which he left with Mrs. Leslie. It ran thus:

16, Minto Street, January 4, 1847.

MY BELOVED WIFE,—As I am going on a journey tomorrow and considering the fragility of human life, I leave this with you, to request that you pay that maternal care towards all our children which you have ever so faithfully evinced towards them, and that no other person be allowed to have any interference with you in this respect. As you promised to me in your recent change of religion from that in which you were brought up to that of the Church of Rome (and I know that you made this change from the purest motives alone) that you would not attempt to bias their young minds, which I implore you not to do, and knowing you as I do in every relation of life, I should prefer them to be under your guidance to that of any other person on earth. I leave this in case of need, at your request, but hope we may yet live some happy years together. I am ever your affectionate husband,

To Mrs. Leslie. ARCHIBALD LESLIE.

As regards the manner in which Mrs. Leslie's own relations viewed the step she had taken, the results were various. Her brother's attitude was entirely neutral, owing to his complete aloofness from every form of religion. And he was at least consistent in this, that he considered every one free to follow his own bent, whether that bent inclined towards infidelity or Catholicism. Opinions among her three sisters were divided. Mrs. Maxwell's strong Protestantism caused her to write with indignation expressed in no measured terms. Madame de Pambour had herself become a Catholic and could sympathise heartily with Mrs. Leslie, and her youngest sister Emily, married to the Rev. Henry Dowson, an Anglican clergyman of no great mental weight or decided views, could only echo her husband's feeble protests. But every post brought letters expressing sympathy or displeasure. Mr. Aitken's ultimatum was characteristic of the man. His letter ended as follows :

> You will be damned, I believe, eternally. I remain yours affectionately, ROBERT AITKEN.

CHAPTER VIII.

REUNION.

MARY and Charlotte Leslie meanwhile remained firm in their determination to follow their mother into the Catholic Church. They were so visibly unhappy at the delay in their being permitted to do so that Mr. Leslie was distressed, and puzzled how to act. At last he determined to seek counsel, and, having fallen upon a paper written by the two girls in which they stated their reasons for wishing to become Catholics, he called upon Bishop Terrot, as the highest authority in the Episcopal Church, to ask his advice. The bishop tried to shirk the interview, but read the paper—so admirably clear, reasonable and forcible a document, drawn up as it was by the unaided intelligence of two mere children, aged respectively fifteen and thirteen, that it is worth reproducing.

> About six years ago [they wrote] one of the curates of Wandsworth, Mr. John Gordon, who has lately become a Catholic, gave us several little books which contained a great deal of Catholic doctrine. A short time after, another very kind Roman Catholic friend gave us a little Catholic story called "The Young Communicants," explanatory of the sacraments of penance and of the Blessed Eucharist, which made a deep impression on our minds.

REUNION.

In August last our brother came from Oxford, and, being much interested in Catholicity, read a great many books on both sides of the question, and repeated to us what he had read. On going to St. Margaret's Convent one day, Sister Agnes Xavier lent papa several books, among others "Dr. Wiseman's Lectures," which Mary read; and the result of our investigation during the months of August and September was this: that the Roman Catholic Church is the Church referred to in Scripture and in the Creeds (where but one is spoken of), and consequently the only true one.

We then formed our resolution of becoming Catholics as soon as possible, *wholly unknown to Mama;* in fact, we had many doubts how best to communicate to her our resolution, when to our great joy, she told us that she was going to join the Catholic Church, and then we began to entertain hopes that we might be allowed to follow her steps. While we know that in everything we owe the greatest respect and obedience to our dear father's wishes, we *never could* agree with his belief even in the Anglican Church; for, as long as we can recollect, he has always denied baptismal regeneration and regarded that sacrament merely as a form by which a name is given, and as one proper to be complied with for the sake of being registered. When we were confirmed, two years ago by Bishop Terrot, he told us in his address, that we were then made responsible beings for the way in which we followed out our own conscientious convictions of right and wrong. This being a matter of conscience, we hope that we may not be forced to act against our convictions which we were then told were to be the rule of our actions. Any violent attempt to make us renounce our faith in the Catholic Church, or to separate us from Mama would, we feel, break our hearts, and injure our health, while our faith would be confirmed by opposition, and rendered firmer than ever.

We cannot help feeling the greatest love and respect for the Blessed Virgin Mary; and being sure that her prayers must be far more acceptable than ours, we daily ask her intercession with our Lord at this time (as we ask the prayers of our earthly friends) that we may be delivered from our present trying situation. If we were on our deathbeds tomorrow, all our cry would be to see a Catholic priest, and that we might be received into the Church, in order to receive the benefit of the last sacraments and the prayers of the Church for the rest of our souls.

Having been always instructed in religion by Mama, and holding in *all* respects the same faith as she does, is it not more natural that we should wish to remain under her instruction rather than under that of Papa, whose faith is so entirely opposed to our own, as he constantly affirms that he considers the Presbyterian the best form of religion, while *we in all things hold the Catholic faith?* Should he be disposed to listen to our earnest supplications, we can only assure him of greater love and gratitude than any other gift or indulgence could call forth.

MARY MARGARET LESLIE.
CHARLOTTE CUMMING LESLIE.

After reading the above uncompromising confession of faith, Bishop Terrot recommended that the two girls should be dealt with by the Rev. Mr. Salter of St. George's and the Rev. Mr. Alexander of St. Columba's, whose High Church principles were more likely to commend themselves to those leaning towards Rome. But Mr. Leslie was firm, insisting that as his girls had been confirmed by Dr. Terrot, he was the proper person to reason with them. A day was therefore fixed, and the interview took place.

The bishop's advice was that they should "search the Scriptures," and that by so doing they would be led into all truth. Charlotte quietly remarked that they could not be expected to decide on the explanation of certain texts which were disputed by the most learned men among Protestants, and that even the bishop himself and several of his clergy would give different explanations of the words "This is my Body," and of many other passages in Scripture. The bishop was unwilling to continue the discussion, and repeated his injunction to "read and pray."

The children's next interview was with Mr. Suther, and this took place on the feast of the Conversion of St. Paul, in the little vestry at St. George's, after the morning service. It was the last time that Mary and Charlotte went to the Anglican service, and on this occasion they occupied themselves with reciting the Rosary instead of following the Protestant prayers. When the Congregation had dispersed, the clerk conducted the party to the vestry, where Mr. Suther received them in all the borrowed dignity of surplice and hood. He took an entirely different line from the bishop, insisted on the duty of loyalty to the Church of one's baptism, and declared that the Anglican Church possessed all means of grace as fully as the Romish Communion, and was in fact the same thing, excepting the supremacy of the Pope, which he sneeringly said, he supposed could be dispensed with.

Mary replied, "We will listen to anything you say to us if you promise that the other clergymen of your Church will say the same thing."

He then declared that St. Cyprian had denied the supremacy of the Pope and had written : "The other apostles were vested like Peter with an equal participation of honour and power." Here he stopped, and Charlotte, who had seen the context in the book "An Irish Gentleman in Search of a Religion," and had committed it to memory, completed the sentence from St. Cyprian: "But the beginning is built on *Unity*, and therefore St. Peter was made the head of the others, to secure unity."

Mr. Suther owned that this was substantially correct, and added, "St. Cyprian even said something still stronger elsewhere; but I have not studied the Fathers much lately, I must confess." He then urged the children to receive communion again in his church. This they positively refused to do, and becoming more and more embarrassed, he got into fresh difficulties at each step.

"If the Pope is not head of the Church, do you acknowledge the Queen as such?" asked one of the children.

"Certainly not," replied Mr. Suther.

"Who is then the head of your Church? Is it the Archbishop of Canterbury?"

Mr. Suther supposed it might be he. His

parting words were said with an air of real distress: "I hope you will stay with us, because——" The conclusion never came, and so they went away. Mr. Leslie, in spite of the signal defeat of the disputants on his side, could not disguise his pride in the intelligence of his children, and described the visit afterwards with a humorous appreciation of the scene that was extremely amusing.

After the above proof of the strength of the enemy, Mr. Alexander elected to call and see Mrs. Leslie in preference to interrogating her daughters. His arguments, which of course ended in nothing, consisted mainly of reproaches for having abandoned the Church of her baptism.

"If," answered Mrs. Leslie, "my baptism as a child was valid, I was by that fact admitted into the Catholic Church, as there is but '*one faith, one Lord, one baptism.*' Hence she is my true Mother. I have been in the position of a child that has been changed at nurse; and by circumstances beyond my control I have been brought up in estrangement from my Mother. When once I recognized this and found out where she was, could I do otherwise than return to her?"

Mr. Alexander declined to argue with the children, and took his leave. Here the matter seemed likely to end, for Mr. Leslie still withheld his consent to their reception into the Church.

Bishop Gillis then wrote out the following instructions for their conduct:

> Let the two children cast themselves at their father's feet, and with every affectionate expression of respect and obedience represent to him in the most unequivocal and firm manner that, much as they would grieve to appear even to slight his parental authority, they cannot in the present instance abstain from declaring to him the utter impossibility for them to receive Communion in the Church of England without feeling themselves chargeable before God, and on evidence of their own conscience, of an act of gross hypocrisy. Let them then implore him through the value he sets on their immortal souls, and through his love for them as a parent, not to drive them to say that they feel this to be an occasion in which they are called upon to declare that they must obey God rather than man; but that, taking into consideration their temporal as well as eternal happiness, he will kindly permit them to have the subject reconsidered by their father and by themselves, in the presence of the bishop, to whom he has been already so condescending as to listen to on this matter in their presence. That as to their not being fit as yet to judge for themselves, they feel that God may call them out of the world before they are much more so in the eyes of others, and that were such to be the case to-morrow, they cannot help believing as Christians, and feeling as human beings, that they would be considered by the Almighty *old enough to be judged*, and that they must be judged according to their works and the faithfulness with which they would have followed out their conscientious convictions, however limited the development of their intellectual faculties."

But before the two girls had time to act on these directions, an unlooked-for intervention of Providence made all further persuasion unnecessary. Mr. Leslie was engaged in some business with a gentleman at Leith, and in returning home on foot one evening in February was knocked down by a cab, the approach of which, as he was partially deaf, he did not hear. Escaping without injury beyond a slight shock to his nerves, he said nothing of what had happened until Mrs. Leslie, noticing that night that he was not sleeping as usual, asked if he were unwell. He then told her of the accident, and said that he thought his life had been spared in order that he might offer his children to God. He withdrew his opposition, and the next day went to Dalkeith to consult Mr. Robertson as to the steps to be taken. Mr. Robertson advised him to allow the two children to enter the Catholic Church at once; and when their father returned, and told them that such was his decision, their joy knew no bounds.

Eleanor was then staying with Sir Ord and Lady Honyman, and they were taking her with their own daughter to one of the Edinburgh Assemblies that evening. Mr. Leslie had promised to be one of the party. He drove round by Greenhill, and had an interview with Bishop Gillis to inform him of his altered purpose with regard to his two youngest children. The bishop promised to call in Minto Street the next day, to arrange for their immediate reception into the Church.

Nothing could have been more satisfactory than this interview; but to provide against the possibility of Dr. Gillis being absent when her husband called, Mrs. Leslie had written the following letter, which he took with him:

> My Dear Lord,—Mr. Leslie hopes to see you himself this evening. In case he should be disappointed, he requests me to say that he commits his beloved girls May and Chattie to your care, desirous at once to do so as a thank-offering to Almighty God for His most providential care of him last night when his life was in imminent peril, and as the best atonement he can make to yourself for his unkind misconstruction of your advice. I did not see Mr. Alexander this morning, as he had already left his chapel, but I have written him a careful and polite note this evening. My dear girls desire more love and thanks than this note will carry, and with our kindest regards to Miss Maxwell,* believe me, my dear Lord, your very grateful and obedient servant,   Eleanor Leslie.
>
> 16 Minto Street, Edinburgh, February 4, 1847.

No further time was lost. It was arranged that the two girls were to go to Greenhill on Saturday, the 6th, to make their general confessions, and that they should receive conditional baptism, holy communion, and confirmation the next day, which was Sexagesima Sunday.

They were left in the dining-room at Greenhill to prepare for confession. Presently the bishop opened the door and asked them if they were ready. Charlotte was nearest to the door and answered in her

---

* A lady who lived at Greenhill, and kept house for the Bishop.

downright way: "I'm as ready as I shall ever be," and he took her to the chapel. They were thus at last at the goal of all their desires, and who shall describe the touching scene as they knelt during Mass and communion the following morning beside their happy mother? With them were confirmed Mrs. Leslie, and a Mrs. Henshaw Jones, a recent convert and a real confessor of the faith. She was the wife of a Protestant clergyman, and for a time suffered much on account of her religion. Then she was left a widow, and was able to lead a peaceful and useful life.*

On the evening of the day on which his daughters were received into the Church, Mr. Leslie dined at Sir Ord Honyman's, and was as usual cheered and encouraged by his old friend's kindness and sterling good sense. "Be a man, Archie," said his host, "and show the world that you can live as happily with your wife and children now, as you have always done hitherto." The advice, however well-meant, was scarcely necessary, for nothing could exceed the generosity with

* One evening at her house, Russell, editor of the *Scotsman*, and Dr. Shain, Archbishop of Edinburgh, were playing cards together, and the game ended by the archbishop winning one penny. Russell said: "Now that penny will be spent on some vile superstition." "Yes," replied the archbishop, "I will buy a *Scotsman* with it."

which Mr. Leslie had made his sacrifice. On that very morning, when he had heard his wife and children going out, he had left his room and with touching tenderness embraced them, begging that their affection for him might suffer no change or diminution by their change of religion. They had assured him that on the contrary it would only be increased, and that they would be more dutiful and loving to him than ever. He was indeed a most affectionate father, excellent in all the relations of life, a loyal friend, beloved and esteemed by all who knew him.

Since the reverses of 1843, the Leslies had never had a settled home, but had lived in furnished houses and lodgings when not paying visits to their many friends and relations. This was inconvenient in many ways, and in the spring of 1847 they looked out for an unfurnished house, and finally settled to take No. 2 Fingal Place, on the south side of the Meadows. For the Catholics of the family its nearness to St. Margaret's Convent and to Bishop Gillis was an attraction, and for all, the position and the beauty of the views were a recommendation. Mrs. Leslie had a talent for making her surroundings pleasant and homelike wherever they might be; but now she could at last have her own furniture as far as it sufficed, and choose what was necessary over and above. They took possession of their new abode with great thankfulness, the young members of the family rejoicing to have at last a home bearing some resemblance to that of their childhood. If Minto Street left many happy souvenirs, Fingal Place was to perpetuate and intensify their gratitude.

In the holidays came Mrs. Leslie's son. After shooting with his uncle, and taking a walking tour in the Highlands, books came in for a share of his attention. He had already seen Milner's "End of Controversy" on one of his former visits to Edinburgh, and had devoured it, thinking at first that it was a Protestant book and would show that one religion was as good as another. When he had returned to Oxford he tried to get a copy of it, but failed. Burgon of Oriel told him that it was "an unknown book." On this occasion Mrs. Leslie would answer any objections which he made to the Catholic religion. She gave him Bossuet's "Exposition de la doctrine de l'Église Catholique," Fénelon's "Letters to a Protestant Gentleman," and Butler's "Lives of the Saints." These books had a great effect in showing forth a high Christian standard which had no counterpart in Anglicanism. He was sick of controversy and wanted to have done with it, and was disgusted with the divisions in the Church of England. At Oxford High Churchmen used to meet on Tuesday evenings at Oriel; and, as young Leslie had many friends among them, he was invited. It was thought a great privilege that any one not a University man should be admitted to this select circle. But in spite of some attractions he was repelled by the disputes, the sneering tone adopted towards Low Churchmen, and by the simpering style which, to him, savoured of anything but religion. He went to the priest at Oxford, a gentle, simple old man, who, when he heard the name of his visitor, told him that that mission had been founded by a Father Leslie.* But his conversion was not yet. The branch theory of Anglicanism was then sprung upon him, and several Fellows of Oriel, learned men, among whom were Burgon and Charles Marriot, gave him to understand that if he read the Fathers he would see that the Church of Rome had gone wrong, and that the Church of England was like that of early Christianity. Upon this came Mr. Allies' book, "The Church of England cleared from the charge of Schism," which deterred

* One of the Leslies of Fetternear. This branch of the family had always remained Catholic. Several of them had been members of the Society of Jesus, and notably the founder of the Oxford Mission, who had settled there during the suppression of the Society.

a good many people at that time from swelling the number of "Rome's Recruits." With these counter-influences at work, it was natural for a sensitive conscience to become persuaded that "loyalty to the Church of one's baptism," a cant phrase which misled many about that time, was the first of virtues, and that to seek communion with the parent stem was to be unfaithful to the branch. Young Leslie determined, therefore, to avail himself of every means of grace the Church of England offered, going to daily prayers and to Communion every week, for which he prepared himself carefully by reading through the whole fourth book of the "Imitation."

He was scrupulously exact about his debts, and having owed a few pounds to his tailor for two or three terms, although the man did not press for his money, was in doubt whether he ought to write home about it. Feeling at last very uncomfortable, he applied to Eden, Fellow of Oriel, to hear his confession. Eden referred him to Rew, of St. John's, the clergyman of his parish. Mr. Leslie accordingly sent Eden's letter on to Rew, who answered that he might come to him the next morning. When his penitent appeared, Mr. Rew, looking very wretched and as if he had not long been out of bed, placed a chair for him and listened with a deprecating air while the young man told him the cause of his troubled conscience. He at once generously offered to lend him any money that was required to pay the tailor without enquiring about the amount needed. "No," replied Leslie, "that would never do; but must I tell my father?" "Yes," that was inevitable, and being too late for breakfast at the surveyor's, Mr. Leslie turned into Christchurch Walk, where he presently became very contrite and very hungry. It occurred to him to go to breakfast with Ffoulkes, of Jesus College, and as he walked in there was a shout from the party assembled which took away his appetite.

"Why, Leslie, you are eating nothing!" exclaimed Ffoulkes. "Don't you know," said Dean,* "he is the most mortified man in Oxford?—never takes anything for breakfast but a sheet of note paper and a glass of water."

Then to his horror in came Rew. They exchanged a few words, and Leslie got away as soon as possible.

When he had made a clean breast of his debt to his father and had got a reply, he sent to ask Mr. Rew if he might come to him for absolution. Rew answered that he might safely apply it to himself when it was read out in church.

* Fellow of All Souls and vicar of Lewknor.   He became a Catholic later on.

Although put back by the branch theory, he never altogether dropped Mr. Newsham, the good Catholic priest on whom he had once called, and driving one summer's evening in a small trap with his friend Dean, saw him looking very poor and shabby, and took off his hat as they passed. Dean did the same, and Leslie asked him if he knew to whom he had bowed.

"Not in the least," answered the other; and when his friend told him that the shabby stranger was a Catholic priest he became alarmed for Mr. Leslie's Anglicanism.

The time was indeed approaching when the object of so many fervent prayers could no longer content himself with a system of compromise and shallow theories. Having completed his time with the Oxford surveyor he returned to Edinburgh. He tried to explain the branch theory to his mother and sisters, and, hoping to convince them of the truth of it, he told them of his intense sensible devotion in receiving Holy Communion. But when they asked him what he believed that he received, although he *felt* a great deal at the moment of Communion he could explain nothing. He read Newman's "Essay on Development," and one day as he was walking near the Grass Market he began to think over his Oxford friend's advice to read the

Fathers. He went to the Advocates' Library and set about studying, but soon found out that reading the Fathers would be a long and, to him, an impossible undertaking. Then the thought struck him that our Lord gave a religion to poor, unlettered, though, of course, reasonable people, and that if, say, a pagan carpenter wanted to know something about the true religion it would be absurd to tell him to read the Fathers. He might very well protest that what he required was a plain and simple explanation, fit for the ignorant and for those who had no time to spend in diving into huge tomes, or wit to weigh subtleties and to pronounce on questions intended only for theologians. The carpenter would say, "If you had good, plain reasons suitable for me you would not tell me to read the Fathers."

The young man then reflected as to what he would say if such an unlearned pagan came to him for instruction. First he would ask him whether he believed that our Lord Jesus Christ was God. If he got an answer in the affirmative, he would then ask, "Did not Jesus Christ give us a religion and promise that this religion should not go wrong?" The conclusion was evident, and reasoning thus he overcame the difficulties raised by his learned friends, and on September 8, 1848, was received into the Catholic Church at St. Margaret's. It is almost superfluous to add that Mrs. Leslie looked on this as one of the happiest days of her life.

Her daughter Eleanor was meanwhile becoming softened towards the Catholic members of her family, and would sometimes do little acts of kindness which were keenly appreciated. One cold morning, knowing that her mother was going out early, she got up and had a cup of coffee ready for her when she came downstairs. But Mrs. Leslie was going to receive Holy Communion and could not therefore accept the graceful offering; but it pained her to refuse the first act of kindness she had received from her eldest daughter for a long time, the girl not understanding why. In other respects Eleanor had many of the charming qualities which endeared the other members of the family to all who came in close contact with them. She shared their intense love for the poor and would spare no pains or self-denial to help those in distress. A pretty example of this was her self-imposed study of a method of reading for the blind, in the hope of teaching an old man who, but for Mr. Atlee's timely intervention, would have fallen over the cliff at Brighton. Eleanor succeeded in mastering the system while still in her 'teens and in communicating it to her aged pupil, who wept for joy the first time that he could read a few words from the Gospels for himself. His daughter's sight was also failing, and Miss Leslie did not rest until she too had learned the art that was to be a consolation in the dark days to come. She was not rich enough to pay the debt which was a crushing weight on the minds of the blind man and his daughter, but she interested her friends in their behalf and, helped by her grandfather and others, she was able at last to take the required sum to her protégés.

By degrees she was led to take an interest in the numerous charities in which her mother and sisters were engaged, and was thus drawn into intercourse with Catholics outside her own family. A visit to the Monteiths of Carstairs, who had recently been converted to Catholicism, also helped to dispel prejudices and to prepare her mind for the reception of the truth. She had some interviews with Protestant clergymen either to satisfy her doubts or to content relations and friends who would in the sequel have blamed her doubly had she not done so. One of these divines, the Rev. Berkeley Addison, so completely lost his self-control in an argument that he ended it by kicking a hassock across the drawing-room.

Unknown to every one she at last applied

to the Rev. James Monaghan for religious instruction, and it was not till she was ready to be received into the Church that she told her mother of what had been passing in her mind. Mrs. Leslie, totally unprepared for so speedy a grace, could at first scarcely believe it to be true; but this too was granted, and on the feast of St. Joseph, 1850, Eleanor Leslie made her abjuration, and Father Monaghan received her into the Church.

There now remained of the whole family only Mr. Leslie's conversion to be prayed for.

For the last sixteen years he had suffered from partial softening of the brain, a condition which, although painful in the loss of memory it entailed, and on account of the occasional confusion of his ideas, yet left him at other times perfectly clear-minded and alive to all that was going on around him. A few extracts from the diary which he kept during the last year of his life, and which Mrs. Leslie transcribed into her notes of the year 1851, will show better than any explanation that her husband's conversion was no mere half-conscious act of a worn-out and dying man, but was the culmination of a conviction that had been steadily growing for some time.

Sunday, February 17.—Stormy day with high wind. I find that Eleanor, who has been keeping me back, has joined, or is preparing to be received into the R. C. Church. This being the case, I see no cause to hinder me from at least inquiring into its doctrines, which, if I find as represented to me, there is no impediment to my embracing them, *altho' late—very late.*

February 18.—Health better. Still valiant about my proposed change, altho' I see I have much to do and to learn; but thanks to God I have nothing else to do or to learn, and everybody kind and encouraging.

Sunday, 24.—Suther's (church). Perhaps for the last time.

25.—Had a conversation this morning with wifie, who has thrown a wet blanket upon me in respect to my wished-for change!!! Ann Shaw still with us for three or four days. Hope she will stay longer and help to convert me.

Sunday, March 10.—Suther's, who seemed to preach at me all the time he was delivering his sermon.

Tuesday, March 12.—A strong determination has again come over me that I am called upon to become a Roman. May God help me to keep firm and steadfast in my determination.

Mrs. Leslie in her touching account of the conversion and death of her beloved husband says:

His fervent, honest prayer was heard. Without even consulting with me (since fearing the respect he had formerly shown to his Protestant friends, and thinking him incapable of forming an act of judgment on so momentous a subject, I had refrained from urging him to do anything hastily) he from time to time sought out Mr. O'Donnell, walked and talked with him, and at last, on Tuesday, July 16, met him by appointment at St. Margaret's and went to the sacrament of penance. He remained in the chapel for some short time afterwards, engaged in prayer and much affected. From that day he was settled and tranquil, never returned to a Protestant chapel, nor did he ever join in making an unkind remark against Catholics, which from the imperfect state of his memory and the force of early prejudice was to me most surprising. Without much controversial reading he always appeared struck with the force of Catholic reasoning, and was ever ready to use my books of devotion or hear me read from them. Although unfit to attempt theological study, he was capable of judging whether our religion was a source of happiness to us, whether its effects were those of happiness upon himself. He was also in a position to judge whether our profession and practice were consistent, and of the soundness of the tree by its fruits. He was also aware from daily personal experience that Catholics neither thought nor did the many foolish things imputed to them, and that, in truth, the Catholic standard was so high and holy that in his simplicity and humility he often expressed a fear that he should not make "a good Roman." During the Jubilee he would gladly have attended the lectures at St. Patrick's, but I feared the crowd would be too great both for him and myself. On the feast of the Immaculate Conception, Sunday, December 8, and the following Sunday we went to St. Mary's and heard Father Cooke preach, first, on the claims of the Blessed Virgin to our love and veneration, and, secondly, on the love of God. He liked both discourses very much and was quite overcome by the latter, so that whilst he listened with the most profound attention, the tears rolled in streams down his face.

Mr. Leslie's children supplement some interesting details of this truly wonderful conversion. Both Mary and Charlotte had, unknown to each other and of course unknown to him, begun a novena for the conversion of their father, to end on the feast of our Lady of Mount Carmel. Every day during the novena he went to the Reverend Mr. O'Donnell's house. Mr. O'Donnell was puzzled, and on the eighth day, though he too knew nothing about the novena, said to Mr. Leslie: "Sir, if you will come to the sacristy of St. Margaret's at nine o'clock to-morrow morning, I will receive you into the Church."

He said this to satisfy him, but thought that it would be impossible for him to carry out the instructions, knowing the utter failure of his memory. Another difficulty, of which the priest was unaware, was that Mr. Leslie never finished dressing till about two o'clock, when he generally went out. But to Mrs. Leslie's surprise and alarm, the next morning he got up early, dressed and went out without saying where he was going. He went straight to his appointment, and when he had made his abjuration, Mr. O'Donnell took him into the chapel and fetched his daughter Charlotte, who was then at school at St. Margaret's. She found him in tears, but very happy and peaceful, and said some prayers with him.

All that day his memory was perfectly clear, and when later on several of his old friends called to see him he would say, "I am a Roman," and look amused at their surprise.

For the remainder of his life the one thing he remembered was that he was a Catholic, with all the concomitant circumstances. Mrs. Leslie thus continued her narrative :

December and January passed very happily and healthfully. On February 4 he was taken ill; I little thought how ill. Still our devotions in private went on as usual, for he was ever ready to attend to the voice of prayer and praise ; and the last night that circumstances permitted me to stay by his side, in the most silent hours he asked me again and again to repeat that beautiful Psalm, "The Lord is my Shepherd." Once I added the "Te Deum," to which he also attended. A few days after he bade me send for a priest. I asked, "Which?" and he replied, "All six," showing his clear recollection of their number. In consequence of a letter from one of my Protestant sisters I asked him one morning when he seemed better whether he would like to see a Protestant clergyman. He said decidedly, "No." I then inquired if he would see Mr. O'Donnell, and he said, "Yes." He never wavered, and after the second and third stroke of paralysis, though almost inarticulate, the evidences he gave of a firm, humble faith, calm submission to his severe sufferings, fervent contrition and patient thankfulness were indicated in ways equally unmistakable and satisfactory to all around his dying bed. He kissed my little crucifix affectionately about three hours before he died. His last word was "Hope," his last look expressive of love. There was no struggle, and a calm, sweet smile immediately settled on his lips. His whole appearance in death was most amiable, dignified and peaceful, inviting us again and again to contemplate his dear countenance and beautiful hands whilst we gathered round his coffin to offer our prayers for the repose of his soul.

The last night but one before his death, Mr. Leslie, seeing one of his daughters sitting by his bed, bade her come close to him, and although his articulation was difficult, said quite distinctly: "Do be good to your mother when I'm gone. No words could ever tell all she has been to me through our whole married life. It would be impossible to be a better wife than she has been. Promise me to be a comfort to her." He continued thus to speak in her praise as long as his failing breath permitted.

CHAPTER IX.

VOCATIONS.

EVENTS have been somewhat anticipated in order to bring into focus the different ways in which the various members of Mrs. Leslie's family were led into the Church. We must now return to the year 1848, when her son, having become a Catholic, was considering his next step. But while serious thoughts of the future occupied his mind, the present moment was not without charm. Apart from the happiness of belonging to the one true Church and the pleasure caused by the ever freshly unfolding beauties of the faith—blessings which the new converts enjoyed with all the zest and relish of minds more than commonly sensitive to every form of beauty—there was the satisfaction of welcoming many old friends to share with them the treasures of the Catholic religion. Then there were new friends to be made and new experiences to learn; and although their conversion had estranged some of their relations, others were staunch and loyal. Mr. Cosmo Innes, the historian, a distant cousin, interested himself in young Mr. Leslie's future career and even encouraged him to cultivate his taste for art. He induced him to draw and lithograph Runic stones for a work on the subject, and, had the young man chosen to pursue that or any branch of draughtsmanship, would have helped him with his advice and influence. He had strong Catholic tendencies, and his daughter, Mrs. Hill Barton, subsequently became a Catholic. Nothing ever alienated old Lady Caithness from any member of the Leslie family, and beyond her usual "Gude be here!" when she heard of the conversion of yet another Leslie, it made no difference between them. She lived in a kind of faded splendour, surrounded by a state and circumstance impervious to change, and her kind heart always kept a warm welcome for her young relatives whenever they came to see her. Her eccentricities were those of an age long since passed away. The family doctor called on her every morning to inquire about her health, and entered the drawing-room making so profound a bow at every few steps that he might have been attending a court ceremony. She was a great stickler for all that concerned her rank and position, and knew every ramification of the family history to the remotest branches. One day the young Leslies found her in deep mourning, and, on asking who was dead, were informed that she wore black for the Duchess of Portland. But the relationship was so distant that they had never even heard of it. On the other hand, the humblest offshoot of the genealogical tree obtained the same recognition, and when a sergeant in Edinburgh Castle who claimed relationship with the Sinclairs died, the old lady would have been glad if her great-nephew had gone to his funeral. Sometimes her idiosyncrasies were grotesque. One afternoon Eleanor and her brother were overtaken by a heavy shower and went for shelter to their great-aunt's, knowing that she would be out driving. They were, however, caught before the shower was over, and Lady Caithness insisted on their remaining to dinner. There was no help for Eleanor, but her brother, who knew that if dinner had been announced while he was there he would have been walked down, managed to make his escape, promising to call for her later in the evening. As soon as he had gone, the old lady, feeling her blind brother's watch, began to walk up and down, saying it was "verra strange—sax o'clock and nae dinner."

"It's nae struck sax, my leddie," remonstrated her companion, Miss Willie Sinclair. Lady Caithness then cleared her throat in the customary way, betokening wrath, making a sound that was something between a mild grunt and a mild scream; but when she had repeated several times: "Sax o'clock and nae dinner," Miss Sinclair in desperation, for she always defended the servants, said with great decision: "It's nae struck sax, my leddie, and that's a fac!"

At last they went down to dinner, and the old lady, who seemed to wish to impress Eleanor with the greatness of the banquet, that she might let her brother know what he had lost, turned to the butler, after the soup, and with her most majestic air said, "Bring up the pie," as if it had been a boar's head, or at least a haunch of venison. A pie was accordingly put before her, but it looked as if it had been doing duty for six months, and as she plunged the knife into it the servant looked anxiously over her shoulder as if he expected worms to come out of it.* The rest of the dinner was in the same style, ceremonious but unattractive.

While in Fingal Place the lines appeared to have fallen in pleasant places, the time was rapidly approaching when Mrs. Leslie was called upon to endure the sharpest pang she had ever yet experienced; and from that moment, at shorter or longer intervals, one sacrifice after another was required of her, till

* Eleanor's version—no doubt somewhat coloured.

at last she might well have said that she had nothing left to give.

But she had, if the expression may be allowed, a rare supernatural aptitude for suffering, which not only prepared her at all times for whatever God should send, but enabled her to leap forward as it were and welcome trials as if they had been joys in disguise. One illustration will suffice to show with what readiness she was prepared to embrace the cross at the slightest indication of what appeared to be the divine will, without pausing to consider whether the matter were really an obligation or not. Her love for her children has been called "excessive,"* and there is no doubt that all that concerned them touched her to the quick; but she never hesitated whenever it seemed as if God might be asking her to give them up. Her Catholic sister, Madame de Pambour, had been staying with her on a visit, and just before her departure proposed to take her youngest niece Charlotte back with her to France, wishing for her as a companion to her only daughter. Although the pain of the separa-

* The Rev. H. J. Coleridge, S.J., who loved and reverenced her so much that, before he died, he said that the only persons he very much wished to see again were Cardinal Newman and Mrs. Leslie, once alluded to her "excessive love for her children." He stopped, and then added: "Yes, it is *excessive*."

tion would have been acute beyond words, Mrs. Leslie was on the point of consenting, thinking that it might be of some advantage to the child, when her son interfered, exclaiming:

"My dear mother, you are so greedy of suffering that the moment it is put before you, you fly at it and lose your judgment."

"Yes," said her sister, speaking of the matter next day, "that is true; she is *greedy* of suffering."

To say therefore that she was ready for all the crosses that might be sent to her is to express but half the truth, for like her favourite saint and patron, Francis Xavier, she could truly say that there was henceforth no cross to her so great as to be without the Cross.

The first sacrifice required of her was her son's vocation.

He was not long left in doubt with regard to his future. Belief in our Lord's Real Presence in the Eucharist had been very sincere and fervent even in his Protestant days, but as a Catholic his devotion was deepened and intensified a hundredfold; and when once he had realized what that devotion meant, he was constantly kneeling before the tabernacle in the chapel of St. Margaret's.

We needs must love the highest when we see it,

and thus vocation followed quickly on conversion. He spoke one day to Madame de Pambour of his hope of becoming a priest, and her answer is eloquent of the bond that united the whole family in the closest and tenderest love and sympathy.

"I cannot imagine," she replied with deep feeling, "how it will ever be possible to break up this happy home."

But when Bishop Gillis was consulted, he dissuaded him, for he much wanted good Catholic laymen in his diocese. However, he agreed to a retreat, and the young man decided to make it at Hodder, the Jesuit novitiate, near Stonyhurst. Whatever there might be decided as to his future course, he was to return to Edinburgh and pay some promised visits with Mrs. Leslie before carrying out any decision. As he walked down the avenue to start for Hodder, his father watched him, and with a strong presentiment declared that he would never return. Mrs. Leslie reminded him in vain that the absence was only to be a short one, but she could not convince her husband. However, from Hodder, in the midst of the retreat, came the first intimation of what was before them. Not as a secular priest, in which vocation there need be no very sharp line of separation, was their son to be taken from them; but the offering was to be whole and entire and his mother was to give him to God as a religious.

"I feel as if caught in a holy trap," he wrote to her; and soon it was clear to him that his vocation was to the Society of Jesus. But there were difficulties; so short a time had elapsed since his conversion, and his studies, especially as regarded mathematics to the neglect of classics, had been directed more towards fitting him for the army than for a religious order devoted largely to education. At Hodder he had found his old friend George Bridges, who had just ended his novitiate, and advised him to go to London and see the Provincial of the Jesuits, Father Cobb. The Miss Nutt, already mentioned in a previous chapter as one of Mr. Leslie's friends had also become a Catholic, with one of her three sisters. They had taken a house in Queen Square, London, where they lived very simply, devoting themselves and their large income to a life of charity. When they heard of any recent convert to the Catholic religion being, as was not uncommon in those days, turned out of house and home for religion's sake, the Misses Nutt would with the utmost simplicity come forward and take the convert in, as if it were a matter of course, and make him one of the family. Mr. Harris, whose health had grown still more feeble as years went on, lived entirely with them and was cared for in the most devoted, loving manner till he died.

To them Mr. Leslie went during his short stay in London, and proceeded from their house to interview the Provincial of the Jesuits. Father Cobb handed him over to his predecessor, Father Lythgoe, a very remarkable man, who in a few minutes vivisected him with questions, and then uttered the decisive words, "I don't see why you shouldn't try." And so the matter was settled.

It was the day of the opening of the London Oratory in King William Street, and Newman was to preach. Mr. Leslie went to hear him, and there he saw Miss Gladstone, sister of the famous Prime Minister, who had lately become a Catholic. She invited him to dinner but he declined, thinking that it would be worldly to go to dinner-parties just as he was leaving the world. He did not even venture to return to Edinburgh and pay the proposed visits, dreading the ordeal of again leaving the beloved home, to him a heaven on earth, with the full knowledge that it was for ever. He therefore went straight back to Hodder and entered the noviceship.

It was perhaps the least painful way of severing ties that were as tender as they were sacred, but to Mrs. Leslie the suffering was intense.

"If I could but see him once again!" was the continued cry of her heart, as the tears streamed down her face.

But a meeting between the mother and son would not have been encouraged during the first months of the novitiate for obvious reasons, and when her kind friend the Rev. Mr. O'Donnell offered to go himself to Hodder, she accepted gratefully. He brought back a report that softened and alleviated the pain, although the wound was to bleed for many a long day.

In the course of the year 1851 it was arranged that Mrs. Leslie should make a retreat at Hodder under her son's Novice-master, the Rev. Father Clarke, staying for eight days at the small inn at Hurst Green, the nearest village.

By an accident, she arrived on a Saturday evening, too late for her son to welcome or even to see her that night. The people at the inn told her that if she waited at the church door the next morning she would see him as the novices filed in to assist at High Mass. She did so, but although their eyes met, she quickly understood that it would be impossible to exchange a word with him then. The novices were forbidden to speak between leaving the noviceship and returning to it, and in his excess of zeal for obedience, he had not considered that such an occasion would certainly form an exemption from the rule. They were however soon rewarded by a message from the guest-master at Stonyhurst to Father Clarke, asking him to send Mr. Leslie at once to see his mother, and give him a special injunction to be affectionate.

This was Mrs. Leslie's first visit to Stonyhurst, but by no means the last, and the friendships then made there were lifelong. In speaking of this retreat Father Clarke said, "She went through it like a formed man," meaning a formed Jesuit; and the guest-master, Father Waterton, half-brother to the celebrated naturalist of that name, declared that "no such lady had been at Stonyhurst for a long time."

The next meeting between Mrs. Leslie and her son was at his father's death-bed. Hastily the young novice had been summoned, when it became apparent that the sufferer's hours were numbered. Mr. Leslie lay weak but perfectly conscious, with his face turned towards a beautiful print of the Crucifixion, after Albrecht Dürer, which hung on the wall opposite his bed, and which his son had long before bought and placed there. As long as he could see, his eyes sought the picture at intervals, and a look of love would steal over his face as he gazed on the tortured form. When Dr. Gillis, seeing how weak he was, proposed to send him some claret, the dying man said earnestly, looking at the print, "*He* had no claret."

All his faculties were clear, and his individuality pathetically unchanged, since the days when he was a notable figure in London society and was the joy of so many devoted friends. Pleased as he was to see his son, he was characteristically distressed at the wear and tear of the novitiate on his outward appearance.

"Very ungentlemanlike hands," he complained, noticing at once the signs of manual labours on hands which had learned among other things to black boots and sweep corridors. We have read in Mrs. Leslie's own words how the devoted wife ministered to her husband's every need till she had folded his beautiful hands in death, and had prayed round his coffin till it was committted to the earth. Like the strong and valiant woman that she was, she did not allow herself to luxuriate one hour in grief, but appeared immediately after the funeral in her widow's cap, and embracing her son, asked him to pray God to bless her widowhood.

Her duty now lay in doing her utmost for her remaining children, and as it was thought that a short time spent abroad would be advantageous, she took them to Tours, choosing that place as affording objects of interest to them and as being near her sister Madame de Pambour. While there, they were joined by Mr. Falconer Atlee and his family, and spent some quiet peaceful weeks together with them.

In days of tranquil reflection especially, Mrs. Leslie braced herself for further stages on the road to perfect self-abnegation and submission to the Divine will. Very early any one who watched her inner life closely must have remarked her conformity to every act of Providence in her regard. To the end of her life this was the dominant note of her spiritual development and progress. A little book in which she wrote some favourite prayers and reflections contains the following beautiful lines composed by St. Alphonsus Liguori, which she had made her own constant aspiration:

> Solo voglio il tuo volere
> O bel cuor del mio Gesù
> Sol mi piace il tuo piacere
> Amo sol d'amarti più.

An ejaculation of St. Philip Neri's was also a frequent one with her:

> Vi ringrazio o mio Dio
> Che non vanno le cose
> A modo mio.

Besides these she was extremely fond of the prayer of St. Ignatius, "Do with me, O Lord, as Thou knowest and as Thou willest, for I know that Thou lovest me."

With these desires and intentions in her heart she was extraordinarily calm, equable and brave in times of trial, danger or sorrow, and it was only when uncertain of the direction in which God's will pointed that she hesitated or seemed to vacillate. At these times she would postpone matters, pray anxiously and consult others, but when once she saw clearly she would act promptly, whatever the sacrifice might cost her. Like the Magi of old she could truly say, not only at each solemn crisis of her life, and of the lives of those closely united to her, but on every occasion when an important decision had to be made: " We have seen the Star in the East and have come."

With such dispositions therefore, it may easily be imagined how she received the new trial that came to her in her daughter Mary's vocation to be a nun. She knew indeed and could appreciate the happiness of religious life, and the blessing of always knowing the Will of God in the voice of superiors, and the following of a holy Rule; yet for all that, or perhaps rather on account of her great faithfulness to grace, her heart was all the more sensitive and more truly loving than if there had been any selfishness in her maternal affection. The depth and earnestness of her feeling made the thoughtless congratulations of some converts on her daughter's vocation hard to bear, and she wrote about this time, "Our Lord's ascension into heaven is not counted among His Mother's *joys*, but among her *glories.*"

It seemed fitting that St. Margaret's Convent which had played so large a part in the conversion of every member of Mrs. Leslie's family should claim one of her children for its own, and this beloved daughter was accordingly received there as a postulant on October 15, 1852.

Warm-hearted Sir Ord Honyman, who associated himself with every possible event in the Leslie family, went to see her at the convent soon after she had entered. As she came into the parlour looking bright and glad to see her old friend, he stretched out his arms, saying, "My dear darling Mary!" and when the nun who came with her held up her finger, he said, "Why I've had her on my knee since she was a baby!"

For many years the health of Mrs. Leslie's youngest daughter was such as to cause grave anxiety, and in the autumn of 1853, a serious chill having greatly increased her delicacy, a milder climate was recommended for the winter. Happily there were no difficulties in the way of carrying out this advice, and Eleanor having recently been married to Mr. Fraser

Gordon, Writer to the Signet and a devout Catholic, Mrs. Leslie was free to devote herself henceforth exclusively to the one child who now needed her care. With no very settled plans she started southwards, en route for Paris and Tours, intending after a visit to Mr. Atlee in the one place, and to Madame de Pambour in the other, to decide on their future movements according to circumstances. It will be remembered that her brother was professedly an infidel, his faith having been undermined when he was still very young. But when Mrs. Leslie met him and her sisters at her father's death-bed, after her conversion, he, feeling for her in the midst of the unequivocal marks of disapproval in nearly all her family, came to her room one evening to cheer her up, saying:

"Nellie you must not mind their black looks. I for one think you did perfectly right to become a Catholic. I lived for some time in Switzerland, alternately in the Protestant and Catholic Cantons, and observed closely the influence of the two religions. And my conclusion was that no other religion than the Catholic can satisfy the wants of the human heart. I wish you could get Emma and the girls to follow your example. Men can do without religion, but it is absolutely necessary for women."

With the hope therefore that some opportunity might occur for furthering this object, Mrs. Leslie and her daughter paid Mr. Atlee a visit at his house near the Champs Elysées, and met with the same warm welcome as formerly at Midshields. His eldest son Falconer had already been appointed private secretary to Lord Cowley, the younger, Albert, being still a pupil at some lycée. One of his daughters was married, and two others were growing up at home. It was a very well ordered, happy and most amiable household. Of religion little was apparent except that on Sundays it was considered the proper thing for the ladies at least to attend the chapel at the British Embassy, Falconer being an attaché. There was a pleasant absence of prejudice or bigotry among them, and even Mr. Atlee would often take pleasure in visiting hospitals, and in going to churches where grand funeral rites were performed. There were also a few books of a religious character which he sometimes looked into. Once, one of his daughters was playing part of Rossini's *Stabat Mater*, while he followed the words in a Catholic prayer-book. After the verses

> Pro peccatis suæ gentis
> Vidit Jesum in tormentis
> Et flagellis subditum
>
> Vidit suum dulcem natum
> Moriendo desolatum
> Dum emisit spiritum

he turned to his niece, and with a burst of tears said, "What wonderful words!"

His son Albert, too, a frank, open-hearted boy, full of fun and high spirits seemed to be strangely open to Catholic influence, and one day, seeing his aunt and cousin ready to go out, he said, "If you are going to Benediction you will do well to pray for me, because I don't pray much for myself."

Sometimes the cousins had games and romps together, as in their more childish days at Midshields, and Albert tore Charlotte's dress in the mêlée more than once. She laughingly told him that he ought to mend it. He agreed, and did it after his own fashion, declaring that now she owed him something for his trouble; upon which she promised him a present. Her mother took her to Notre Dame des Victoires to get some miraculous medals blessed, and to ask for some Masses. When Albert claimed the promised present, Charlotte gave him a medal, with the request that he would wear it, and he accordingly undertook to do so. His high sense of honour made her hope that he would be as good as his word, and years afterwards she found that she had not been mistaken. But on this occasion the visit ended with no visible progress towards Catholicity having been made by any member of her uncle's family.

The Château de la Filonnière, where Mrs. Leslie's brother-in-law, the Comte de Pambour, lived, was at some distance from Tours, and quite in the country. Madame de Pambour had become a Catholic through the influence of the celebrated Père de Ravignan, but as she lived far from a church, and could only hear Mass on Sundays, she had few spiritual advantages and looked forward to her sister's visit as a great consolation and help. Her husband, although born a Catholic, had been brought up without any religion, but at the time of his marriage with Miss Harriet Atlee he had approached the Sacraments, perhaps the only time in his life till he was a very old man. Thanks to the many prayers offered in his behalf, he made a good death. He was very clever and agreeable, and took much pleasure in Mrs. Leslie's society.

At Tours the travellers met some old friends and made new ones. Madame de Bodenham introduced them to the D—— B——s, who, converts like themselves, shared their tastes and occupations. Together they worked for poor churches, visited the places of interest in the neighbourhood and laid the foundations of an intimacy that was to be lifelong.

Charlotte was ordered to spend the winter at Pau, and Mrs. D—— B—— gave them letters of introduction to Mdlle. de Castelbajac

and others likely to render their sojourn agreeable and advantageous. Mdlle. de Castelbajac gave them a welcome that was duly appreciated after the long journey in a diligence over the dreary Landes, and took them to an apartment adjoining her father's house.*
There was an immense concourse of strangers at Pau that winter — English, Russian, American and French, and in nearly every family there was an invalid. Among those whose acquaintance Mrs. Leslie made were: Lady Acton, who had come with her grandson, young Throckmorton, dying of consumption; Mrs. Bolton with her daughter and son-in-law, Monsieur d'Abadie and Père Hermann. All who came in contact with her were attracted by her charm of manner and by the wonderful power of sympathy which made people trust her and count on her in sorrow or in any emergency as if she had been an old friend.

At Pau she was awakened one night by a pebble being thrown up against her window. On looking out she heard a voice which she recognized as belonging to one of her new acquaintances, saying:

* Monsieur de Castelbajac was one of the Royalists condemned to death during the first Revolution. Disguised as a printer's boy he printed his own condemnation. The fall of Robespierre saved him from detection.

"Mrs. Leslie, Ellen* has a baby girl. The layette ordered in Paris has not yet arrived. Can you give me anything to dress the child in?"

Mrs. Leslie was one of those happily constituted people who always happen to have what is wanted; she provided the necessary garments, and the child thus clothed by her in its earliest infancy grew to be a Catholic and a Religious.

Apart from the friends she made there, Pau was not at that time a congenial place. The churches were ill cared for and neglected in appearance and the society was worldly. Mrs. Leslie had, however, a genius for finding out and tracking saintliness to its most hidden retreat. At Gélos lived a holy priest bearing some resemblance to the Curé d'Ars, whose church was a model of cleanliness and neatness, the services being conducted with the utmost reverence; and she would frequently undertake the long walk thither in order to counteract the disedifying impressions of her immediate unspiritual surroundings.

In the spring an excursion was made to Notre Dame de Bettharam, a very ancient place of pilgrimage in the Pyrenees; and they passed a night at Argelez. The evening devo-

* Mrs. Maxwell Lyte.

tions of the month of Mary were going on in the village church when they arrived. It looked as if it were full of monks, for all the peasant women wore white capuchons.

An errand of charity made Bagnères de Bigorre their next halting-place, and on returning northwards a night was spent at Poitiers to visit the tomb of St. Radegonde. They were in Paris for the octave of the Fête Dieu, and at the Madeleine there was a procession of the Blessed Sacrament. As it passed down the church Mrs. Leslie saw mothers holding up little children to be blessed, and looked imploringly at the priest* as he drew near. Reading her unspoken desire in the earnestness of her gesture, he placed the Monstrance on Charlotte's head.

Leaving Paris they returned to Scotland by easy stages, paying a visit to Stonyhurst on the way.

* M. l'Abbé du Guerry, the holy Curé of the Madeleine, who was shot with the other hostages during the Commune.

CHAPTER X.

THE CATHOLIC REVIVAL IN SCOTLAND.

WE have several times in the course of this Memoir alluded to some of Mrs. Leslie's many friends, and as the story of her own life has been gradually unfolded, several of those who were associated with her in the pursuit of truth have necessarily been mentioned at some length. But after she had become a Catholic their number greatly increased; and as she was set free by the death of her husband from the tenderest and most absorbing of her domestic ties, she was now at liberty to turn her attention to others in a way that would not formerly have been possible. In her choice of friends she had always a high standard before her eyes, and never formed a trivial or an unworthy friendship.

About the time of her own conversion and that of her family there was a distinct movement in Scotland towards the Church. Amongst the first Scottish converts, who were also the first of Mrs. Leslie's new friends, were Mr. and Mrs. Monteith of Carstairs.

Mr. Monteith's father was a great Glasgow merchant, descended from a laird of no considerable estate. He made a large fortune in business. In those days the trade of Glasgow was growing apace, and the merchants grasped their opportunity. They built Port Glasgow at the mouth of the Clyde and then deepened the river, so that mighty trading ships could float up to the quays, where boys used to walk across the river at low water. These lands were wanted for the factories, and an agent was sent to the Highlands to induce the Macdonnell clan to leave their mountains and come to the city. They consented on one condition. The entire clan was Catholic. Could the agent promise them a Catholic church in Glasgow? He referred the matter in the form of a petition to the merchants, who at first refused. But afterwards Mr. Monteith signed the petition and then others followed his example. The Macdonnells came with their priest, but suffered so much annoyance on account of their religion that after a time they emigrated in a body to Canada.* Upon this followed the potato rot in Ireland; the poor Irish took the places vacated by the Macdonnells and re-

* The account of the Macdonnells' coming to Glasgow is given by Dr. Gordon in the appendix to the "Scotichronicon," under the years 1790—1800.

mained, so that now about one-fourth of Glasgow is Catholic, with twenty churches and a population of 250,000 souls. Perhaps Mr. Monteith's action in being the first to advocate the building of a Catholic church in the city may have helped to merit for his son Robert the gift of faith. Robert went to Cambridge and there became acquainted with Tennyson, with whom he formed a life-long friendship. He was a man of large intellect; he wrote good poetry, and his oratory was of so high an order that although Glasgow people are bigoted, they asked him after his conversion to deliver a speech on the occasion of a sword being publicly presented to Lord Campbell of Clyde. And he was no half-hearted Catholic. He built the beautiful church at Lanark, and with the help of his friend, Mr. Hope Scott, bought Smyllum and turned it into a Catholic orphanage and hospital. He also contributed largely to the building of the convent of the Good Shepherd at Dalkeith. His hospitality was no less magnificent than his charity, and when he came into possession of Carstairs, he loved to fill his house with guests, Catholic and Protestant. Mrs. Leslie and her daughters stayed there frequently.

In the same county lived Colonel and Mrs. Gerard, intimate friends of the Monteiths, and a little later of the Leslies also. They were received into the Church about the same time. Colonel Gerard and Mrs. Leslie were confirmed on the same day at St. Margaret's Convent by Dr. Gillis.

The following account of the Gerards' conversion is contributed by their eldest son, the Rev. John Gerard, S.J. :

How my father and mother were first drawn into the High Church movement I do not know. They were both by education Scotch Episcopalians, but I know that at one period after their marriage (in 1839) they made a point of attending the Presbyterian Church when it was impossible to attend their own. In the Holy Week of 1844 we were at Rome, and by that time the edge of their Protestantism must have been rubbed off, for they were indefatigable in their efforts to see all they could of the Pope and the papal functions. On the occasion of the benediction *Urbi et orbi* in the piazza of St. Peter's, we children (my brother Montagu and myself) were sent in a carriage to witness the spectacle. my parents having gone on foot to get as near as possible to the Holy Father. I remember that we were right at the back of the crowded piazza, and that our Catholic nurse, an old Highland woman, made us get out and kneel down to receive the Pope's blessing, and that I was much bewildered with the whole affair, having a general impression from my Scotch education that the Pope was a species of monster, and finding it difficult to believe that the little white figure pointed out on the balcony (Gregory XVI.) was really he and not one of the fans of peacocks' feathers on either side of him.

My recollections begin to be coherent about 1846, when we were living at Chesters on the Teviot in Roxburghshire, by which time both my parents had thrown themselves heartily into the High Church movement. The great centre of its activity was Lady Lothian's beautiful church at Jedburgh, the pastor of which was Mr. White, assisted by a deacon, Mr. Campbell I think, who afterwards became a Catholic. The services were of course purely Anglican, but conducted with great solemnity, and there was an excellent surpliced choir of men and boys.

I remember hearing it said, as instancing the bigotry and prejudice then commonly prevalent, that according to popular belief a live dragon was kept under the altar, which Lady Lothian and Mr. White used regularly to feed.

In 1847, early in the year I fancy, we flitted from Chesters to Rocksoles. My father had hitherto resided in the Border country for the sake of hunting and salmon fishing, and the neighbourhood was certainly more attractive than the coalfields of Lanarkshire. My mother was greatly distressed at the thought of the change, and asked me if I could guess what it cost her most to leave. I failed to do so, and she explained that it was "the little church," and that she could not hope to find anything like it where we were going. Certainly Episcopalianism was not well represented in our new quarters. The only available church was at Coatbridge, and there the services were conducted in a fashion that I soon learned was anything but pleasing to my parents fresh from Jedburgh. The clergyman, whose name I quite forget, but who certainly was from Ireland, appeared to be particularly obnoxious to them. After a time he disappeared, and we were without a pastor. During this interval my father exerted himself to obtain casual assistance, and on one occasion the Sunday work was undertaken by a person styling himself the Hon. and Rev. Mr. ——, who stayed with us and preached two sermons which were considered exceptionally good, but he proved to be no clergyman at all. Meanwhile my father took much trouble to secure the services of a permanent minister who should instruct his flock in sound High Church doctrine. To this end he made a journey to Leeds to take counsel with Dr. Hook, whose authority was great with Episcopalians of his school. By Dr. Hook's advice he then paid a visit to the Isle of Man, and there prevailed on the Rev. Robert Aitken to take pity upon us and come to establish himself at Coatbridge. Mr. Aitken was certainly a remarkable man, a powerful though violent preacher, and exceedingly imperious. I remember hearing my father, after his return from his mission, recounting an expression used by Dr. Hook, that before recommending him for the place he should know what sort of flock he would have to address, but that if they could be dosed with raw brandy, Mr. Aitken was the man.

I infer that by this time my parents were thoroughly imbued with Newman's Anglican teaching. My mother was at great pains to instruct me—I was then between seven and eight—as to the distinctive character and position of the Anglican Church, and the impression produced on my mind I afterwards fully recognized when I came to read of the *Via Media*. Our Coatbridge church stood on the middle of a hill, on the summit of which was the Presbyterian "Mount Zion;" and at the bottom a Catholic chapel was building. I used often to think that this situation exactly typified what I had been told of our position between Calvinism and Popery. In the winter of 1847-8 my father paid a visit to the West Indies. During his absence my mother began, if she had not previously begun, seriously to study the Catholic claims; for I remember being startled to notice that she was reading a book called "The Faith of Catholics." A scriptural difficulty which presented itself to her mind she proposed for solution to Mr Aitken, who endeavoured at once to crush the spirit of enquiry by assuring her that if she presumed to entertain such thoughts she would infallibly be damned, and so terrified her that, going out immediately afterwards driving by herself, she was run away with and had a bad accident. His reply however chiefly upset her as being altogether inconsistent with the system of private judgment which he loudly professed.

Shortly afterwards we all went to Ireland on a visit to my mother's brother-in-law, Colonel Nugent, in Westmeath, a zealous Protestant. In passing through Dublin she paid a visit to Gardiner Street and saw Father St. Leger—I do not know which of the brothers of that name,—to whom she proposed the difficulty to which Mr. Aitken had refused to listen. Father St. Leger at once explained the Catholic doctrine on the point, my mother being as much struck by the reasonable procedure of the Church of authority as by the unreasonableness of that of private judgment.

In the country district where the next few months were spent she was much impressed by the faith and devotion of the Irish people. She also formed a fast friendship with a good parish priest, Father Eugene O'Rourke, whose simple piety and earnestness she never forgot. All this time, however, she attended the Anglican church, and although undoubtedly much shaken in her conviction, had not, I believe, as yet seriously contemplated the possibility of becoming a Catholic. It was, I suppose, when we got back to Scotland that she began formal discussions with Mrs Monteith, who with her husband had visited us at Chesters as an Anglican, both having since then become Catholics. Mrs. Monteith had unquestionably much to do with my mother's conversion, but I never heard any particulars of their conferences on the subject, save for a casual remark of the former, that although it was hard work arguing, yet it was a satisfaction to have to deal with a person who never looked back, and with whom a point once gained was gained for ever.

By the time that my father returned from the West Indies, my mother had practically made up her mind to go over, but I fancy that she did not at once tell him of her resolve, and certainly she went to church at Coatbridge with him on one occasion at least. But in no long time she took me out one day for a walk, and after reminding me of her former religious teaching, told me that she had been led to enquire further, and from all she had heard and read she had resolved to become a Catholic; that my sister (there was then only one) was to be a Catholic too, but that we three were to remain Protestants with my father. I was greatly distressed at the idea of this separation, and thenceforth she taught me no more catechism, and I remember, in our English history lessons, insisted on skipping over the Middle Ages. On the first Sunday when she went to Mass at Airdrie we drove round to drop her there on our way to Coatbridge, and found that Mr. Monteith had come over from Carstairs to support her under what he felt would be a trying ordeal. She was much rejoiced to find him there, not having expected his coming. We never were told when she was received, but my sister, then quite a child, one day described a ceremony she had gone through, which we understood to mean her baptism. My mother's reception into the Church and baptism took place at St. Margaret's Convent, Edinburgh.

My father afterwards gave me some slight account of his own progress. When my mother told him of her determination he was startled, but said that he would make no opposition to the step she proposed to take, and that after what she told him of her experiences he would make it his immediate business to enquire further for himself. As a first step he at once wrote to his old counsellor, Dr. Hook, that he felt it his duty to obtain all the information he could on the subject, asking for advice as to the books he should consult. Dr. Hook replied that not being sufficiently acquainted with his capabilities in respect of intellect or education, he did not know what to recommend, but would suggest the reading at least of Tom Paine and Voltaire, that he might have the opportunity of becoming an infidel as well as a papist. Naturally, this response did not serve to satisfy my father's mind, and he began his researches for himself, and, as he said, at once discovered that he had hitherto known nothing of the true state of the question. Of all this, at the time, we of course knew nothing.

At this juncture my mother was taken suddenly ill, and lay for some time in great danger of her life. This brought the Airdrie priests frequently to Rocksoles. They were a Mr. McNabb and a Mr. Jeremiah Buckley, both of whom, and especially Mr. McNabb, we got to know and to like, and I could not help observing on what good terms they appeared to be with my father. We ceased our visits to Coatbridge, and presently he dropped a remark one Sunday showing that he had been that day to Mass. I felt sure that something was coming.

Soon afterwards, my mother, who was still in bed, sent for me and told me that we were all going to be Catholics, asking me whether I understood the great difference between the two Churches, namely, that Catholic priests could, and other ministers could not, consecrate the Body and Blood of Christ so as to be really present on the altar. How much influence Newman's writings had exercised upon her was made clear by her subsequent habit of reading to me passages from his Catholic sermons which had then begun to appear. She was particularly fond of the passage (in the sermon entitled "Saintliness the Standard of Christian Principle") describing the sensations of one born and bred in a pit, underground, and suddenly introduced to the upper air and the light of day, which he applies to a soul brought from error to the true Church.

We boys were present when my father was confirmed, in the chapel of St. Margaret's Convent, I think on the feast of St. Francis Xavier, whose name he took (December 3, 1848); and on the 27th of the same month, the feast of St. John the

Evangelist, my two brothers and myself were conditionally baptised by the Rev. John Macdonald in the sacristy of St. Mary's, Edinburgh.

(Signed) JOHN GERARD, S.J.

The first link between the Leslie and the Gerard family was formed at the baptism of Mrs. Gerard's little daughter Emily, soon after her own conversion, when Mary Leslie, then a pupil at St. Margaret's Convent, acted as godmother.

Passing years have not dimmed her recollection of those beloved friends of her youth, and she writes from St. Margaret's after a long interval of religious life:

> I always think of Mrs. Gerard as the most highly gifted woman I ever knew. Whatever she undertook she carried through perfectly and seemingly without effort, whether it were music, drawing or languages, though she applied herself to each with unflagging energy and interest. I well remember how she devoted herself to the training of the very unpromising choir of the chapel at Airdrie, and how immensely it improved under her care. She was ever ready to help the clergy by providing vestments and altar linen, her devotion to the Blessed Sacrament rendering all her work a labour of love.

Great was her joy when leave was given for a chapel at Rocksoles, wherein the Blessed Sacrament might be reserved, and henceforth the sanctuary lamp shone through a cross of red glass in the oratory window as a beacon, showing forth to the world a real Catholic home.

Mrs. Gerard's love for and interest in the

poor were heartfelt, and her children were trained from their earliest years to take pleasure in depriving themselves of little dainties for their benefit. The hospitality at Rocksoles was proverbial and was extended to Catholics and Protestants alike. It was no uncommon occurrence for the Presbyterian minister, the Anglican parson and the Catholic priest to meet there at dinner. It was probably the only house at which they were all three to be seen together. On such occasions the conversation would be skilfully led to such topics as were of general interest, no opportunity, however, being lost of creating a better understanding of the Catholic religion by bringing in a useful explanation in the right place or by dispelling a time-honoured misapprehension.

The following anecdote illustrates Mrs. Gerard's energy in the cause of religion, her large generosity and truly Catholic spirit.

A Parliamentary Commission had been appointed to investigate the state of religious instruction in Wales. The report, printed in *The Guardian* newspaper, revealed appalling ignorance in the Principality. Mrs. Gerard was then living in Ireland, and on her brother-in-law's property was a row of cottages inhabited by poor Catholics, the Catholic chapel being some miles away. With *The Guardian* in her hand, she questioned the poor

Irish children dwelling in these cottages on the subjects of which the Welsh children had shown such deplorable ignorance, and the answers she received were admirable for correctness in every instance. As she was returning home, at the first town she came to she gave an equal sum of money to the Protestant clergyman and to the Catholic priest for their poor. The clergyman merely thanked her, the priest asked for her name. She made some difficulty, but gave way when he said: "We like to write the names of our benefactors in a book, so that we may pray for them."

Colonel Gerard had been in the Scots Greys, and had a soldierly appearance, combined with great gentleness and even sweetness of manner, which won all hearts. One exceptionally cold, hard winter a committee was forming at Airdrie for the relief of the poor. As so many of them were Catholics, he proposed that a Catholic should be put on the committee. The motion was carried at once, and a Presbyterian minister brought forward the name of one Catholic while another minister immediately proposed that of another.

The extremely good terms on which he lived with his Protestant neighbours owed nothing to the sacrifice of Catholic principle, as the following story shows.

He had been invited during one Advent to a shooting party in Arran by the Duke of Hamilton. On the first fast day, a Wednesday, a gentleman observed that he was eating no breakfast. In the middle of the day luncheon was brought for the shooters on to the hill-side; but there was no abstinence food, and Colonel Gerard could eat nothing. His friend remarked this, and when they assembled at dinner said to him as they sat down, "What a dinner you will eat!" But again there was scarcely anything he could venture upon. Some one whispered to the Duke, and he looked distressed, but on Friday the same thing happened again; the Duke sprang up, rang the bell, and had a long conversation with the steward behind a screen. Colonel Gerard felt sure that it was all about food for him on abstinence days. After that he was not only well provided for, but a mutual understanding sprang up between himself and his host, and from that day he was perhaps the best friend the Duke ever had. The Duke of Hamilton, who held himself to be little less than king of Lanarkshire, supported a man in an election for office in the police, and was much put out when Colonel Gerard, knowing the man to be unfit for the work, opposed him. The Duke's candidate was not elected, and Colonel Gerard rode over to Hamilton and explained to the Duke that he had done him a good turn in opposing his man, who, if he had been elected, would have disgraced his patron. The Duke was wise enough not to resent this sturdy act of friendship.

Colonel Gerard was a remarkably good artist; his sketches which now cover the walls at Rocksoles are delightful. Mrs. Gerard's talent for drawing has already been mentioned. She had learned of an old Scotch artist who had taught Queen Victoria, and who used to say, "The Queen is a verra sensible person and no wi'out talent."

This Colonel Gerard's father, also a Colonel Gerard, had gone to Tours some time after the battle of Waterloo and had bought some pictures there of which the old drawing-master disapproved. When he heard of anyone wanting to buy good pictures, he would say drily, "Go and buy them at Tours. Colonel Gerard has bought all the bad ones there."

Early in the fifties Mr. and Mrs. Caswall came to live in Edinburgh, and were soon counted among Mrs. Leslie's greatest friends. They were recent converts, although they cannot be exactly said to belong to the Scotch revival of Catholicism. Mr. Caswall had been at Brasenose College, Oxford, and had written clever little books which had a certain vogue at that time. These were "Sketches of Young Gentlemen," "Sketches of Young Ladies," and "The Art of Pluck," in imitation of the style of Aristotle, which passed through several editions. A prize was offered at Oxford for the best essay on a method for converting the Brahmins. Caswall wrote an essay but brought himself to a Catholic conclusion. He thought this must be wrong and threw his paper aside. After some time he made a fresh start, and again arrived at a Catholic conclusion. He had married by this time, and both he and his wife were interested in Catholicism. He wished that she should become a Catholic, but they waited for each other. Long afterwards he said : "Whenever I wanted to be a Catholic she did not, and when she did, for some reason or other, I did not." At last they made up their minds that they had had enough theory and would like to see the Catholic religion in practice. Just then there was no political disturbance in Ireland, so they went there and took lodgings in Dublin. As they meant to be very impartial in collecting evidence they provided themselves with two note-books, in one of which they intended to put down all they saw in favour of Protestantism, in the other all they saw favourable to Catholicism. The landlady asked Mrs. Caswall if she would like to witness the ceremony of a nun's clothing. At the convent they were put into a room overlooking the chapel with the father of the young novice who was to be clothed that day. Mr. Caswall asked him if he were not sorry to lose his daughter in such a manner. But the man replied earnestly, "Sir, I am not worthy of it;" and Caswall said afterwards, "I put that down."

One Sunday they passed a thatched hovel. It was a Catholic chapel; Mass was going on, and it was pouring with rain. The chapel was full to over-flowing, and outside men were kneeling among the puddles. Caswall said, "I put that down."

They were received into the Church and went to Edinburgh, where Mrs. Caswall was at once attracted to Mrs. Leslie, and being an orphan she begged that she might call her "mother." This was one of the many instances in which Mrs. Leslie's motherliness appealed to a want in others and made itself practically felt.

While in Edinburgh Mr. Caswall occupied himself with his translation of Breviary hymns, now so well known and admired. Later he went to Bangor, where Mrs. Caswall died. He never forgot Mrs. Leslie's sympathy in the time of trouble and bereavement that followed. After a time he joined the Birmingham Oratory, and died at Edgbaston. In one of his letters Newman mentioned him as among his dearest friends.

From Mr. Caswall Mrs. Leslie heard a great deal about the conversion of his friend Ambrose Lisle Phillips, and the kind of persistent annexing of every fragment of Catholic truth remaining in the Church of England which led him up to it. When a boy he read something in Edward VI.'s first Prayer Book about a cope. He went to the old parson and said to him, "Sir, I find you might wear a cope." "Oh, yes, my dear boy, but it's never done." "But sir," he persisted, "I should like to see you in a cope. I'll get you one." Another time he went to him and said, "Sir, I find I might go to confession." "Yes, my boy," answered the parson, "but no one does now." "But, sir, I'll come to-morrow and make my confession." He was as good as his word, went to the old man's study and knelt down. In terror the parson urged him not to say a word, but the boy got his way, and, having made his confession, asked for absolution. The parson asked him which he preferred, as there were two in the Prayer Book—the general absolution and the one *in articulo mortis*. The boy answered, "Please, sir, I would like the best." The next thing young Ambrose suggested was a cross on the

Communion Table in the church. He got one made, and a procession of the school children followed him, carrying it through the park to the church, the poor old parson, a maiden sister on each arm, bringing up the rear. The boy put the cross on the Communion Table, and heard the parson say to his sisters with a sigh, "Ain't it awful!"

At Carstairs Mrs. Leslie became acquainted with Colonel and Mrs. Macdonell. They were perhaps the first of her friends who had always been Catholics. Colonel Macdonell had seen hard fighting, and was a gallant soldier, very warm-hearted and impetuous, ardent in his faith and also in his devotion to the Bourbons. His pretty courtesy to his wife, who was slow in her manner of speaking, was very pleasing. He would check his impetuosity and wait for her to finish speaking in the most high-bred manner. They lived in Edinburgh in a very simple, quiet way, observed the fasts of the Church when past sixty, and went to Mass every morning. One day Colonel Macdonell found the Duchess of Parma kneeling on the floor among the poor at St. Mary's. She had been driven from her home in the revolutionary crisis of 1848 and had arrived in Edinburgh the night before. Colonel Macdonell waited for her till she came out of church, welcomed her with a shout, and walked with her to her hotel, talking politics all the way. She afterwards drove from Drumlanrigg, where she was staying on a visit to the Duchess of Buccleuch, to call on Mrs. Gerard, whom she had known as a child, Mrs. Gerard's father having held some office at the court of Charles X. The Duchess of Parma was not a stranger in Edinburgh either; she had been at Holyrood Palace with her father, and had made her first Communion at St. Mary's.

Another of Mrs. Leslie's Catholic friends was the widow of a Colonel Hutchinson, a charming old-fashioned lady, who had been an Irvingite, and who, when she first became a Catholic, was described by Dr. Gillis as "stiff as buckram." But the warm genial heart soon melted the stiff manner, and nothing could exceed the child-like simplicity and eagerness with which she sought to learn ever more about her religion. When Mrs. Leslie's son went to the Novitiate and sent home his gold watch, Mrs. Hutchinson sent him a silver one. She was extremely charitable and gave largely to the poor. When she died, she left her house to the Sisters of Mercy with some money. Sometimes as she talked she would wave her right hand, turning out the palms in an odd way. In her last illness she was often visited by Sister Mary Sales (Mary Leslie), and one day said to her, "Well, my dear, Mr. Monteith has been here. I've told him where I am to be buried, and he's quite delighted," with the usual wave of her hand.

Mr. Robertson, whom the reader will remember as having belonged to the Portobello days, had gone to live at Dalkeith, where the beautiful chapel built by the Duke of Buccleuch, within the park gates, was finished. He was highly appreciated by the Duke and Duchess, as also by the Marchioness of Lothian. To all of them he spoke much of Mrs. Leslie, and before long she was invited with her two younger daughters, who were about the same age as Lady Lothians' daughters, to stay at Newbattle. Thus was formed another friendship which suffered no diminution when Mrs. Leslie became a Catholic. Mr. Robertson continued to study and pray, and the more he studied and prayed the less was he contented to remain in the Church of England. Mrs. Leslie also helped to solve his difficulties, and he spoke to the Duke of Buccleuch about giving up his chaplaincy. But the Duke would not hear of it, and for a time persuaded him to remain where he was. Then the longing to be a Catholic returned stronger than ever, and he said to Mrs. Leslie, "I am sick of saying that 'Dearly beloved brethren'— it is immoral." At last one Saturday afternoon he came to Mrs. Leslie's house and went with her son to St. Margaret's Convent. The nuns were singing the Litany of Loreto. After a few invocations Mr. Robertson sang, "Ora pro nobis," and our Lady helped him to take the final step which reconciled him to the Church. Immediately after his reception his children received conditional baptism, and his aunt, Miss Cunningham, who kept house for him, also became a Catholic. She still treasured in her old age her first Catholic prayer-book, the gift of Mrs. Leslie.

It was natural to expect that Lady Lothian and the Duchess of Buccleuch, who had been influenced by Mr. Robertson's teaching as an Episcopalian, should follow him into the Church. But this hope was not at once realised. Lady Lothian used to carry her difficulties to Mrs. Leslie, who could not understand why she did not decide. One day she asked her, "How many hours will you be before you are received?" She took her to the chapel at St. Margaret's, and Lady Lothian threw herself on her knees before the Blessed Sacrament as she entered. Soon after this she drove one day to Fingal Place with a paper in her hand, and reading from it asked for an explanation of certain things which were not clear to her. She was perfecly satisfied with Mrs. Leslie's answers to one question after the other. Her last doubts were now dispelled and she made her abjuration. She had feared that her children might be taken away from her, and suffered greatly in anticipation of the wrench, but after her first Communion she declared that God had abundantly repaid her for all she had gone through.

Lady Lothian had so often repeated to the Duchess of Buccleuch facts that Mrs. Leslie had told her about the Catholic religion that, although the Duchess did not make her acquaintance until after her own conversion, she always considered Mrs. Leslie as her mother in the faith. It was in recognition of the help she had afforded to herself and to many converts, especially at that time in Scotland, that the Duchess exclaimed some years later, on the occasion of Lady Lothian's death, when addressing the children of Mary at Roehampton: "Mrs. Leslie is the mother of us all!"

All these conversions in a short time produced the effect of completely changing the religious aspect in that part of the Lowlands and Border country. A few years before the only Catholic place of worship had been at Traquair. Now churches sprang up in all directions. Mr. Monteith built a fine one at Lanark; Lady Lothian another at Dalkeith, which serves for a population spread over a wide area. She had been persuaded as an Anglican, by a Mr.

Laing of Jedburgh, to place the church which she had already built there in the hands of trustees, he fearing that she would become a Catholic. In thus doing Mr. Laing was hoist with his own petard, for he and his family were also ultimately brought into the Church. Afterwards Lady Lothian built the present Catholic church at Jedburgh. The Duchess of Buccleuch erected one at Selkirk, and Mr. Hope Scott another at Galashiels, and also a chapel at Kelso. By his means too, Mass was said at St. Andrew's and at Oban. The chaplain at Traquair built a church at Hawick. At first there was no one to go to it; but soon after it was built a colony of Irish navvies came to the neighbourhood and filled it. All these edifices sprang up without opposition, the fact presenting a startling contrast to the struggle which it had cost the Vicar Apostolic, Dr. Scott, a few years previously to build St. Andrew's Church at Glasgow. So great had been the disturbance caused in that city that as the walls rose by day they were demolished by the populace by night. Dr. Scott could get no redress from the provost, and wrote to the Home Secretary. At last compensation was made, and the building proceeded.

A strange scene was witnessed at the laying of the foundation stone of St. David's, Dalkeith. Lady Lothian, her children and a few others were kneeling in the wooden building where the ceremony was taking place. At the door was a crowd of black-faced colliers, all striving to see over each other's shoulders, and facing them was Bishop Gillis, in full pontificals, saying, "My dear brethren, you are surprised at seeing me in this dress. This dress is 1,800 years old." All mouths were agape in astonishment, and the discourse that followed these opening words was listened to in breathless silence; whereas, at first, nothing could be heard but the pelting of stones and lumps of coal against the wooden shed, as a Protestant demonstration against the Popish doings within.

All the churches that had now been built were centres of growing Catholic communities, still small indeed among the upper classes, but with a large population of poor in the manufacturing districts. Lord Henry Kerr, brother of the Marquis of Lothian, and his family had become Catholics in England, but were now living at Huntlyburn, near Melrose, a house on the Abbotsford estate in which later on we shall find Mrs. Leslie as a welcome and frequent visitor.

Lady Lothian's children followed her into the Church with the exception of her two elder sons. Lord Walter was in the Navy, and therefore less accessible to his mother. When he was at Portsmouth she took her two daughters to the Isle of Wight, and when suddenly his ship was ordered to Gravesend before he was ready to be received, she left them there and went to complete his instruction. Lady Alice wrote an amusing account of her brother's conversion to Charlotte Leslie up to the time of his ship leaving Portsmouth, "when Mama flew up to London like a fiery dragon, leaving me and Cecy here praying like mad bulls."

CHAPTER XI.

FOUR YEARS IN ROME.

Mrs. Leslie returned to Edinburgh with her daughter Charlotte in the summer of 1854, and there were many besides her two elder daughters, the one married, the other a nun, who would gladly have seen her settle there. But the same reason that had obliged her to seek a warm climate the preceding year made it again necessary to fly southward before the long bleak Scotch winter set in, and this time the choice of a sojourn was not difficult. On December 8 was to be defined the dogma of our Lady's Immaculate Conception, and all Catholic hearts were turned Romewards.

The Italian railroads being still unfinished and the journey over the Alps a far more complicated one than the present younger generation can remember, Mr. Monteith introduced Mrs. Leslie in Paris to three ladies who were bound for the same destination, who would share with her the responsibilities of the route. They met at Lyons in October, and started in the diligence that crossed the Mont Cenis. It rained heavily all day. A diligence coming from Turin met theirs, and the driver told them that the rain in the valley was snow in the mountains, and the road scarcely passable. Towards evening the rain ceased; they stopped for supper at St.-Jean de Mourienne at the foot of Mont Cenis, after which the ascent began with two horses and a team of fourteen mules. A fine sunset tinged the snowy heights with rose colour, and every step revealed some new beauty. It was dark when they reached the top. At the frontier the mules were left behind, and the descent began with two horses only. The barriers were completely hidden by the accumulation of snow, and the driver kept close to the side of the mountain lest the horses should go over the precipice. Here and there large crosses marked the spot where some fatal accident had occurred. They had not gone far when the wheels of the diligence became embedded in a snowdrift, and the horses were powerless to extricate them. After many fruitless efforts a messenger was sent back to the frontier and brought a mule. The struggle recommenced, but in vain. A second mule was sent for and was harnessed in front of the first. At last, with the united efforts of horses, mules and the male passengers, who helped to shovel away the snow from the wheels, they got clear, and a fresh start was made, but not before one of the mules had his fore-legs over the precipice, to the imminent danger of dragging the whole party into the abyss. They reached Susa without further accident, but long after the last train had left for Turin, and the travellers passed the night there. At Genoa they were detained for some days, the river Magro being so swollen by the floods that it could not be forded. When it was supposed to have subsided, they set out for Pisa, taking the beautiful coast road, but they were forty hours in reaching it owing to the floods. A sultry afternoon was followed by a tremendous thunder-storm with torrents of rain, which continued all night, and on reaching the Magro in the morning it was found that the crossing would have to be effected partly in boats and partly on the men's shoulders. On the other side broken-down vehicles replaced the sound one that had come from Genoa. Pisa, and still more Siena, with its memories of St. Catherine, delighted their taste for the beautiful and stimulated their devotion, but they pressed on towards Rome with great eagerness and longing. All the public conveyances being crowded, they engaged a carriage with the understanding that the Eternal City should be reached in thirty-six hours.

There is no greater test of a person's

amiability than the test of travelling; and in this as in all other journeys Mrs. Leslie displayed the most perfect unselfishness and thoughtful care of others, always sacrificing her own convenience and pleasure to theirs.

At last the cupola of St. Peter's could be seen rising as it appeared out of the midst of the Campagna, and the hearts of the travellers thrilled with faith and gratitude as they beheld it. Soon their carriage dashed through the Porta del Popolo and clattered over the paving-stones of Rome.

Mrs. Leslie's first care was to find a suitable apartment for herself and her daughter. She wished to be near the Gesù, and was directed to No. 13, Via dietro il tribuno del Tor dé Specchi, which in spite of its long name was a most insignificant street. But when the door of No. 13 opened, the charming countenance of the woman within was like a sunbeam, and there was a refreshing vista of orange trees and azaleas in the small garden behind the house. A particularly clean flight of stairs led to bright, sunny rooms above, and Mrs. Leslie was induced to engage them. The circumstance that they had once been inhabited by Cardinal Acton and Cardinal Weld increased their interest. The house belonged to Count Demakolis, a Greek; his second wife, Liberata, Contessa though she was, had been his servant and worked like the most faithful and devoted sick nurse. She was invaluable to her lodgers. A small apartment reached by another flight of stairs was inhabited by Miss F. Taafe, and afterwards by Mr. William Palmer, brother of Roundell Palmer, first Lord Selborne.

The approaching solemnities on the occasion of the definition of the Immaculate Conception had attracted a vast number of foreigners to Rome that year. Among the English were many of Mrs. Leslie's friends. Lady Lothian had come with her younger children; the Philip Stourtons, the Scott-Murrays, the Fitzgeralds, the Mannings were also there, and were met at the various festas and stations. At the Academia and the English College were many well-known names—Cardinal Howard, Fathers Wynne and Coleridge, Gilbert Talbot, Dr. Patterson and others. Mr. William Palmer was also in Rome at that time, and many were hoping that he would give up his cherished scheme of uniting the Anglican and Greek Churches and become a Catholic. During Shrovetide a retreat for ladies was to be given in French at the Convent of the Sacred Heart. Many of the English Catholic ladies wished to attend it, and one evening they met at Lady

Lothian's at tea, and the conversation turned chiefly on the coming retreat. Father Wynne and Father Coleridge were present, and also Mr. Palmer, who listened attentively to what was being said. Presently he asked what a retreat meant. Father Coleridge explained, adding: "You should make a retreat yourself." Mr. Palmer said his purpose in coming to Rome was a very different one, that he wanted every hour of his spare time for his researches in the libraries and museums, and that he could not give up eight or ten days to a retreat. "But if," pursued Father Wynne, "we engaged a room for you at the Roman College, and arranged with a Father to give you the Spiritual Exercises, would you still refuse to make them?" "I suppose," answered Mr. Palmer, "if you had been to so much trouble, I could hardly persist in refusing." That evening it was difficult to say whether he had seriously undertaken to make a retreat or not, but Mrs. Leslie and her daughter with many of the other English ladies made his conversion a special intention of their own retreat, and it was therefore with great joy and gratitude that they heard before leaving the convent that he had been received into the Church. He had gone to the Roman College and had begun the Spiritual Exercises under Father Passaglia's direction. Instead of the usual meditation on the choice of a state of life, Father Passaglia proposed the choice of a Church, carrying out the rules of St. Ignatius for a wise election. The result was so clear a light and so profound a conviction that further hesitation was impossible. Mr. Palmer was then and there received into the Church, and continued his retreat as a Catholic.

A violent epidemic of measles broke out in Rome. Scarcely a house was spared, and people of all ages were attacked. Grandmothers and grandchildren were often laid up under the same roof, and some took the disease for the third time. Lady Lothian's daughters did not escape, and Miss Taafe had it dangerously. Mrs. Leslie's hesitation between charity to the sick and her duty to her daughter was only momentary. Charlotte had never had the measles, and her delicate state of health made the greatest care necessary; but the mother's common sense told her that the air of Rome and the very house they were in being strongly impregnated with the disease, precautions to avoid it would avail little if there were any predisposition to take it. There was no one to nurse Miss Taafe, who had for a long time lived the life of a recluse, spending her days in prayer before the Blessed Sacrament, and only leaving the church at the hours when it was closed. She cared little for personal comfort and still less for society. But she had been from the first greatly drawn to Mrs. Leslie, and before her illness would occasionally come to her rooms in the evening, her conversation, always unworldly and tinged with a certain blunt originality, making her a welcome guest. Her isolation was entirely owing to her devotion, and appealed therefore doubly to Mrs. Leslie's charity. The sick room resembled the cell of a religious in its simplicity; there was not even a curtain to the window to protect the invalid from the fierce glare, which was intolerable. Mrs. Leslie suggested that a curtain should be put up, but Miss Taafe answered in the blunt way in which her mortifications were disguised:

"What do I want a curtain for? Can I not close my eyes if I dislike the light?"

Thanks to the good nursing, she got over the danger and recovered, and gratitude cemented the friendship between her nurse and the Taafe family. She afterwards went to live in a convent, and Mr. Palmer occupied the now vacant rooms in the Via Tor de' Specchi.

Mr. Palmer was a very valuable friend to have in Rome. He knew of all the best opportunities for seeing things of interest, and was always ready to help others to avail themselves of such opportunities. At one time he would organise a visit to the Catacombs, under the guidance of Padre Marchi; at another, to the recently discovered basilica of St. Alexander, with the Cavaliere Rossi as *cicerone;* or to the Colisseum by moonlight or to the Capitol, where by appointment Padre Secchi would show him and his friends the wonders of the heavens through the powerful telescope belonging to the Observatory. If Ostia was to be visited, Mr. Palmer would be ready with the history of the place interspersed with anecdotes, stories of St. Augustine and St. Monica, odds and ends of archæological lore suited to the capacity of his hearers. Learned though he was, he was never pedantic, and delighted in sharing his knowledge. But he hated pretension, affectation or worldliness, and made no secret of his dislike. A young lady, not a Catholic but often to be seen in Catholic society that year, was very much admired for her somewhat showy style of beauty. Mr. Palmer was one day heard to murmur a kind of dissent from what was being said in praise of her looks. Some one put the direct question to him: "Mr. Palmer, do you not agree in thinking Miss So-and-so very handsome?" He answered almost fiercely: "No, I never could see anything to admire in her. I can't bear the way she swivels her great black eyes about."

He enjoyed the pleasant evenings at Mrs. Leslie's after working hard all day at his book on Egyptian Chronology, sometimes playing chess, or listening with Father Coleridge to a symphony of Beethoven's or Haydn's which he would laconically pronounce to be "nice." These gatherings took place in what the Romans call the *prima sera*, as most of the English colony elected to dine early, and Cardinal Howard and the students from the Academia would often drop in, when the conversation would take a serious or an amusing tone.

Liberata never could master English names, so she announced them with a description. Father Coleridge was ushered in with a slight wave of her hand over her head and the words *l'alto*. Father Wynne she called *il più alto* with a higher wave, and Father Talbot was *l'altissimo* with a still higher wave. Sometimes Charlotte would give Mr. Palmer an open volume of Dickens, saying, "Now, Mr. Palmer, you are to read *that*," while she and her mother would sit quietly at work and enjoy seeing him shake with laughter.

The winter of 1854-5 was one of exceptional privileges, in honour of the Immaculate Conception. Unusual facilities were afforded for seeing the great relics, and on account of the large number of bishops and prelates then in Rome, ceremonies that would otherwise have taken place in the Sistine Chapel were performed in St. Peter's. This was notably the case on the occasion of the *Quarant' ore* in Advent, and of the Blessing of the Candles on the feast of the Purification, when Pius IX. was carried on the *seda gestatoria*, holding his enormous wax taper aloft and preceded by a vast number of bishops from all countries, including Archbishop Polding, Dr. Hughes of New York, Dr. Walsh of Halifax, Mgr. de Goesbriant, and many others, known personally to Mrs. Leslie. Cardinal Cullen presented her and her daughter to the Holy Father in a private audience. Scarcely had they crossed the threshold when the Pope called to his "carissimo figlio" to come near him, and those whom he introduced were affectionately welcomed.

Conspicuous among the strangers at all the great religious functions was an American lady, a Mrs. Peter of Cincinnati, not yet a Catholic but an intelligent and sympathetic observer of all that was passing around her. Her object in coming to Italy was to collect pictures and other works of art for the

"Ladies' Academy of Art" in her native city. When she arrived she was possessed of the ordinary Protestant misconceptions regarding the Catholic religion, but being remarkably fair-minded, when personal observation convinced her of the injustice of the usual accusations brought against the Church, she at once set about correcting in her letters to her friends the prejudices in which she and they had been brought up. Moreover, having a natural love of fair play she was inclined to interpret favourably what she did not yet understand in Catholic devotions and practices. While she was in Rome letters reached her containing the information that the funds on which she had counted to meet the expense of her purchases for the above-mentioned institution were no longer available, and the primary object of her visit to Italy had to be abandoned. But another and far more engrossing matter had begun to occupy her attention.

Mrs. Peter's clear, observant mind and right intention gradually brought her to the threshold of the Catholic Church, but it was not without intense suffering that she recognized the necessity of breaking with the religious traditions of the past. At a point where her convictions were on the side of Catholic truth, but her courage to take the now necessary step scarcely equal to the effort, Archbishop Hughes suggested that she should make a retreat at the Convent of the Sacred Heart. She consented to this, and here at the *Trinità dei Monti* she was introduced to Mrs. Leslie, who better perhaps than any one could enter into her difficulties and sympathize with a struggle in which the associations of a lifetime, family affections, doubts and fears were so many temptations threatening to make shipwreck of a strong and noble nature. At this time Mrs. Peter wrote to an intimate friend a letter of which the following is an extract giving a remarkably clear account of her position:

> I have for years been restless and unhappy on finding that the views held and taught by our Church (the Anglican) could not satisfy me, and my unhappiness arose from my own self-accusation because I was not satisfied. Many others, I doubt not, live and die with the same habitual self-condemnation, yet never suspect the cause. And now as I come nearer to the clear light of truth I wonder that I should always have been so near and yet never have discovered it. . . . I have had excellent opportunities to learn, and fearful interior difficulties to overcome before I could separate my better judgment from the mass of error which overlaid it. I say nothing of the struggles in my conscience, my terrible fears of being misguided by illusions, but which seem gradually to be dissipated by the light of a clearer faith.

The "illusions" vanished at last like the morning mist before the vivifying rays of the noontide sun, and Mrs. Peter became a fervent Catholic. At the ceremony of her conditional baptism, Mrs. Leslie was her godmother, and the two became devoted friends, Mrs. Peter going over again with her the hallowed places of Christian Rome, seeing the things she had seen before with a larger, clearer vision and a superadded sense of their inner meaning and beauty. Together they made the pilgrimage to Subiaco ; together they assisted at the most affecting of all Rome's solemnities, the procession of Corpus Domini through the colonnades of St. Peter's, Pius IX. carrying the Blessed Sacrament, borne along above the heads of the kneeling crowds. In an audience with his Holiness the Pope was so much interested in all that Mrs. Peter told him about the state of religion in America, and of her own plans for its advancement by means of her ample fortune and the devotion of the rest of her life to its cause, that the interview surpassed in length all that was customary. At last, without waiting for the Pope to dismiss her, she took leave of him, apologising for having trespassed so long on his time, a solecism which no doubt amused the Holy Father greatly.

In a subsequent visit to Rome Mrs. Peter found herself in the midst of a conclave of Cardinals ; Pio Nono perceived her not far from his throne and remarked to those nearest to him with evident satisfaction, "Ecco la nostra cara Signora Peter!" On another occasion she was kneeling in front of a rail with a number of other people to receive the Pope's blessing. In her emotion she dropped the staff which she at that time used to lean upon when walking, and it fell on the other side of the rail, startling his Holiness. He looked round, and seeing what had happened stooped and picked up the staff, saying pleasantly as he handed it to its owner, "Signora Peter, you have done what all Europe has failed to do — you have stopped me in my career."

Mrs. Peter was again in Rome during the Vatican Council, and, as a member of the American pilgrimage, presented the homage of the Catholics of the United States to the Holy Father. On each occasion of her visits he welcomed her in the warmest manner and sent her back loaded with gifts, the tokens of his high esteem and fatherly affection. Her good works in the land of her birth, extending over a period of twenty-three years from 1854, the year of her conversion, to 1877, the year of her death, were prodigious. By dint of unflagging energy, perseverance and lavish generosity she succeeded in founding convents of the Good Shepherd, of the Franciscan Order, of the Little Sisters of the Poor, of the Sisters of Mercy, and

of the Sacred Heart in Cincinnati. She was the
head and life and soul of innumerable pious
institutions and charitable organizations, and
during the war in the United States she became
a second providence to the sick and wounded,
neither obstacles nor ingratitude, doubt nor
suspicion, tempting her to look back when once
she had laid her hand to any work.

Some disappointments fell to her lot; she
was denied the happiness so ardently longed for
of seeing her beloved children within the fold,
and this was an abiding sorrow; but the general
impression which she produced on all who came
in contact with her was one of intense joy—joy
in her faith and in her works. She was actively
engaged in planning out still further spheres of
usefulness when she was called to inherit her
reward. Her death, apparently the result of
a slight accident, left many to mourn her loss,
in society, among the poor, and in the fourteen
religious communities which she had founded.

Another convert helped into the Church by
Mrs. Leslie during her first visit to Rome was
a Mrs. W——. Her husband had already
become a Catholic, but she was kept back by
timidity and a certain want of resolution more
than by any remaining difficulties. She
accompanied him to Mass and other religious
ceremonies, but although she seemed to believe
all that was necessary she could not make up

her mind to the plunge. On one occasion she was greatly distressed to hear the peasants in a country church whisper to each other as she passed them, "Poveretta, non è cristiana!" Father Coleridge applied to Mrs. Leslie for a suitable book to lend her, and after hearing Mrs. W——'s state of mind described, she chose one of the Clifton Tales. Father Coleridge carried it straight to the table d'hôte at the Minerva where the lady was staying and said, "Mrs. W——, I have brought a book which will exactly suit you, 'Winefride Jones, the Very Ignorant Girl.'" Mrs. W—— took the book with great sweetness and humility, and soon became a fervent Catholic, not called indeed to play a conspicuous part like Mrs. Peter, but to edify many by a life of hidden virtue, patience in suffering and fidelity in small things.

When the summer heat had driven away most of the foreigners, Mrs. Leslie left Rome to return to Scotland, taking with her as far as Marseilles Madame de Ferron, one of those ladies who had accompanied her from Lyons, and who was a great invalid. They went by sea as the least fatiguing hot-weather route, and remained at Marseilles long enough to visit the celebrated sanctuary of Notre Dame de la Garde, proceeding the same day to Avignon. The Hôtel de l'Europe had been strongly recommended by friends in Rome, and the landlady turned out to be a second Liberata in point of kind-heartedness, piety and charity. The hotel, which was a model of good order and neatness, was very full, for numbers of French, English and Russian officers were returning from the Crimea. Among the Russians was the celebrated Prince Menschikoff. Besides these were the homeward-bound tourists from the south, usually to be met with at that season. The next morning, to the dismay of many of the travellers, it was found that none could leave Avignon, as no train for the North had come in, and it was feared that an accident had happened. Later on the news came that a bridge over the railway had been swept away by the rising of the Rhône. To Mrs. Leslie and her daughter the delay caused no great inconvenience, but as the day wore on the townspeople grew anxious. The rain came down in torrents, and the military were hastily sent out to strengthen the dykes and ramparts near the river. An open-air banquet given to the officers of various nationalities then in the town came to a sudden end. Soon cries of terror were heard; people ran wildly hither and thither panic-stricken. Forty metres of the river wall had given way, and the Rhône rushed into the town, carrying all before it. The turbid waters could be seen from the hotel windows rising every moment higher. The landlady never lost her presence of mind; she forgot nothing, did the best for everyone, and even remembered the aviary of little birds in the courtyard, unlocked it and set the inmates free. But soon, like Noah's dove, they flew in at the windows, finding no resting-place anywhere outside in the world of water. The black muddy stream filled the basement and the ground-floor, and continued to rise till it reached the *entresol*, then the first-floor. From the second-floor landing three dry steps were to be seen, all the rest below being dark water. The travellers had removed their luggage to the top of the house, and were obliged to make the best of the accommodation left by the invading waters. The scene from the windows was not easily to be forgotten. People in boats, on rafts or in tubs steered themselves along as well as they could, trying to reach their homes or put their goods in a place of safety. The contents of shops, suites of furniture, meat, vegetables and household stuff were swept along the street, now a deep and rushing river. With them came hundreds of rats swimming or drowning. Presently large boats passed along filled with soldiers and engineers, testing the strength and condition of the buildings to resist the rush of water. As the day wore on the current flowed less rapidly, the water found its level, and there was hope that the flood would subside without further damage. But the inhabitants of the city had to remain for some time in their upper storeys, many of them in dire want of food and of water fit to drink. All the first night the greater part of Avignon was in total darkness, the street-lamps being of course submerged. Early the next morning boats plied about distributing aid. The weather was brighter, the water clearer, and from a corner room commanding views of cross-streets the Bishop and his clergy were seen in small barks carrying necessaries from house to house. It would have made a fine picture had any *genre* artist been on the spot. Food was brought by steamer from Marseilles, and the landlady of the Hôtel de l'Europe managed in some miraculous way to cook it for her numerous household; but how it was done remained a mystery, the kitchen being deep under water. Her politeness and good temper kept up the spirits of her guests and underlings, and barring a little confusion, such as Prince Menschikoff mistaking Mrs. Leslie's bedroom for his own, there were few *contretemps*.

But the greatest anxiety was felt concerning the fate of the Jesuit Father, who had preached the Lenten sermons in Rome that year, at San Luigi dei Francesi. It was known that he had gone to remove the Blessed Sacrament from a church that could not possibly escape inundation, had taken refuge in a room over the sacristy, the window of which was at so awkward a height that it was scarcely possible to reach it from below, while all means of escape from above were cut off, and he was himself without food. The ingenuity of the landlady of the Hôtel de l'Europe invented a way of introducing supplies through the window, and as soon as he could be rescued he was brought in a boat to the hotel. Sunday came, but to get to Mass was impossible, and all the Catholics in the hotel assembled to offer the Holy Sacrifice in spirit as best they could. Gradually the flood subsided, and at last the higher part of the town could be reached partly in carts partly in boats. The Leslies made their way up to the Rocher where the ancient palace of the Popes still stands, and viewed from thence such a scene of desolation as it does not often fall to one's eyes to witness. A vast expanse of water stretched over the whole plain; only the tops of poplar-trees and the tallest chimneys might be seen above the flood, while the Rocher itself was covered with a heterogeneous mass of carriages, household furniture in vans, livestock and all kinds of provisions that had been brought up there for safety. Communication with the North having been re-established, there was of course a general exodus from the city of waters. Mrs. Leslie and her daughter were among the first to leave in a railway omnibus well filled with passengers. Before long the driver recommended the travellers to put their feet up on to the seats, and scarcely had he done so when the horses began swimming and plunging and the omnibus became a kind of large bath. Considering the above circumstances it is not to be wondered at that Avignon did not leave a very pleasing impression.

The rest of the summer was passed in visiting relations and friends in France, England and Scotland, and when the first cold weather was felt in Paris, after their return thither, Mrs. Leslie hastened her preparations for taking Charlotte back to Rome. Before starting she one day met an old friend, Admiral Belcher, who enquired about their route and asked what day they intended to sail from Marseilles. On hearing their plans he said:

"Well, you can go on board that evening without fear, though there will be a heavy gale. At ten o'clock it will go down, and the voyage will be calm. From my experience of the moon's influence, I know as an old seaman that it will be so," and he quoted several examples in favour of his theory. His prediction as to the gale proved true. It was blowing hard when they reached Marseilles, and towards evening the wind became so terrific that all the intending passengers by the boat were afraid to venture on board and elected to remain where they were for the night. Mrs. Leslie, in spite of her faith in the old admiral's weather lore, did the same, but exactly at the hour he had foretold, the storm ceased and a beautiful star-light night followed, which made every one regret not having gone by the boat. The service between Marseilles and Civita Vecchia was far less frequent then than now, and instead of waiting for another boat, Mrs. Leslie took the Riviera route to Genoa, travelling by vetturino from thence to Florence, with two English ladies, a Miss Roskell and a Miss Plowden. This mode of travelling was the most enjoyable of any. In Italy at every halt there is something interesting to be seen—a church, a remarkable picture, a lovely view, as the case may be, and to be able to stop at leisure, to visit the Blessed Sacrament, hear Mass, and enjoy the freedom which travelling by vetturino secured, more than compensated for bad inns, poor fare and the want of home comforts.

At Florence some English Protestants at the table d'hôte were one day heard to speak most offensively and most untruly of Dr. Newman, accusing him of having remained in the Church of England to secure its emoluments long after he was a Papist in heart and to a great extent in practice. Mrs. Leslie's travelling companions begged her to contradict the statement, which although not addressed to her or to any of her party, had been spoken so unnecessarily loud that it was unmistakably intended for the four Catholic ladies at table. It would have seemed wrong to let such an accusation go unchallenged, and Mrs. Leslie, who was ever ready to defend the absent and to forget herself whenever the Catholic cause was attacked, carefully prepared what she wished to say, and with perfect dignity and politeness of form made so able and convincing a defence of the maligned convert as to cover his slanderers with confusion.

The journey from Florence to Rome occupied a week. The travellers stopped at Cortona, at Perugia, and at every other place of interest on their way. The succeeding winter was an extremely happy and peaceful one, a second visit to the Eternal City being perhaps always a source of greater joy than the first. The excitement of novelty gives place to a more peaceful feeling and there is less of curiosity and more of devotion in revisiting the sacred places.

Pius IX. was still free, and often on a sunny afternoon he might be seen walking outside the walls with a small group of attendants, among whom was Mgr. Talbot nearly always beside him. The papal carriage would be following slowly at a little distance. Mrs. Leslie delighted to meet him thus, to stop and kneel as he drew near, to see his kind smile of recognition, and to hear him say in his fatherly tones, "Iddio ti benedica, figlioula mia." She had the happiness, with her daughter, of assisting at his Mass and of receiving Communion from his hand on the day he left Rome for his tour through the Pontifical States and Tuscany. Afterwards they witnessed the touching affection of the crowd gathered in the great square of St. Peter's to take leave of him. Many were weeping aloud at the thought of the separation and the fear lest some evil should befall their beloved pontiff during his absence. None who saw the faithful Romans that morning, or on the day when they went out to meet and greet him on his return and heard their enthusiastic welcome could ever admit that they were indifferent to the Pope.

During a retreat, made by the mother and daughter in the spring of 1856, Charlotte Leslie began to feel the premonitory symptoms of an illness which proved to be a serious attack of pleurisy, and declared itself immediately on her return to the Via Tor de' Specchi. Her convalescence was long and tedious, and left great delicacy behind it. The greater, therefore, was the need for care, in choosing a suitable villeggiatura for the summer months. After much deliberation Mrs. Leslie agreed to join the Contessa Borgogelli and her daughters, who were going with Miss Martha Taafe, the Contessa's sister, to Spoleto. One reason for the choice of this place was its reputation for salubrity, the cholera, which was causing ravages in many parts of Italy, being hitherto unknown at Spoleto, and the beauty of its scenery, the easy distance from Rome, and the facility with which Assisi, Montefalco and other interesting places might be visited from thence, added weighty inducements. The party left Rome on June 22, the driver of the vetturino promising to be at Narni by nightfall. The weather was bad and the roads were heavy, so that their progress was very slow. It was growing late when the carriage ceased the melancholy trundle which it had kept up for some hours, and came to a sudden halt before an unpromising roadside inn. The driver announced calmly that his horses would not reach Narni that night, and that the ladies must put up at the inn. In vain Countess Borgogelli remonstrated. With Italian coolness the man unharnessed his horses, and assured the travellers that they would be *molto contente* with their quarters. There was no appeal, and they entered a dark, bare kitchen with a cavernous chimney, in which lay heaps of wood ashes, the remains of the whole winter's fuel, making a comfortable bed for three ugly dogs that were sleeping there. The landlord appeared, looking very wild and excited, as he asked what their requirements were. When told that seven beds were wanted, he clutched his black locks with a gesture of despair, and declared the impossibility of supplying them. He ran about ejaculating, "Sette letti! Santissima Vergine, sette letti!" At last he calmed down sufficiently to understand that he was wanted to show what accommodation he could offer. He exhibited three bedrooms with brick floors, one bed in each, made up of planks laid on tressles, a palliasse of Indian corn leaves and a mattress. The breadth of these beds would have allowed of four persons sleeping abreast. Contessa Borgogelli and her eldest daughter Polissena took possession of one, Miss Taafe and her niece Caterina of another, Mrs. Leslie and Charlotte of the third. The maid was to have a bed found for her. The washing apparatus was as primitive as the beds, and the demand for seven towels was evidently considered as exorbitant as the first. But after much parleying and gesticulating on the part of the landlord, who saw that no abatement in the number would be made, he produced seven towels, and after another short delay supper was served for seven in the kitchen. At the far end of the long table, in the dark, bare room, some waggoners were having their meal, and no fewer than ten famished dogs prowled round the table, poking their noses into the plates, snapping at every mouthful, pushing in between the guests, and nearly upsetting the dishes. There was no inducement to sit up after supper; nothing was to be seen from the window but a bit of ruined castle and some fields, and the party retired at once to their respective rooms. As there was no fastening to any of the doors, they barricaded them with their luggage and some of the scanty furniture, and when they were ready for bed found it prudent to clamber in simultaneously, from opposite sides, as the whole structure threatened to tilt over without some such well-combined movement.

The next day, in bright weather, they reached Spoleto, which fully realized their expectations as to natural beauty and other advantages. The party was a happy one, sufficiently numerous to be agreeable, and a similarity of tastes made each other's society delightful in the various expeditions which were planned. One day, they went to Montefalco, a poor mountain village which did not even boast of an inn, but contained a priceless treasure in the *Corpo Santo*, the incorrupt body of St. Clare. They saw it lying in its calm beauty, not dark like that of St. Rose of Viterbo, not even bronzed as St. Mary Magdalen of Pazzi, but quite white, the feet only being a little discoloured. They went to Assisi and the Portiuncula, and in their daily walks visited the churches, convents and shrines nearer to Spoleto; the spirit of St. Francis, his simplicity, his gentleness even to animals still seemed to pervade the country side. On one occasion, the three girls with their maid set out to visit a monastery on the top of a high hill. They stopped at a mill to enquire whether they could hire a donkey to help them up the ascent. The miller's wife agreed to let them have one, and while they were waiting a flock of sheep came by. She gave them each a handful of salt, and the animals crowded round them, licking their hands and making friends with them, evidently accustomed to the kindest treatment and exhibiting not the slightest fear. Towards evening, the girls were walking in the upper town, when they saw two women talking to each other excitedly. Polissena's quick ears overheard one saying to the other that a case of cholera had broken out in their street. In a few days it was public news, and a panic ensued among the peasantry. Mrs. Leslie and her friends decided that it would be useless to leave only to be placed in quarantine, and made up their minds to wait. But the epidemic increased daily, and at last the authorities forbade the tolling of bells at funerals, so great was the terror that reigned. A cart was sent round every evening to collect the corpses and bury them at night outside the town in a cemetery blessed for the occasion. The weather was intensely hot, but in order to purify the air, huge piles of brushwood were stacked at the corners of the streets, and every night the whole town was illuminated by blazing bonfires, the sparks flying in at the open windows, to the great risk of setting the houses on fire. Fruit and ices were prohibited, and the doctors and priests were worn out with attendance on the sick and dying. The cholera did not, however, prevent the arrival at Spoleto of numbers of pilgrims, bound for Assisi, to gain the Portiuncula Indulgence on August 2, the *Perdono di San Francesco.* Many, as could be seen by their costumes, came from the kingdom of Naples, and these weary, footsore pilgrims slept for the most part in the streets or under some archway. If they should fall a prey to the ravages of the cholera, at least they would be well prepared to die after visiting Assisi and Santa Maria degli Angeli.

Mrs. Leslie's practical common-sense was

of great help while the cholera raged. She always knew exactly what to do for the sufferers, and never lost her head. She sent to Rome for stores of arrowroot for the convalescents and those who were in the early stages of the disease; and to distribute and administer remedies became her daily work of charity. Peaceful, and even cheerful in the midst of the prevailing terror, she also exercised a beneficial effect upon her surroundings by her calm and equable temperament, a quiet mind being the greatest preservative from danger. One evening, after their return from a walk, Countess Borgogelli became suddenly ill. The doctor at once prescribed twelve powders of flower of zinc, a remedy which had been tried with great success that year at Ancona and other places. The little party gathered that night round the supper-table was more grave than usual. Polissena and Caterina soon went to replace their aunt by their mother's bedside, and in crossing the landing heard moans in the hall below. It appeared that one of the hotel servants had imprudently walked to the top of the Somma in the great heat, had returned exhausted, and had fallen a prey to the epidemic. All remedies proved unavailing; it was a case of cholera *foudroyant*, and the man died before morning. Five other persons in the hotel were attacked that night, but recovered. A poor girl in a neighbouring street happened to go to the window as the dead cart was passing, was seized with a shivering fit, and was dead in a few hours. Public prayers and processions were ordered, and at last a storm accompanied by heavy rain cooled and purified the air and arrested the further progress of the disease.

Towards the end of August it was ascertained that there would be no difficulty in returning to Rome, and no delay, beyond a halt for fumigation at Narni. A carriage was engaged for the journey, and the party set out, Mrs. Leslie intending to go to Albano, the Borgogellis to some other country place till October. At the foot of the steep hill on which Narni is built the carriage was stopped, the luggage taken down, and the travellers were ordered by a number of police officers to follow it into a small hut and unlock the trunks. They were then hermetically closed in, the door was locked, and they were not allowed to emerge till they were half blinded and nearly choked by the thick smoke of some very powerful disinfectant. They were then suffered to continue their journey. After spending one night in the Via Tor de' Specchi, Mrs. Leslie and Charlotte proceeded to Albano, to pay a long promised visit to the Tollemaches. At Albano they found a whole colony of English friends, among whom were Lady Fitzgerald, Mr. Palmer and Lord Clifford, with whom they made the pilgrimage to the Sanctuary of Our Lady of Galloro, as well as excursions to other places of interest among the Alban hills, promising themselves a longer sojourn on some future occasion. During the following winter in Rome, Mrs. Leslie's charitable offices were claimed by Miss Gladstone, who had always been deeply attached to her since an illness she had had in Edinburgh in 1848, when Mrs. Leslie had nursed her with great devotion. They had often met since then in London, Scotland and Rome, and Miss Gladstone had introduced her to the celebrated Dominican, Père Besson, for whom she had the most intense veneration, as well as for the whole Dominican Order. She subsequently entered a Dominican convent in Rome, but the attempt at religious life was beyond her strength, and when laid prostrate by some dangerous kind of fever she sent for Mrs. Leslie. Thanks mainly to her care, the patient recovered, but to her own great regret was obliged to leave the convent.

As during the two previous winters, Father Wynne and Father Coleridge were frequent evening visitors at Mrs. Leslie's. They looked upon her as a mother—a way many people had—and they both confided to her their intention of entering the Society of Jesus. It will easily be imagined, that such an intention awoke her tenderest sympathies and constituted a fresh bond between them. The two young priests were devoted friends and companions, Father Coleridge having an immense admiration for Father Wynne, who to a large, grand, and almost royal manner, united great warmth of heart, generosity, and rare mental endowments. He was a convert of the Newman school, and had given up a large fortune, and his inheritance to an estate, on becoming a priest. No one was more careful about his dress, which in his worldly days was always exquisite, and contributed with his fine face and figure, his charming manner and delightful conversation to make him a notable personage in society. One evening, as the two friends were leaving the house in the Via Tor de' Specchi, Mrs. Leslie gave Father Coleridge a light, fearing that there might be none at the bottom of the stairs. As he took it he looked affectionately at his companion, saying, "I am not worthy to hold a candle to Wynne."

On the day when they left Rome for England, to put their design into execution, Mrs. Leslie went, in motherly fashion, to see them off and say a last "God speed" as they got into the diligence. Father Coleridge had been of great use to her in introducing her to the "Life of our Lord" by Ludolph le Chartreux, a book which became the food of her daily meditation. He used to say that he always considered he had done a good work when he had persuaded anyone to adopt this book for habitual use. He also gave her something of his own devotion to St. Anne, the mother of the Blessed Virgin.

When the time again came round for choosing a summer resort Mrs. Leslie, remembering the beautiful scenery of the Alban hills and the freshness of the air, arranged to go with her daughter to Castel Gandolfo. They took some rooms commanding wide views of the Campagna, the Mediterranean and Rome, in the house of the Arciprete's sister, within a few minutes' walk of the Duomo, the Pope's summer palace, of Miss Plummer's pretty villa on the edge of the lake, and of the old ilex avenues, known as the *galleria di sopra e di sotto*.

Mr. Palmer had chosen Rocca di Papa as his summer residence, where he lodged in a peasant's family, contenting himself—he cared nothing for comfort—with their poor fare. Oftener than not he supped on Indian corn slightly roasted. Each member of the family picked out the dry grains with his own fork and ate them with a little sugar, salt or butter. On Saturdays Mr. Palmer generally went over to Castel Gandolfo, early in the day, and remained till Monday. In the afternoon he would ride to Galloro with Charlotte, and after going to confession, they would remount, ride round the lake of Nenni, or to the Basilian Abbey of Grotta Ferrata, or call on his Russian friend, young Princess Gargarin at Genzano. It was sometimes near nightfall before they returned, when, fearing that her mother would be anxious, Charlotte would propose a canter. But Mr. Palmer never would agree to this if they were near a village or hamlet, objecting that it was very bad-mannered to ride fast through a town, and that no civilised people ever did so, except the Greek Court at Athens, which always set off at a hand gallop.

On Monday, when he returned to his hermitage for another week of study, the peasant, his host, would arrive on an old horse to fetch him, bringing a donkey for Mr. Palmer to ride. Then a well filled basket of provisions would be tied to the horse's saddle, for Mrs. Leslie distrusted the régime to which he had condemned himself, and did all she could to supplement his meagre fare, fearing that his health would break down. On these Mondays, she and Charlotte accompanied him on foot, as far as they could walk, the donkey being taken in tow by the horse, while the peasant sauntered along carelessly by the side of his animals. Once the donkey tugged so violently that the basket was thrown to the ground, somewhat to the detriment of its contents.

Mrs. Leslie's apprehensions regarding Mr. Palmer's health were not without foundation, and at each of his visits she grew more uneasy. At last, one Sunday, he nearly fainted during High Mass, and seemed ill all day. The next day he was so much worse that he was unfit to return to Rocca di Papa, and finally yielded to the necessity of being nursed. A serious illness laid him prostrate for many weeks, during which time Mrs. Leslie was not only his faithful and indefatigable nurse, but also his secretary. She communicated by letter with his nearest relations, and gave them details of every stage of his malady. Her anxiety increased as his state became more alarming, and at last she sent for Baron Schrœter, who was always to be found at Rome, whatever the season might be, and who was not only Mr. Palmer's friend, but the friend of all who were in trouble and in need of one. He came at once, and his presence was a great relief, although his opinion of the patient was not encouraging. After seeing him, he exclaimed in his broken English, "Palmer will die, yes, he will die. But I do the right thing. I go back to Rome, and bring out Small."

Dr. Small was an English physician, whose advice for all concerned it would be a satisfaction to obtain, even if the doctor from Albano in attendance on him were treating his case suitably. The consultation was eminently successful, and after some time anxiety gave place to thankfulness, for "Palmer" did not "die," but in due course got well. His gratitude, and that of his people, especially of his mother and brother, for all that Mrs. Leslie had done for him may be imagined.

The history of the next winter is a touching chapter in the family records. Mr. Falconer Atlee had written to his sister from Paris that his son Albert's health was extremely delicate, that an attack of bronchitis had left his lungs in a susceptible condition, and that a winter in a southern climate was judged advisable for him. The letter ended with the request that Mrs. Leslie would undertake the care of her nephew in Rome. Her answer was not long delayed, and in December Albert Atlee, now a very tall, delicate-looking youth of about twenty, joined his aunt and cousin in the Via Tor de' Specchi. There was little in the weary and somewhat querulous valetudinarian to remind them of the light-hearted boy of former days, but Charlotte ascertained that he still wore the medal which she had given him five years before.

Beyond his having kept his promise in this, there was little to encourage hope of his conversion. He avoided any allusion to religious topics, and seemed unfavourably impressed with the ceremonies and practices of the Church that came under his notice. He appeared to be irritated if his criticisms provoked an explanation or any approach to an argument, so that his doctor, fearing that excitement might bring on hemorrhage from the lungs, forbade the discussion of any subject bordering on controversy. Nevertheless, he grew steadily worse, and on New Year's Eve had a very bad hemorrhage, the cause of which could be traced to no irritation whatever. His increasing weakness distressed him greatly; he shrank from the prospect of death, and was painfully affected by anything that reminded him of it. Mrs. Leslie and her daughter could only pray silently, while they surrounded the poor boy with all that the tenderest love and sympathy could devise to cheer and comfort him. Mr. Palmer joined them in all their prayers for his conversion, and contrivances for his comfort, even giving up his own room to the invalid. They made novenas to St. Joseph, but March slipped away leaving the situation unchanged.

"It will be for the month of May," they said hopefully, and when Charlotte, who had hitherto escaped the penalty to which so many visitors to Rome fall a prey, was seized with Roman fever, it was to her only something more that could be offered up for her cousin's conversion. The saving of his soul had become an all-absorbing intention. But April was almost over when he became restless, and announced his resolve to return to Paris. He even engaged a courier to accompany him, and made plans for starting immediately, although he was totally unfit to travel, and it seemed more than likely that he would die on the road. The case was desperate, and Mrs. Leslie, who remembered hearing in her visits among the poor of the Trastevere that when they were in despair they prayed to St. Jude, determined to make a novena to St. Jude for this almost despaired-of grace. Many of the English Catholics in Rome joined in the novena. Before it ended, Charlotte urged her mother to speak to Albert on the subject nearest to their hearts. Mrs. Leslie, after much deliberation, decided that written words would be less likely to excite or annoy him than any spoken ones, however carefully chosen, and she accordingly wrote :

ROME, April 25, 1858.

MY DEAREST ALBERT,—Whilst I am waiting with the idea that you may presently ring for me, I cannot resist writing you a few lines, for my heart is indeed very earnestly and affectionately preoccupied about you. Four months have now elapsed since you came to Rome—months of disappointment and suffering, during which your chief consolation has been the attention and care of your medical friend. While we naturally regret that his efforts and the climate have not been crowned with the success we had desired and most fervently prayed for, we can only submit to the overruling decrees of Divine Providence, commend the results of the unknown future to His all-wise and all-merciful disposal, and, since the present alone is in our power, make the best use of it that we may be able to do. And how is this to be done? There is an old saying: "Hope for the best, but be prepared for the worst." And what is really to "hope for the best" but to wish and desire that the holy will of God may be done—not in a vague and general way, but *in all things concerning ourselves*, whether as regards health or sickness, wealth or poverty, life or death? But what is *essentially* the will of God towards every living soul? It is, as the apostle says, "our sanctification," our becoming holy, for if without faith "it is impossible to please God," so, as the same apostle writes, "without holiness no man shall see the Lord."

Just consider then, the supreme importance of a right faith and a solid holiness, based on a foundation that shall not fail us under any conceivable circumstance of trial and temptation, being based on that eternal truth which is the same yesterday, to-day and for ever. Our blessed Lord not only came to suffer and to die for us, but to teach us, and He left us a Church, the depository of His doctrine, which He commanded us to obey. This Church must have certain attributes, and whatever separated sects may assume, and whatever pious opinions may assert, these attributes can only meet in the one true Church, which at the same time must be Catholic, Apostolic and Holy.

You might have known more of the claims of the Church upon your regard and obedience, since you have been here (an opportunity granted to comparatively few of our countrymen), but you rejected the simple offer I one day proposed to you on the score of its consolations, and I have since refrained from pressing the subject. But now, my dear Albert, when the day of our parting is drawing nigh, permit me to use the privilege of a very near relative and of a very warm friend, of one who has watched over you very anxiously for some time, and who feels deeply interested in all that concerns your welfare of soul and body, and who grieves that she has not been able to do more for either. Permit me, I say, to urge you to look into this all-important question *now, without delay*, whilst so many opportunities and facilities surround you, whilst in short, as our divine Master said, "it is called to-day," lest the night overtake you, in which no man can work, and these things shall be hidden from your eyes.

Justly viewed, this consideration is both easy and reasonable. Be assured, you would be all the happier for it, and I believe all the better, for even if it should please God to continue the trial of your sickness, a true religion and the sacraments of the Church would certainly support and cheer you. Even if you were called to pass through the valley of the shadow of death you would not be dismayed by the summons; and were you restored to health, you would be all the better able, having learned to know God (where and how He has specially appointed to make Himself known to his poor, weak, blind and ignorant creatures) also to love Him and serve Him. And having, by the help of His grace, loved and served Him here, you would be united to Him in the joy of a blessed eternity.

Oh, my dear Albert, what a joy is this! It is meant for you; will you not have it? I pray that you may, and all whom you love, and that without delay. May Almighty God then dispose you so to seek that you may find, so to ask that you may obtain, this pearl of great price, and evermore vouchsafe to guide and guard and bless you. It is now late, so I hope, as you have not rung, that you are sleeping, and will awake refreshed. I will say "good night," and beg you to believe me always with every good wish,

Your most affectionate aunt,

ELEANOR LESLIE.

Mrs. Leslie read this letter to her daughter, who was disappointed with it, exclaiming: "Dearest mother, you could have written something far better and more convincing than that!"

"It may be," her mother replied, "but I mean to give it to him just as it is, because I prayed so much about it before beginning."

The letter was placed that night on a table in the young man's room, where he could not fail to see it when he awoke.

The next morning he came to breakfast as punctually as usual, looking moreover brighter and more cheerful than his wont. When his cousin had left the room, he said, going straight to the point:

"Auntie, who is your confessor?"

She told him that it was Padre Cardella, an Italian Jesuit; and when Albert thereupon enquired what kind of a man he was, and whether he spoke English, she was able to give the most satisfactory answers.

"I should like to see him, and have a talk with him," he said next, adding, "not of course with any idea of confession." Padre Cardella was asked to call, and when he came, was left alone with Albert. Two hours passed, and he was still there. When at last he left, the boy looked transformed.

"I told Padre Cardella all my difficulties," he said, "and he put before me all the truths of the Catholic religion, and I can accept them all, and he is to return to receive me into the Church, but he says he looks upon me as a Catholic already." Beaming with his newly-found happiness, his whole thoughts were now intent on preparing himself for the step he was about to take. Padre Cardella received his abjuration, and gave him his first Communion. Dr. Brown, Bishop of Shrewsbury, came to confirm him a few days later. Of his own accord, Albert sent for the courier, and told him his services would not be required, as he intended to remain in Rome. He wrote to his parents, told them that he had become a Catholic, and had given up his intention of returning to Paris. On receiving this news, Mr. Atlee at once left for Rome. He was shocked to observe the change which disease had wrought in his son's looks, but inexpressibly thankful to find him peaceful and happy, even with the knowledge that he was dying. All his horror of death had disappeared with the fret and worry which inaction had always caused him; and when he had received extreme unction his old light-heartedness and something of his boyish fun returned. His intense love for his father made Mr. Falconer Atlee's presence a joy to him, and he never tired of hearing him speak of his mother, his brother and sisters; but he never expressed a regret for the sacrifice he had made in not returning to Paris. All sorrow, dread or pain seemed merged into the perfect joy of faith, hope and charity, and

Mr. Atlee was so persuaded that the change in him was due to religion, that for a moment his own scepticism seemed to waver. An extract from one of his letters to his elder son will better show his state of mind than any description :

> Dr. Tramo has just been. He says to-day will be a bad one, and what that means is now too evident. God grant that it may be his last, for he suffers dreadfully. He has turned Catholic, and is to receive the last Sacraments presently. He is tranquil and prays for his release. "I am brisé," he says, "from head to foot," and "Heaven and my poor, dear mother alone engage my thoughts." Your aunt and Chattie's devotion to him surpass all description. He is patient, thankful and full of thoughtfulness. No alarm, no anxiety. With regard to his conversion no unfair influence has been used—far from it. It came upon him spontaneously, slowly, and so manifest has been its solace to him, that *it almost persuades me to be a Christian*. He has no excitement, but quiet, philosophical serenity. I ask him again and again if he would wish to have his mother here. He says, " No, no ; it would be too much for her, too much for me. Better as it is ; of that I am as certain as that I am dying. I would scarcely trust myself to die in her arms, for it would break her dear, dear heart. But she and I are to meet again." I had no idea that he possessed feelings of such exquisite tenderness.

On May 18 Charlotte was so ill from Roman fever that she too received the last Sacraments, and a nursing Sister was engaged to attend her. The next day she was better, it being the day of interval between the fits of tertian ague ; but after rising as usual Albert became faint, and a marked change came over him. Father Cardella was hastily sent for. While he went to fetch the Blessed Sacrament, Charlotte prepared the altar, and in a short time the ringing of the church bells announced that the *Santissimo* had come forth. In those days a devout crowd accompanied the Blessed Sacrament to the house of the sick, and remained praying outside while it was within. Albert could hear the bells and the procession passing through the Palazzo Campitelli into the quiet street as he sat on the couch, dressed with scrupulous neatness, his energy never having allowed him to fall into the negligent habits so excusable in an invalid. The bright, sunny drawing-room had nothing of the aspect of a sick-room, and through the open windows the sweet May air floated in, loaded with the scent of orange blossoms, and of all the thousand flowers which make Rome fragrant at that season. As Father Cardella entered, Mr. Falconer Atlee knelt respectfully with the others; the priest said a few words and some short prayers before administering Viaticum, and after taking the Blessed Sacrament back to the church, returned to say the prayers for a departing soul. When they were ended, Albert, who had been suffering great pain, revived a little; his face grew bright, and he threw his arms round Padre Cardella's neck, embracing his aunt and cousin also very affectionately.

His father, with tears in his eyes, said gently,

"Will you not kiss me too, Albert?"

"Oh yes," he replied fervently; "but these have opened Heaven to me."

The rest of that day and the next passed calmly, but another attack of fever having prostrated Charlotte, Contessa Borgogelli insisted on taking her away, Mrs. Leslie's strength hardly sufficing for more than the anxiety of one invalid at a time. The farewell between the cousins each knew to be final. It was the case to say with the Italians, "Arrivederci in Paradiso."

The nun who watched by Albert's bed during the night saw him turn to a picture of the Madonna hanging close to the bedside. Showing it to her he said, "Elle est ma mère." In the morning he asked what feast it was, the bells had been ringing so joyfully all night. He died on May 22, joyful and peaceful to the end, and Polissena Borgogelli, with her robust Italian-Irish faith, ran into Charlotte's sick-room saying, "I bring you good news. Your cousin has gone to heaven."

His body was taken to the Church of Santa Maria in Campitelli to pass the night before the funeral in front of the Blessed Sacrament. Franciscans chanted the Office for the Dead, the last rites being performed with devout solemnity.

A marble slab put up by Mr. Palmer at the cemetery of San Lorenzo bears the following inscription, composed by Padre Cardella:

☧ Positus in Pace heic est ☧
Albertus Joannes Falconer Atlee nat Anglus
Qui corporis valetudinem Romæ quæritans
Æternam Incolumitatem.
In germana Christianorum veritate est adeptus
Et præsidiis salutaribus fretus
Sit cum gaudio ad Deum
XI. Kal. Jun. an. MDCCCLVIII. æt S XXI.

CHAPTER XII.

GREETINGS AND FAREWELLS.

In various ways Mrs. Leslie's work at Rome seemed to be finished. The years which she had spent there had been abundantly productive of results in her own interior life, in the many valuable friends she had added to her circle, in the immense help she had afforded to those in need, body and soul. After long years her memory was still green in the eternal city, and her son, who went there for his Tertianship* ten years after she had left, heard her spoken of as "quella santa donna." Moreover, Father Cardella, who knew her perhaps best of all, once said to him, "I look upon your mother as a saint," testimony the more remarkable from the fact that Jesuits are slow to speak of people in that way. But, indeed, this opinion was universal among those who came into contact with her. Before starting on his journey to Rome, Father Leslie called on the Bishop of Southwark, Dr. Grant, to ask for his blessing, and because he was so great a friend of the Society. But

---

*The third year's Novitiate made by Jesuits after they are priests.

when he found himself in the Bishop's room, he discovered that he had nothing particular to say, and apologised for troubling him. Instead of answering, as he probably would to any other of the Fathers, that he was glad at all times to welcome a Jesuit, the Bishop said cordially, "We all respect your mother so much," as if that made his coming quite natural. Again, in Paris at another stage of this same journey, Father Leslie was glad to see Père Fessard who had been very good to him when he was studying theology at Laval. But at the first moment Père Fessard did not remember his name, whereupon Père de Ponlevoy recalled it to him by saying, "Il a une sainte mère—une sainte mère."

But in 1858, the good which Mrs. Leslie was to gain, and the good she was to do was no longer in Rome. The state of her daughter's health necessitated a prompt departure, for it seemed probable that the Roman fever from which Charlotte was suffering would only leave her on the other side of the Alps. There was yet another reason for hastening to Paris, where a great work of charity awaited her, left by Albert as a legacy. He had entreated his aunt to take up the conversion of his mother and sisters, and did not even despair of her influence with his father and brother. And meanwhile also, the bereaved mother needed the consolation of her presence. Mrs. Leslie and Charlotte had paid their farewell visits, had gone for the last time to the sanctuaries where they had obtained so many answers to prayer, and were ready to start on their journey northwards. But at the last moment there were difficulties about their passports, without which it was in those days unsafe to travel. Mrs. Leslie, in general so patient, was disconcerted at a delay which might cause anxiety and inconvenience to others, she having announced their arrival at Dijon and in Paris at a certain date. She was so exact in keeping engagements that a *contretemps* of this kind was doubly vexatious. Moreover, every day in the great heat increased the danger from Roman fever, and Mrs. Leslie was considerably troubled about it. "Dont be distressed," said Mr. Palmer, who had undertaken all the arrangements for the departure and the journey, "there is no sin in it," knowing well that to her, an annoyance in which there was no sin could not long be considered an evil. When at last the consul delivered the passports, they set out by way of Siena, Genoa and Turin. The crossing of the Mont Cenis was very different to the last they had experienced. Instead of the deep snow-drifts there were green hollows and beautiful Alpine flowers; and little children laden with blossoms ran by the side of their carriage. The travellers pushed on rapidly to Dijon to meet Mrs. Leslie's youngest sister, Mrs. Dowson, whose favourite son had lately perished in the massacre at Cawnpore. The two sisters had not met for years, but sorrow is a bond that quickly bridges over the gaps caused by absence, and Mrs. Leslie had the gift of carrying consolation wherever she went. Differences of religion seemed to be forgotten, and the week passed together was for all concerned a blessed time. The meeting would doubtless have been prolonged, but for the other grief-stricken mother in Paris, who was longing for those numerous minute details of her son's last months on earth, little nothings which yet say so much to a mother, and which her beloved sister-in-law could alone communicate. So they hastened on to Paris, and with the story of her nephew's wonderful conversion and death, Mrs. Leslie inspired gradually in Albert's mother and sisters a desire to share his faith, and to be instructed in the religion which had surrounded his deathbed with such peace and joy. Having done what she could for them, and leaving them in good hands to be prepared for their reception into the Church, she went with Charlotte to Ryde, to stay with her sister, Mrs. Maxwell. At Ryde, among other interesting people, they met a Mrs. Wood, the authoress of sundry books for children which had been given by Mr. John Gordon to Mrs. Leslie's children at Wandsworth to replace the depressing dissenting literature to which they had before been accustomed. These charming books had been written in Mrs. Wood's Anglican days, and she had since become a Catholic. Her son, who was in the navy, was absent from England at the time of her conversion. He returned unexpectedly, and arrived at his mother's house one day when she was out. To pass the time until her return home he took up a book which he found lying on the table in her drawing-room. It was Mr. Allies' "Journal in France and Letters from Italy," in which the author describes his visit to the Ecstatica and the Addolorata in the Tyrol. Captain Wood happened to open the book at these pages, and after reading the description, resolved to verify the statements for himself. He did so, became a Catholic, then a Jesuit, and died a holy death comparatively young at Malta.

From Ryde Mrs. Leslie went with Charlotte to Eartham, on a visit to Mr. and Mrs. Charles Manning. Lady Cecil Kerr and her cousin Francis were already there when they arrived, but the visit was cut short by the sudden illness of Mrs. Manning, and they went on to London taking the Kerrs with them. On coming out of Farm Street Church, one afternoon after Benediction, they met Lady Fitzgerald in the porch. When Mrs. Leslie asked her whether she would be in Rome the next winter, her answer, a decided negative, showed plainly that some other plan had been resolved on. A little later it became known that she had followed her two daughters to Roehampton, and had become a Sacred Heart nun.

Mrs. Leslie passed the rest of the summer in Scotland, and after a pleasant stay at Carstairs travelled south to Mexbury Rectory in Berkshire, a living held by Mr. Palmer's father. Ever since their son's illness at Castel Gandolfo Mr. and Mrs. Palmer had greatly wished to make the acquaintance of his devoted friend and nurse, and this visit was in fulfilment of a long-standing promise. In the hours of convalescence he had described Mexbury and the different members of his family, dwelling with much affection on the portrait of his mother, whom he represented in such choice colours, that it was a test of her singular charm when reality only confirmed the impression he had given of her. The visitors arrived in the midst of an evening party, the carriages coming and going in the neighbourhood of the Rectory causing a great stir in the place. They received, however, a warm welcome, but Mrs. Palmer's white silk dress, and the gay attire of the assembled guests made the new arrivals so conscious of their wraps and travelling gear, that they were glad to accept the offer of retiring to rest. The next morning, on hearing a gong which they supposed meant breakfast, they went downstairs, but finding the dining-room door locked understood that family prayers were going on. It appeared afterwards that the door had been locked in order to spare them the embarrassment of an excuse or apology, as it was understood that as Catholics they would not take part in an act of religion conducted by an Anglican clergyman. It was only such thoughtful reminders as this that accentuated any difference of religion between the guests and their hosts, and the visit passed most agreeably. On St. Michael's day Mr. William Palmer drove early in the morning with the Leslies to the Catholic church, situated at some distance from Mexbury. They all went to confession to the venerable old priest in charge of the mission, and Charlotte never forgot the earnest way in which he said to her, " Keep the world far from you, and draw as near to God as you can." It was the echo of an inward voice which had been whispering to her ear since early childhood and had lately become more sweetly importunate. She realized vaguely that all those pleasant summer visits were last ones, and that many of the farewells she had spoken might be final. Nevertheless, even if her health presented no obstacle, for the coming winter, at least there could be no question of entering a convent. The work which Albert had entrusted to them was still incomplete, and she must help her mother to bring it to a happy conclusion.

On leaving Mexbury they returned to Paris. Their plans for the winter were to be shaped according to circumstances.

At that time the Atlee family presented a curious combination of religious elements. Mrs. Falconer Atlee and her two youngest daughters were nearly ready to be received into the Church, to the great satisfaction of the head of the family, who saw too clearly the inconsistencies of Protestantism to have any respect for it, and at the same time was convinced of the absolute necessity of religion— at least for women. He was also convinced that the Catholic faith could alone satisfy the craving of the human heart for some form of worship, and although he was still a professed unbeliever, he gave his wife and daughters every facility for receiving instruction. One single embargo was put upon their reception into the Church. They must all take the final step together, and if one were not sufficiently prepared, the others must wait for her to be ready. This command, a very positive one, was a fertile source of delays and difficulties. If one of them had a doubt which an explanation easily removed, the next day another would crop up in the mind of another member of the trio, and when further instruction had shown the futility of this, it would be the turn of the third to bring forward some objection. And so things went on, till Mrs. Leslie had recourse to Notre-Dame des Victoires, as on the occasion of Charlotte's giving the medal to Albert. A Mass was said there for the intention that all three might be of the same mind together, and wish to embrace the truth without further delay. This desired result was at last obtained, and they were all received into the Church at the Sacred Heart Convent, Rue de Varenne, on All Saints' Day, 1858, by Père de Ponlevoy. They remained at the convent nearly the whole day, and on their return home, Mr. Falconer Atlee entered so fully into their joy and enthusiasm, that after dinner, in spite of their remonstrances on account of the intense cold, he insisted on starting off to thank those who had helped them to so great a good. His satisfaction was, however, not shared by other members of his family. His son Falconer, while devotedly attached to his mother and sisters, was frankly indifferent to whatever religion they adopted, but his eldest daughter and her husband were extremely gloomy and unhappy at the change. There was a strain of absurdity in the manner with which they would mark their dissent, when any Catholic topic was introduced, by frequent heavy sighs and laboured depression. Mr. Atlee nick-named them "the Albigenses," and joked good-naturedly about the view they took of the Catholic religion. But Mrs. Leslie, intensely sympathetic as she was, could find it in her heart to be sorry for their evident grief, and felt more affectionately towards them than ever. Although there seemed little hope of their own conversion, she would by no means despair of it, often quoting a favourite word of Père de Ravignan's, "Il faut toujours prier et ne jamais désespérer."

She had now become, if that were possible, more dear and necessary to her brother's family than before, and as it was the great wish of all to remain together as long as they could, it was agreed that they should spend the winter at Tours. Taking her daughter with her, Mrs. Leslie started before the others to seek an abode that should be large enough to accommodate the whole family. This was ultimately found in a house opposite the beautiful church of St. Julien, long desecrated by being used as a coach-house and stables for the diligences, but which had now been restored to its original uses.

They passed a peaceful and tranquil winter at Tours, Mr. Falconer Atlee entering amiably into the new Catholic life of his family, welcoming their Catholic friends at all times under his roof, and extending his friendliness and charity to priests and religious without reserve. In the month of May, seeing that his daughters wished to erect a little altar in honour of the Blessed Virgin, he worked like a carpenter to help them, and often during the month would accompany them to the flower-market to buy plants and bouquets to place before their image of the Madonna.

Towards the end of May Mrs. Leslie and her daughter went to the convent of the Sacred Heart at Marmoutier, to make a retreat in preparation for Pentecost. Charlotte hoped that the moment might be come for settling her vocation to a religious life; but the Jesuit father who gave the Spiritual Exercises did not encourage her to pursue the idea. Practically, he considered her in the light of an only child, with regard to the most devoted of mothers, who had already given her only son and another daughter to God. But in taking this view, he did not know the whole extent of that mother's generosity and her capacity for making sacrifices. She had been for some time past preparing herself in secret for a possible separation from her youngest child, and the first initiative came from her own brave heart.

Just before going to Marmoutier she said to Charlotte one evening, "My dear child, I think it likely that while you are in retreat you will be anxious to decide your vocation. At your age, and at such a moment it is almost impossible that it should not occupy your thoughts. Now, if you feel that God calls you to a religious life, do not let me be any obstacle. However much it would cost me to part from you, I should be happier to see you settled and happy during my life than if your devotedness to me should cause you to postpone taking such a step till you were beyond the age when it is customary and comparatively easy to follow conventual rules. Therefore, do not let affection for me be a hindrance. God gave you to me, and He has the first right over you—a right which I could never venture to dispute."

With a mutual agreement to pray for light during their coming retreat, and with tender expressions of love and gratitude on her daughter's part, the understanding between them was complete. When the Father who was giving the Exercises pronounced against

Charlotte's entering a convent, another opinion was taken, that of Père Rubillon, who had been her confessor in Rome and knew both mother and daughter well. He considered that from motives of health, delay was to be recommended, and thus for a time the subject was suffered to drop. Charlotte went with her mother to La Roche Posay in the department of the Indre, where Madame de Pambour was taking a course of mineral waters.

It was a primitive little place, not much frequented, but not altogether without attractions, the approach to it on one side being very picturesque. The modern bridge crosses the Indre a little lower than the ancient one, of which the ruined masonry resembles rocks of a fantastic form, rising up out of the bed of the river, which at this point is like a rapid torrent. High up, above the surrounding buildings, rises in the centre of the town an ancient tower or keep, probably a part of the fortifications of olden times. The mineral waters are supposed to have been discovered by accident. This is the story. A favourite horse, too infirm and diseased to be of any use to his master, who could not make up his mind to have him shot or see him suffer, was turned out to shift for himself. One day, the man was passing by a marshy spot and saw a horse struggling to get out of the morass. He went to help him, and recognized his own invalided beast restored to health and beauty. The waters of the marsh were analysed, found to contain medicinal properties, and four of them directed into channels for the convenience of sufferers from various maladies. The old church, which was very ill-attended in those days, retained some curiously primitive customs. Before High Mass on Sundays, two boys were employed in ringing the bells, the ropes of which came through holes in the roof between the transepts, each boy in turn flying up some six feet into the air clinging to his rope. As one came down, the other went up, and the effect, to the assembling congregation, was comical to a degree rather out of place in a church.

While Mrs. Leslie, her daughter and sister were at La Roche Posay Mr. Falconer Atlee went to Paris to see his son at the British Embassy. He called at the Sacred Heart Convent, and saw a very charming American nun, whom he had known for some time as a friend of his family. She extracted from him a promise to go and see Père de Ponlevoy, who on hearing the name of his visitor, interrupted important business to converse with him. Mr. Atlee at first talked like an agnostic, expressing doubt as to the existence of his own soul. But he allowed Père de Ponlevoy to place round his neck a miraculous medal, saying at the same time with great solemnity, "There is a God, and you have a soul, and you are now going to pray for that soul of yours." Suddenly a gleam of faith seemed to penetrate the clouds of unbelief which had hung over him for so many years. He sank upon his knees, confessing with tears the principal sins of his life. For a while at least, he believed, and assisted that afternoon at Benediction with great sensible sweetness and fervour. It was the feast of the Assumption, and at first it seemed as if our Lady had really obtained the gift of faith for this soul, in many ways so noble and generous. But the gleam died away, and other absorbing interests and occupations banished even the memory of it from his mind, so strong was his habit of infidelity.

In the meanwhile, Mrs. Leslie, drawn thither by many tender desires, proposed to pay a short visit to England and Scotland before the winter. The chief of these desires was to see her son after a prolonged absence. He had made his theological studies at Laval and Innsbruck, had been ordained at Brixen in the Tyrol, and had said his first Mass at Innsbruck. To behold him at the altar, and to receive Holy Communion from his hand was now the great longing of her heart. They had reached Paris on their journey to England, whither Father Leslie had now returned, when some travellers who came to the hotel at which they were staying for a night gave such bad accounts of the rough weather in the Channel that Mrs. Leslie resolved to put off their crossing for a few days on Charlotte's account. She was still so delicate that her mother took all possible care to avoid extra fatigue for her or the risk of her taking cold.

But these few days passed in Paris altered the whole course of their future lives. The plans made for their going to England together never came off, and Mrs. Leslie's own journey was delayed by this stress of weather for nearly nine months. On such seemingly accidental circumstances do great events sometimes turn. In the afternoon of the first day they went to the convent of the Sacred Heart, and were urged to take up their abode there during the interval of waiting for a quiet passage to England. This they did, and while staying at the convent made the acquaintance of the venerable Mère Barat, foundress of the Society of the Sacred Heart. Charlotte felt moved to confide to her the ever-burning question of her vocation, and the advice obtained was, first to consult

Père Olivaint, and then, if he considered that she was called to a religious life, to take the opinion of an eminent physician as to the fitness of her health for it. Finally, if all seemed to point in that direction, she was to go to the noviceship of the Sacred Heart at Conflans for a month, and try it, after which the interrupted journey to Scotland might be resumed, and farewell visits paid before definitely beginning the novitiate. This advice was not only kind and considerate, but very practical, especially as the Mother General promised that the month at Conflans should really initiate the young postulant into the daily routine she would be called upon to lead for some time to come, if it should prove that she had a vocation to it. Both Mrs. Leslie and her daughter could not but feel that such a test would put an end to the painful uncertainty that had tried them for some time past. When Madame Barat asked half playfully, "What will you do if Père Olivaint says you have a vocation to the Sacred Heart?" Charlotte's answer was prompt and courageous: "I will go to Conflans next week."

Père Olivaint's decision, after hearing the whole state of the case, was briefly expressed in the words, "Je crois devant Dieu que c'est cela." The doctor's verdict was more cautious, but amounted practically to the same conclusion. "I cannot venture to say whether the patient's health will stand religious life; but I am sure of one thing, that if she has a vocation, and is thwarted in following it, she will die all the sooner, and that the peace of mind and regular life of a convent would give her the best chance of improved health and prolonged life."

This important question was therefore settled at last, and Mrs. Leslie's sacrifice accepted. Once more she could enter into the true spirit of our Lord's Ascension, understanding it in its right sense, and confusing it neither with the joyful nor the sorrowful mysteries of His Mother's life on earth. But all real sacrifice implies pain, and this last wrench cost her no less because she had no other child left to give. Henceforth her life must be lonely, although surrounded by a large circle of devoted friends, the last tie being snapped which bound her to any life on earth. True however to her constant principle of never allowing herself, or those belonging to her, to dwell unduly on the painful side of things, she accepted an invitation to spend their last few days together with her old friends the Wilberforces at St.-Germain-en-Laye.

Mr. Wilberforce was the eldest brother of the celebrated Bishop of Oxford. He was then still a Protestant, but his wife had become a Catholic, and there was a bond of sympathy the more between them both and Mrs. Leslie, since she had assisted at the death-bed of his brother Robert at Albano. Full as were the hearts of mother and daughter at the thought of the approaching separation, Mr. Wilberforce detected no shadow on Mrs. Leslie's face, but he was struck with something not hitherto there in Charlotte's, and exclaimed, "What has happened to my little friend Chattie that has made her so serious?" And partly as a diversion, partly because it was one of his hobbies, he took her to the kitchen and gave her a cooking lesson, showing her how to hash mutton on the best principles. He also took great interest in his garden, devoting much time and taste to its cultivation, so that his lawns were as smooth and velvety as the finest English turf, and his flower-beds did justice to his artistic combination of colour and design. But these things were only adjuncts to his more serious occupations. He was a singularly clever, interesting man, learned in all sorts of out-of-the-way subjects, and his conversation, whether tête-à-tête or as one of a party, was always extremely interesting to the Leslies, and made their stay a pleasant souvenir.

September 14 had been fixed as the day for Charlotte's going to Conflans. The Wilberforces did all they could to persuade their guests to prolong their visit, but in vain; and on the feast of the Exaltation of the Cross, Mrs. Leslie drove with her daughter through a heavy downpour of rain to the noviceship. She would not try the courage of either by lingering over their farewells, but with a last embrace and blessing, and promising to return shortly, went on to Paris, where she purposed awaiting the result of the month's trial of convent *régime*.

Since none of her relations had returned to their winter quarters, and since she dreaded the new experience of solitude at an hotel, she took rooms at Mrs. Murray's house for converts till she could decide on her next step. Then came the inevitable reaction which follows a sacrifice, however nobly made. It was not regret, or any desire to take back what she had so generously given, but the pain of separation in all its poignancy, a keen sense of loneliness and desolation, of having broken with the happy past, and with that *vie à deux* to which she had clung, she knew not how much till now. She thought of the delightful hours they had spent together, the books, the scenery, the friends they had shared, of the thousand little humorous touches which had made their companionship so perfect, and their understanding of each other so complete. Doubts as to the prudence of what she had done, crowded in upon her. The welfare of this dear child had been the first consideration in every plan she had formed, in every journey undertaken, for the last five years and more. How would this trial of religious life end? If it succeeded, the child would be gone for ever; if it failed, she would come back with shattered health and disappointed aspirations, and those nearest and dearest would perhaps blame her mother for having consented to the test. These thoughts, combined with uncongenial surroundings, made the next few days a kind of purgatory. The following letter, written thirty years later, shows what she went through as the immediate consequence of the sacrifice, and the good that had come out of the suffering :

MY DEAR, DEAR CHILD,—I must write you a line to-day to meet the anniversary of our journey to Conflans thirty years ago. In the deep anguish of my heart I did not then thank our heavenly Father for calling you into His more immediate service. But now I can sincerely thank Him for all His mercies in this to you and to me. And to-morrow, please God, in Holy Communion I will offer you to Him afresh with all the love and gratitude of my heart and soul. Adieu, my beloved child. That you may be blessed and become more and more dear to the hearts of Jesus and Mary ever prays

Your loving, grateful mother,

ELEANOR LESLIE.

The first gleam of consolation in her bereavement came from the news that Lady Lothian would shortly arrive in Paris, bringing her eldest daughter, Lady Cecil Kerr, to the Sacred Heart. To both mothers the meeting seemed a delicate attention on the part of Divine Providence, for besides their old and tried friendship, the similarity of their actual circumstances made them a stay and support to each other. Mrs. Leslie went early on the day after their arrival to their hotel. The young ladies were still in bed resting after their journey. Each called out on hearing her voice:

"Where's Chattie? Why did she not come?"

On being told that Chattie was at Conflans, the satisfaction of one sister was equalled by the disgust of the other at the desertion of her "early friend."

Madame de T——, whom they had known in Rome, called one day on Lady Lothian after her daughter had gone to Conflans, and found Mrs. Leslie with her. Asking after the two postulants, she was horrified to hear that they were both in a convent. The lady had no esteem for religious vocations, and had successfully hindered one of her own children from following one—a subsequent cause of misery to both. But at that time she had not yet learned her lesson of sad experience, and delivered her sentiments on the tragic event by exclaiming: "Malheureuses mères que vous êtes! Vous allez mourir toutes seules!" Those who knew Lady Lothian can scarcely fail to remember her singularly musical laugh. This melancholy prediction excited her merriment, and she replied: "Oh, Madame, je n'ai pas du tout peur que je mourrai toute seule." In neither case was the prophecy verified. Lady Lothian died in Rome, surrounded by friends, her youngest son being led as it were by inspiration to his mother's bedside, while Mrs. Leslie's last hours on earth were blessed by the presence of the two beloved children whom she had first given to God. If Madame de T—— could have really foreseen the end, her pity would have given place to a feeling akin to envy.

But at that time even Mrs. Leslie's courage needed all her faith to sustain it. Her first visit to Conflans brought little comfort, and one line in her carefully kept diary is an indication of her state of mind: "Saw my dear child, but full of tristesse and ennui; I did not enjoy it."

Lady Lothian, too, though she could laugh at the world's verdict, was none the less a *mater dolorosa* at that time, and the exchange of sympathy between the two mothers might sometimes have ended in tears, had it not been for the presence of Lady Alice, who often rendered good service by giving an original, amusing turn to the subject when it threatened to become serious. Her wit and drollery were perhaps more valuable to both than the most pious exhortations.

A letter written by Mrs. Leslie in her eighty-fifth year to a friend who had lately suffered the loss of a beloved niece to whom she had acted the part of a mother, and who had been called to religion, contains this affecting passage:

> I am not surprised at the depression you speak of. Both for our poor minds and bodies this generally follows some great effort. You made your great sacrifice of dear E—— courageously and generously, and even cheerfully, much better than I did with any one of my beloved children. But then when the loneliness comes, our poor nature suffers under the depressing vacancy. I am now going to say a few words of what I was taught, and what my experience has confirmed. Our natural and affectionate feelings prompt us to think that by living near, and frequently seeing, the being we have cherished, but really given as He asked, to God, we shall become more soothed and resigned. This I now believe to be a mistake, and Rev. Mother Marie Amélie, then Superior at St. Margaret's, taught me this lesson, firmly but kindly. She checked frequent visits to dear Mary as best for *her*; and for myself, enjoined me to look *up* and not *down* as I was doing. But a signal mercy was shown to my pusillanimity, by circumstances taking me away shortly after parting both from her and Chattie, and obliging me to make certain exertions which no doubt helped me to get more out of myself and closer to the will of our heavenly Father.

Another letter to the same friend runs thus :

My very dear Friend,—In heart and mind I have been so occupied with you during the last month that I cannot resist writing to you a few lines. You must know that I understand from a threefold experience all that is connected with the sacrifice which our heavenly Father has asked from you, and which I am sure you have made with a loyal, courageous, loving will. But it is not at the moment when we give up what has been and ever will be nearest and dearest to our whole being that the trial is most felt. No, for that moment a strength is given which lifts us above ourselves. But when the blank comes which follows our sacrifice, though we would not recall it, nature will have her say. And well do I remember, when yielding to some selfish murmurs which I must have made in my exceeding weakness to Père Olivaint, he gently reproved me by saying, "You behaved so well at first—but now!" I think, dear friend, with your firmer faith you are not likely to do so; but I will quote the words of a priest, now departed, who met me looking very mournful. "'If you look upon this trial with the eyes of earth all will be wrong; but if you look at it with the eyes of heaven all will be right." So, dear friend, though I doubt not you have already done so, I will pray that you may steadfastly continue to do it. We cannot now appreciate nor understand all the *love* and *wisdom* that takes a beloved child from us, but I may add that, imperfect as it still is with me, as time goes on we feel both, more and more, and can praise our good God and thank Him for having in *this*, as in all other things, done *well*. Please let me know how you are, and with a fervent God bless you, believe me as ever,

Most affectionately yours,
E. Leslie.

It will be easily understood by those who have followed Mrs. Leslie thus far in her life of singular resignation, fortitude and charity, that the selfishness with which she reproached herself in the above letters was entirely unrecognized by others. She so feared to sadden and unsettle her child by letting her even suspect how intensely she felt the separation, that she appeared cheerful and satisfied with everything, whenever she went to Conflans. Many years indeed were allowed to pass before her daughter knew the utter desolation of her heart at that time. By degrees, the entries in her diary grew more cheerful, and most of them were written in a tone of gratitude, some time before the trying ordeal of waiting in Paris came to an end. "Went to Conflans. Thankful to find my dear child so well," is the refrain of most of her visits there.

Then came the time when Charlotte was to make her election. The Superior General, it will be remembered, had given permission for a trial of her vocation to be made provisionally, and if she succeeded in it, she might resume her interrupted journey to Scotland, pay her farewell visits, and enter the convent definitely in the spring. But just as her brother had preferred, after his first retreat at Stonyhurst, to enter on his religious career at once, without returning to take leave of his family, so Charlotte feared to risk her vocation by exposing herself to the enervating influence of appeals dictated by natural affection to induce her to give up her purpose.

But to give up this journey entailed another costly sacrifice. She had been looking forward intensely to seeing her brother as a priest, to the joy of assisting at his Mass, and of once more renewing the tender associations of the past. She knew what it would be to her mother to have her society on the journey, and she thought of the delight of her sisters in being once more together with her. Then it occurred to her that she might never again have the power to offer such a gift to God as this sacrifice, and it would be a pity to lose the opportunity. She opened her heart to her mother, only to find the most perfect acquiescence and approval of her wish to pursue her religious training without a break. Mrs. Leslie still lingered on in Paris, less perhaps now to be near her daughter than because she had placed herself under the somewhat austere and very supernatural direction of Père Olivaint.

Late in December she had the consolation of seeing her old friend Mr. Robertson and his aunt Miss Cunningham. In January, 1860, came Lord and Lady Henry Kerr and made some stay. Meanwhile, the usual three months' term of probation for postulants had been prolonged to nearly five, and Charlotte began to wonder whether her turn to be clothed would ever come. Others, who had entered after her had received the habit, and she felt rather anxious. At last she was told that doubts had been entertained as to her health ever allowing her to conform to all the rules of community life, and the matter had been laid before the Superior General. Her answer was "Donnez-lui l'habit quand même. Plus tard elle se fortifiera." To this news was added the pleasing information that she, and the friend of her childhood, Lady Cecil Kerr, whom she had helped through her postulancy, were to be clothed on the same day. Charlotte had had a certain amount of training in religious exactness and obedience to bells, as a pupil at St. Margaret's Convent, and had learned many rules and observances which stood her in good stead when she first went to Conflans, preventing her feeling so complete a stranger in a religious house as she would otherwise have been. But her friend had been brought up entirely at home, and would often have been puzzled but for Charlotte, who was allowed to act the part of a good angel towards her, prompting and reminding her when necessary, and explaining small difficulties.

On February 8, which in the diocese of Paris is the feast of the Most Pure Heart of Mary, Mrs. Leslie wrote in her diary:

Went to Conflans for the *prise d'habit* of my beloved child and Lady Cecil Kerr. Let me thank God for *all* his mercies, and ever more and more.

On the 29th she went to the convent and remained for about ten days, and seems about this time to have become thoroughly reconciled and happy about her daughter's vocation. There are daily entries in the diary of "pleasant visits from dearest Chattie and Cecil in the evening." Lent was passed in Paris, and on May 12 she travelled to London with Mr. Palmer, and after several visits in the south, went in June to St. Asaph, to see and for a short time remain near her son who was making his fourth year of theology at St. Beuno's College. Father Leslie met and welcomed her at the station, and obtained leave to say Mass for her several times at St. Asaph. The blessedness of both mother and son in being once more together was too deep for expression save the fervent and reiterated *Deo gratias* of her diary, and she now began to experience the hundredfold reward promised to those who have stripped themselves of all their earthly treasure for the sake of everlasting life. It would be almost irreverent to lift the veil thrown over those heart-to-heart communings, as they two walked together about the pleasant places already sanctified by the presence of great saints; or to attempt to describe the emotion with which the one knelt at the altar while the other reached to her the Bread of Life. But the joy that is born of sacrifice is more unutterably sweet than the joy of fulfilled desires.

CHAPTER XIII.

AUTUMN.

AFTER the completion of his fourth year of theology Father Leslie was sent to the mission at Glasgow, a very struggling one in those days, and chiefly composed of Irish immigrants, exiled by the famine which followed on the potato-rot, and employed in the Glasgow factories. His mother, who had gone from St. Asaph to Edinburgh, visited him soon after his arrival in Scotland, and was much impressed with the faith, piety and fine feeling of the people. They were so poor that the offertory at Mass was entirely made up of pence, and when she dropped half-a-crown into the plate, it was brought back to her four times, as it was supposed that she had given it in mistake for a penny. At another time she also put in half-a-crown, when the old man who was collecting handed it back to her saying, "No, ma'am, you have given your son." When she went to stay at Carstairs and Huntlyburn, Father Leslie, whose health sometimes gave way under the hard life and heavy work of the Glasgow mission, would be sent there for a few days at a time to rest and gain fresh strength for his labours.

The Monteiths and Lord and Lady Henry Kerr were never at a loss to invent some plea for these highly prized meetings between the mother and son, which were to them also occasions of special rejoicing. The distance of Huntlyburn from the nearest Catholic church at Galashiels made it an inestimable boon to have Mass said for them in their private chapel, and as often as there was the least pretext, they asked that Father Leslie might be sent.

During one of these visits, Mrs. Leslie was mainly instrumental in getting a rather remarkable man into the Church. He began life as a saddler, but developed a taste for sculpture, to which he subsequently devoted himself. He had already talked to her about religion, and she went to see him at Darnick, the nearest village, with her son, and found him reading Milner's "End of Controversy." After a little conversation, Father Leslie said, "Now you ought to fix the day for your reception into the Church." His wife, who was present, expostulated, but the man said: "Sir, you are right," and accordingly a Sunday not far off was agreed upon. He had set his heart on being received by an Oblate Father who had been at Galashiels, but who was then at Leith. On the day fixed, he went to Leith, but the Oblate Father was absent. He went to Edinburgh to find Father Corry, a Jesuit, whom he also knew, but Father Corry was away. Then he returned to Galashiels and called on the priest who was new there, and did not know him. He was being put off, when Lord Henry Kerr, who heard him speaking, said to the priest: "You may trust that man," and he was received then and there. Afterwards his whole family became Catholics. Some years later, when Mrs. Leslie was living in Edinburgh, the man came to see her, a little while before his death. When he left he knelt down for her blessing.

All who came in contact with her felt the wonderful power of her sanctity; many, perhaps unconsciously, the charm of her refinement and the singular attraction of her simplicity of manner. She became a kind of standard to many of her friends by which to measure the value of a course of action. If it was instinctively felt that Mrs. Leslie would not like a certain thing, it was abandoned as unworthy. One who met her for the first time at Huntlyburn * in the early 'sixties contributes the following graphic description :

> My brother and I were staying at Huntlyburn—both very, very young people then, although I think I at·least felt more aged

* Baroness Anatole von Hügel.

and more capable of being sure what I was like and what everything else and everybody else was like than I have felt for many a year now past. Yet we had all the freshness really of young people and all the unconscious ignorance, and so could feel vividly the help of the touch of the wonderful fingers on our minds and ourselves in general—even when consciously all we knew was that we were seeing "a most jolly person" or "oh! such a wonderful old lady!"

Did you know Huntlyburn in its royal old days—when through its windows the sun looked in always more gladly, I am sure, than it could do anywhere else—upstairs, through the three long French windows into the quiet roomy chapel, where the lamp never went out as it does in so many a private oratory; where the atmosphere was never chilly, either mentally or physically; where every conceivable footstool made kneeling peacefully easy, where everybody's books and rosaries were happy on the seats as well as oneself; where the perfect taste of perfect instinct made the pictures go right on the walls and the flowers right on the altar; where mostly you found someone else already saying his prayers whenever you went in. Chiefly and oftenest you would see the head, the gracefullest and most characteristic we shall ever any of us see, with a little, light, black silk cap on and a veil over, till we see it again by and by. Father Leslie used to say, "I should like a persecution; I should like to see Lady Henry go to the stake—she would do it in such style!" Downstairs, faded, old-fashioned furniture, ornaments, each with a history: piety and old beauty mixed. And the round face of the beautiful sailor boy looking from a gilt frame on the wall—the face which manhood and keen feeling and eager thought sharpened into such clear-cut strength, when we all knew and answered to it in the long after years. And oh! the wonderful view outwards, downstairs, of the wooded Tweed valley, down to the grey, shining Abbey ruins, from the one window; of the solemn purple Eildons from the others. But from the chapel, only the one of which Melrose Abbey was the leading thought.

Well, I think it was in that bright, faded, delicious drawing-room that I got my first impression of Mrs. Leslie. I think she had arrived just before dinner, and that I came down early and found Lord Henry there. Then presently the door opened and a small figure entered—very crisp, wearing a black silk skirt, shortish, a sort of soft black shawl—China crape I fancy—pinned with precision, just exactly so that it looked best, a cap of soft white tulle or net, with tiny bows, and white close curls against a rosy cheek, eyes which I don't think I noticed, for it was not very light in the room. But strongest of all is my remembrance of small, vigorous, tapered fingers, with long, very careful-looking nails, holding firmly and crisply a small, black silk bag, drawn up with a string and a frill.

I remember a kindly word or two, which gave me a sense of being admitted to good company, and then she began talking to Lord Henry—he with warm, bright, funny eagerness, wishing to get at her thoughts, she with a gentle stiffness of phraseology, calling him "my lord," but giving me, as she said the pretty, old-fashioned words, the sense that everybody was at Court, in good old days; that he was bowing beautifully and she curtsey-ing, and that some kingly king must be near who was going to say to them both, "Pray now be seated." It once and for all made a standard in my mind of manners in speaking to people. Not that we can ever get back to the charm of old-fashioned exactness; but we can still feel something that her exactness gave outward life to. And ever since I have rejoiced in the sight of a bishop for a private reason of my own, as well as for the good of his blessing, because now I too might say "my lord" and copy Mrs. Leslie, and remember the clear, sweet tones that had said it that evening in the firelight at Huntlyburn.

All the rest of the evening is vague to me, except that he asked her to play. "Now Mrs. Leslie, I must have my tune," and that from the tips of the strong, light fingers there ran the most delicious, bright old tunes, played out of a small MS. music book, where the noting was as light and correct and delicate as the music and as the handwriting of the journal.

The same writer goes on to say that after this first meeting the feeling that something gentle and strong was being good to her took hold of her and helped her over some of the puzzling things of life which had begun to exercise her young mind. The things that had seemed to her so tangled became really less complicated when Mrs. Leslie had handled the theme in her simple, direct, bright way. With all her experience and matured judgment, there was, to the end of her life, something of the delightful simplicity of a child in her intense, unquestioning confidence that God's goodness would make all crookedness straight at last, and that meanwhile the crookedness did not matter. She realized so completely that the other world is only just beyond and alongside the turns of this one that she easily convinced those who came in touch with her of the same, while she drew them less perhaps by her words than by that something in herself which was impressing people profoundly, and giving her little playful words the force they had. Once at Huntlyburn, the same eager, impressionable girl was shyly confiding to her her anxiety respecting the soul of a friend who, she hoped, was on the road to conversion. Mrs. Leslie gave her a fragment of glass from a tomb in the Catacombs, and the young girl said how much she would like to twist some of this friend's hair round it, to bring the grace of conversion to him from the prayers of the unknown martyr. Falling in sympathetically with the notion, Mrs.

Leslie replied, "Now I once also got some hair of a friend and put it near a relic. I thought I would pull him in by the hair of his head." The gay laugh which followed this admission showed how the true, earnest spirituality that could pray so wonderfully was equal also to the every-day things of faith, and was not without that merry twinkle which might prompt, as it were, a little trick upon a saint. Sitting very upright on a little stiff old armchair in her bedroom, where these confidences were exchanged, she would flash out bright thoughts, which often afterwards served her listener as a key whereby to move back one or another of the ponderous wards of the lock that barred the solution to so many weary enigmas.

They formed a pretty contrast, and a very instructive one—the soul just beginning its experiences of life, anxiously scanning the untried problems that lay scattered on all sides, and the soul that feared nothing, because it had nothing left to lose, but yet had brought that merry laugh unspoilt through all the years of sorrow and sacrifice, and now on the borders of old age was still gay with the gladness which we are wont to associate with happy childhood or matured sanctity. Perhaps the secret of it is that such souls as hers see heaven clearly, and observe how its laws make sense from its own side, and yet fit on to all that is apparently lawless, useless and vain on the earth side. They met again often in after years, but the most vivid impression was made on the young girl's mind by these early talks, which proved so fruitful in forming her taste and character, perhaps also in deepening and broadening her piety.

About this time occurred Mr. Falconer Atlee's formal submission to the Church. One day at Conflans, his niece Charlotte heard the announcement from the Martyrology for the following day, "the feast of the prodigies of the Blessed Virgin Mary," and immediately thought that she would try to obtain the prodigy of his conversion. She was one of the sub-sacristans, and had the charge of decorating the side altars. She therefore asked and obtained leave to do something more than usual to honour our Lady's prodigies in order to win one.

> It was the time when lilies blow
> And clouds are highest up in air.

The garden was therefore ransacked for what was fairest and most fragrant, and presently the little novice came in with an armful of stately white lilies and rich scarlet verbena, which she arranged much to her satisfaction, thinking that the altar had never looked so beautiful. But the head sacristan, Madame Louise Mallac, instead of praising her work said, "Ma sœur Charlotte, il faudrait oter ces beaux lys, ou vu la chaleur dans l'église ; leur parfum pourrait faire tomber les gens en pâmoison."

It was a disappointment, but Sister Charlotte had already learned that few things are so good but that the sacrifice of them is still better, and before the lilies had had time to fade she heard that her uncle had been received into the Church by Père de Ponlevoy. At the moment of conferring conditional baptism, the priest asked what name he bore, and he answered, "My name is John, but if it may be allowed, give me also the name of Mary." In spite of his good dispositions, it was thought advisable to prolong his religious instruction somewhat before admitting him to Holy Communion. But he pleaded so earnestly, "Oh, mon Père, laissez-moi recevoir mon Dieu," that Père de Ponlevoy yielded, hoping that what was still needed in the way of instruction would be supplied gradually by others. But unhappily, when the first fervour of his conversion had subsided, he gradually slipped back into the old paths. Soon after his abjuration, he removed with his family to Nantes, and for a time Mrs. Leslie wrote hopefully in her diary of his perseverance. Her last visit in Scotland in 1860 was at Carstairs, where Father Leslie was allowed to join her. On September 10, she left for the south, and a few days later wrote at Conflans, where the next few months were spent, "Found my beloved Chattie quite well and happy. Deo gratias."

The beginning of 1861 saw her at Alençon with her niece, Madame de Champfleur, her sister Harriet's only daughter, an excellent Catholic wife and mother, one of whose sons became a priest in the diocese of Paris. During the next few years, Mrs. Leslie divided her time between Nantes, Alençon, Tours, England and Scotland, devoting as much of it as possible to her brother, in the hope of helping him to regain the faith of which he had had so bright if transient a glimmer. But forty years of studied infidelity had established such a habit of doubt and disbelief in his soul that temptations against all revealed religion were frequent and violent. Moreover, the general tone of thought in France was totally anti-Christian, and as he was little grounded in the doctrines of religion, he had no weapons wherewith to meet the specious arguments with which he had been familiar since his boyhood. His wife and two Catholic daughters, recent converts themselves, had not the same kind of influence for good with him as his eldest sister, and they counted on her to lead him back into the right path. Her nieces describe her life with them at Nantes as differing little from that of a good religious, so exact was she in keeping her self-imposed rule, so perfect a model did she appear to all of self-denial and charity. Her day began with Mass and Holy Communion, whatever the state of the weather or of her own health, although, if they convinced her that there was real and considerable imprudence in her leaving the house, she would sometimes give in, and thank them affectionately for their care of her. Her leisure was shared with Mrs. Falconer Atlee in the humble occupation of mending old clothes for the aged men and women under the charge of the Little Sisters of the Poor. Not unfrequently she would be called upon to take part in controversial talks with her brother, and these necessitated not only the defence of Christian doctrine against his infidel objections to all revealed religion, but also the constant remembrance that to convince him she must make that religion attractive and amiable. To this end she was always studying how to contribute to the agreeableness and charm of her brother's home-life, often at the cost of many a personal sacrifice. Sometimes the religious discussions would leave her completely exhausted, and she would ask her nieces, who had been present, with tears in her eyes, whether she had behaved as she ought.

The autumn of 1862 brought a special work. The Marchioness of Queensberry had been received into the Church, and had gone with her children to Boulogne, where she engaged a Catholic tutor for them, M. l'Abbé Bonamy. Finding that their guardians were pursuing her with the intention of taking her children away, she was advised by the Abbé to go on to Nantes, where he knew an old Breton family named de Kersabiec who might be of use to her. The de Kersabiecs were intimate with Mrs. Leslie and her brother's family, and they helped Lady Queensberry to find a suitable apartment and to settle in it. But just as she began to breathe more freely, Mr. Falconer Atlee, who was then British Consul at Nantes, heard sooner than most people that she was still being pursued, and as his house had an entrance and staircase at each end, offering a convenient refuge for anyone wishing to leave at a moment's notice, should unwelcome visitors arrive unexpectedly, invited her to make her home there as long as she required it. The offer was gratefully accepted, and Mrs. Leslie became an immense moral support to Lady Queensberry during the year that followed, helping her with her clear sense and judgment. Together they wrote a letter to the

Emperor,* claiming his protection, and whether in consequence of this letter or from other causes, Lady Queensberry was allowed to keep her children in peace, and bring them up as she pleased. Mrs. Leslie's diary about this time is among other things a chronicle of the principal events in the Douglas family. She writes on November 25, 1862:

First Communion of Lord Archibald.

December 21.—Confirmation of Lord A. Douglas.

January 16, 1863.—Heard of Mr. Wilberforce's conversion. ["This was a great joy to her," writes one of her daughters.]

29.—Letter from Mr. Palmer, telling me of Miss Taafe's death.

March 3.—Lady Gertrude made her abjuration. The twins are baptized. I godmother to Lord James.

March 4.—Lady Gertrude's First Communion. Deo gratias.

But whatever else Mrs. Leslie's hand or head found to do, her almost daily visits to the poor were never left out. Now she would often take one or another of Lady Queensberry's children with her, and initiate them into Catholic works of charity. Sometimes pleasant meetings with old friends would bring an unexpected glow and colour into her life, devoted as it was almost entirely to piety and the service of her neighbour. She usually broke her journeys between

* Lady Queensberry's father had been kind to him when he lived in exile in England.

Nantes and Scotland at Marmoutier, whither her youngest daughter had been sent from Conflans. On one of these short halts, she found Lady Lothian with her daughter Alice, who had come to see their Sacred Heart nun also; and when Mr. Palmer arrived unexpectedly, it was like a return to the happy days in Rome when they were all together.

But peaceful as her life was, the cross was never absent from it in one form or another. In 1861 she had lost her good son-in-law, Mr. Fraser Gordon, and this sorrow was followed by anxiety concerning her eldest daughter Eleanor, who was left with an only child, a boy of four years old.

In March, 1863, she was hastily summoned from Nantes to Edinburgh by the news of Eleanor's alarming illness. Travelling rapidly, Mrs. Leslie arrived in time to cheer her last days on earth, to assist at her holy death, and to perform for her the last sad offices. When all was over, she wrote to Charlotte:

> Not anything could be more peaceful, more painless than that departure. One could only thank God for the tender mercy He had shown in every way, and pray that the precious soul had become most acceptable to Him. The body was very nicely arranged, and I remained with it till the morning, along with Mary Walters [her faithful attendant], when I came on to St. Margaret's for the Mass said on her behalf. She had wished when placed in her coffin to be removed to St. Mary's, and this was done on Thursday night, when many poor good people came and prayed round her. The face remained very sweet and calm

till the coffin was closed. The funeral took place from St. Mary's on Saturday, and she rests, dear child, in the Grange Cemetery. Poor little Mickie [Eleanor's son] had a terrible burst of grief at first, and was quite sick with crying next day; but since I got him out here,* he has been well and happy, and is the delight of everybody. I have been wonderfully supported throughout, but now need repose. For this, and as Mickie cannot yet be removed beyond the jurisdiction of the Scotch courts, we are to go to Lord Henry Kerr's, at Huntlyburn, on Tuesday.

After her daughter's death, Mrs. Leslie was detained in Scotland for some time to make arrangements for the education of her little grandson, for although his two uncles, Colonel and Major Gordon, were his guardians, the responsibility fell practically upon her. Towards the end of the year, Father Leslie fell dangerously ill of typhus fever at Glasgow, and his mother had the unspeakable consolation of being allowed to nurse him. By her thought and care she was able materially to lessen the difficulties caused by so dreadful an illness on a poor mission; and when the case seemed desperate, a suggestion of hers relieved the most distressing and alarming symptoms, and was the beginning of an improvement in his condition which led on to recovery. She afterwards said touchingly, "I never could pray for his recovery, but kept on saying, 'Lord, he whom Thou lovest is sick,' and I left him entirely in God's hands."

* To Greenhill, Bishop Gillis' house, opposite St. Margaret's Convent.

When he was convalescent, Mrs. Leslie took him to Portobello for the benefit of the sea air, and afterwards, when all fear of infection was at an end, to Huntlyburn for a short visit, to complete his recovery. There were other guests in the house, and notably Mr. Palmer and Dr. Patterson, now Bishop of Emmaus. They were all talking one day at dinner about old Oxford days and the High Church movement, and the difficulty they had in getting the poorer classes to take an interest in it. Father Leslie said he was once having his hair cut at Oxford, when he began teaching the barber about the services of the Church of England, and thought he had made an impression, but was interrupted by some other young men coming in. As he was leaving, the barber followed him to the door, and whispered, "Sir, you should come to our Independent Chapel next Sunday night; we have a regular Apostle Paul man preaching there."

Dr. Patterson capped this story by saying that a friend of his had tried to make his college scout an Anglo-Catholic, and to get him to practise abstinence on the proper days. He was quite pleased with his success till one Ash Wednesday, when the scout came and asked leave of absence for that evening, as it was "Hash Wednesday, and I likes to keep the feasts of the Church, so I have got up a little supper-party with some friends."

Mr. Palmer then said that when he had settled down at Magdalen, he invited the French Curé, with whom he had lived while learning French, to pay him a visit. When the Curé accepted the invitation, Palmer and his High Church friends were in great expectation. They thought that he would make such an impression, walking up and down "the High" with them in his *soutane*. It would show the union between the English and French branches of the Church. But when Palmer went to the railway station to meet him, he was disgusted at seeing the Curé get out of the carriage in coat and trousers. Knowing that he was coming to an heretical country, where he imagined that Catholics were still in danger, he had disguised himself. On Sunday morning, he was taken to St. Peter's-in-the-East, but found the service cold and unmeaning, very unlike Catholic worship. Mr. Palmer was greatly disappointed, and in the evening left him to his own devices. The Curé went out, and returned in a state of enthusiasm. Bursting into his friend's room, he declared that he had been among the early Christians. "How they prayed and cried out 'Glory be to God!' and 'Alleluia!'" On being asked where he had been, he said that he had found himself in the Independent chapel, and that if he were not a Catholic, he would be an Independent.

On leaving Huntlyburn, Mrs. Leslie made her way slowly back to Nantes, paying, as was her custom, visits to her various relations and friends on the way. It was about this time that she met with an accident which, but for her brother's presence of mind, might have proved fatal. While dressing to go out, a rug or piece of carpet slipped on the highly-polished *parquet*, and she fell, striking her head violently against the sharp corner of a table and thereby severing two arteries. In a moment she was bathed in blood, but managed to rise and make her way to her brother's dressing-room. Mr. Atlee, seeing where the danger lay, carefully kept his fingers pressed on the arteries till a doctor could be brought to tie them up. The operation was painful, and perhaps unskilfully done, for the instrument broke, but Mrs. Leslie was never heard to utter a complaint, and her patience at that time and during the wearisome treatment that followed was a marvel to all.

The first words which she wrote in her diary on New Year's Day, 1868, are these:

Through the infinite mercy of Almighty God, I am brought to this new year. Oh may it be spent according to His holy will, which is my sanctification !

Early in May, Mr. Falconer Atlee's eldest daughter Julia and her husband came to Nantes; but as there seemed little hope of their conversion, Mrs. Leslie saw no reason for prolonging her stay at that time, and went to Marmoutier, remaining in the convent the whole of the summer. On her arrival she wrote in her diary:

> Left my dear, kind family. May they be blessed for all their kindness to me.

Madame Leslie was no longer at Marmoutier, but had been sent to Mount Anville, near Dublin, where her mother subsequently visited her.

In the meanwhile, Mrs. Leslie was perfectly contented at the convent. She could not be anywhere without making her presence felt beneficially, and here, as everywhere, she found plenty of occupation. She attended the meetings of the Children of Mary, helped in many of the good works carried on at the convent, and was always ready to take any of the English pupils into Tours to confession to the English-speaking priest there. She also took pity on a new arrival, an Irish child, who understood no French, and gave her lessons; in fact, wherever there was a gap, Mrs. Leslie always came forward to fill it.

Madame de Pambour and her daughter arrived at Marmoutier towards the end of

July, and Mrs. Leslie noticed that her sister looked ill. In a few days, indeed, her life was in danger, and the last Sacraments were administered. She passed away very gently on August 5, feast of the Transfiguration. The event, like many others, in which sorrow was merged in spiritual consolation and that supernatural attitude of mind now so habitual with Mrs. Leslie, is noted in her diary with a *Deo gratias*.

A year and a half previously, Lady Cecil Kerr had also died at Marmoutier, having made her religious profession on her deathbed. Mrs. Leslie had been there during the whole course of her illness, and had kept the novice's mother informed of every detail of her malady. Lady Alice, who was in Scotland, wrote in the midst of her grief:

> I can't say what a comfort it is to all of us to think you are at Marmoutier. It is next best to having her at home.

Summoned at last by their devoted friend, Lady Lothian and her daughter arrived before the death of the charming young nun, and were able to spend with her the last precious hours of her short life on earth. She was buried in the convent cemetery. Mrs. Leslie made a sketch of her grave, with its surroundings, and sent it to Lady Lothian for the first anniversary of her death.

In 1869 Mrs. Leslie went to Scotland and

Ireland. She had last parted from her daughter at Conflans after Charlotte's profession, and was anxious to see her again. While in Ireland she made many new friends, all attracted to her by her wonderful personality and those gifts of mind and heart which made her at once a power wherever she was. She was one of those rare souls who create an atmosphere around themselves into which others are irresistibly drawn, and this by the exercise of no aggressive art, but by the strong and gentle individuality that conquers, without appearing to claim anything; for while people were feeling and wondering at her singular influence, she herself was solely occupied with the one absorbing desire to love and serve God ever more perfectly. To some it might appear that having now become free from all ties, the great bar to her sanctity might be the absence of any particular duty in life. But although she seemed to come and go, and to do very much as she pleased, having no longer any great cares or anxieties, her purpose and intention were as clear and firm as in the days when she made her greatest sacrifices—abnegation of self and submission to the will of God. Her favourite prayer was still: "Do with me, O Lord, as Thou knowest, and as Thou willest, for I know that Thou lovest me."

She returned once more to Nantes; then the Franco-Prussian war put an end to her long sojourn in France. Henceforth she could do little but pray for the conversion of that beloved brother whose welfare lay so near her heart; for when the horrors perpetrated by the Paris Commune were at an end and the country had settled down again, Mrs. Leslie had fixed her permanent abode in Scotland, and she only saw him at rare intervals, the weight of increasing years making travelling abroad less easy.

CHAPTER XIV.

AT ST. MARGARET'S.

MRS. LESLIE had been spending a few weeks with the Falconer Atlees at Croisic when the war broke out between France and Germany. On account of the disturbed state of France she resolved to return to England, and as her son had been allowed to go to Croisic he was able to travel with her. After some delays, occasioned by the frequent stoppage of the trains to allow of the troops moving to the seat of war, they arrived at St. Malo, but only to find that they had missed their boat, and would have to remain there a few days. When at last they landed at Southampton, they were met by Mrs. Leslie's sister, Mrs. Dowson. Father Leslie returned to his mission at Liverpool, and his mother went to Mrs. Maxwell at Ryde. After a short visit to Ryde, she went to stay with Lady Lothian's daughter, now married to Mr. Gaisford, at Offington, near Worthing, where she met many old friends, and passed some pleasant days. Before introducing her to the priest at Worthing, Lady Alice spoke of her to him as a lady who had done more than anyone else to help on the

PART OF ST. MARGARET'S CONVENT, EDINBURGH.
Showing the bow window of Mrs. Leslie's sitting-room.

[*To face page 75.*]

revival of Catholicism in Scotland. On leaving Offington, she went to London, and thence to Edinburgh. It had been decided that her future home should be St. Margaret's Convent, where a few rooms were being built for the accommodation of a certain number of lady boarders. Mrs. Leslie helped considerably towards the building of these rooms. She arrived on the feast of St. Ursula, patroness of the community, and superintended the furnishing of her new abode, which consisted of a pretty sitting-room with a beautiful view, and a small bedroom adjoining. Rooms bear in some sense the impress of their occupants, and Mrs. Leslie's rooms at St. Margaret's were characteristic of her. On the walls were hung her favourite pictures—an *Ecce Homo* reputed by Guido, bought in Rome; a view in the Eternal City, by Carrodi; sketches by her son, and by other members of her family. The furniture was simple but comfortable.* Her prie-Dieu stood in the window which faced the convent chapel, and the sanctuary, towards which her thoughts were turned many times in the course of the day. The books she loved were everywhere visible, and contributed their share, with the photographs of her children

* All the furniture which she did not need for her own use was given to the house of the Jesuit Fathers, when they came to Edinburgh.

and dearest friends, to make her surroundings homelike. The loving remembrance of many friends seldom left her without the brightness which flowers bring into a room.

Here Mrs. Leslie passed the remaining twenty-two years of her life, with the exception of short intervals of absence, occupying her time with almost conventual regularity. She had always been an early riser, and to extreme old age, unless prevented by illness, she continued to assist at the half-past seven o'clock Mass in the convent chapel, receiving Communion daily. After breakfast followed meditation and spiritual reading, the rest of the morning being spent with her large correspondence, and in work for the poor. Dinner was served in the middle of the day, and she never omitted her particular *examen* of conscience before it. In the afternoon, she would sometimes pay calls, go to see a poor pensioner of hers, or receive her friends. In the evening she invariably made the Way of the Cross, recited the Rosary, visited the Blessed Sacrament, and read some spiritual book. Long habit no doubt often becomes second nature, but here nature and grace seem to have gone pleasantly hand in hand, and to have prevented a methodical way of life from becoming a mere monotonous groove. There was always so much freshness, gentleness and energy in Mrs. Leslie's manner of going about her pious exercises that they never became tiresome to herself or others. The friends who gathered round her in her charming, quiet room were always sure of a warm welcome, and the keenness of her delight in these visits never wore off.

But sorrows were not wanting; neither of course were those smaller trials which do not bear so dignified a name, but which by their frequency make up quite a respectable bundle of mortifications and penance. The first shadow cast upon her new home was the news of the atrocities committed by the Commune of Paris after the war, and the martyrdom of her friend and valued confessor, Père Olivaint.

In April, 1871, a much regretted change took place at St. Margaret's, in the removal of Father O'Donnell, who had been the devoted chaplain of the community for twenty-six years, and a special friend of the Leslie family, having received both father and son into the Church. He was appointed by the Bishop to the parish of Falkirk, but until his presbytery was put in order he returned frequently to the convent to pack and superintend the removal of such furniture as he wished to have. Mrs. Leslie notes these passing visits in her diary, always with a word of kind regard and esteem.

During many of these years at St. Margaret's Father Leslie was allowed to go to Edinburgh in the autumn. Some work would be found for him, such as preaching in the Jesuit Church, or giving the Spiritual Exercises to a religious community in the north; or he would make his own retreat at Dalkeith, combined with which journey was a short visit to his mother. It would seem as if in this way, God rewarded Mrs. Leslie for the large-heartedness with which she had given up her only son. Neither mother nor son ever came to look on these visits as a matter of course. There was always a degree of uncertainty about them, which made his arrival each year like a freshly bestowed blessing. At first, they would make some little excursion, or pass a few days at Huntlyburn or Carstairs, but as her infirmities increased, and moving about became a difficulty, the whole of the time allowed would be spent at St. Margaret's. In June 1871, Mrs. Leslie went to see him at Liverpool, and from thence crossed over to Ireland, and paid a second visit to the Sacred Heart Convent at Mount Anville. Here she made her usual annual retreat, an exercise never omitted, while the necessary strength for it lasted. Then she returned to her quiet home in Edinburgh. We have still to touch on the most obvious feature of Mrs. Leslie's residence at St. Margaret's—the living under the same roof with one of her beloved children, given long years since to God.

All seemed indeed exceptional, in the result of the sacrifices made by this tender mother. What son, following a worldly career, could have been so much to her, perhaps even so much with her, as he whom she had with most loving hands put away from her? What daughter could have watched over her declining years with greater care than she, who had given up father and mother for the kingdom of heaven's sake? Perhaps the clue to these things lies in the hidden measure of generosity with which the offering had been made.

Among the entries in Mrs. Leslie's diary, relating to her devotional practices, alms, correspondence and passing events, we find on September 8, 1871, the following:

> My beloved and good sister Emma [Mrs. Falconer Atlee] died at St. Helier, Jersey. R.I.P.

In 1872 the usual visits were paid, only Madame Leslie was now at Roehampton, and having gone south to see her, her mother went on to Ryde and Southampton. Mrs. Maxwell's daughter writing from Ryde says:

> It was when dear Auntie spent so much time with us here, that my love and reverence for her became as it were a part of my life. It seemed to me that she carried about with her always an atmosphere of love and strength; and it is much more than a mere pleasure to me to remember that she once told me I occupied a place in her heart, very near her own children.

Before leaving Roehampton, Mrs. Leslie had followed a retreat given by Father Morris, which she ever afterwards remembered and spoke of as one of the best and most helpful she had ever made. At the request of the ladies who were present, Madame Leslie took notes of the meditations. Nearly all Mrs. Leslie's oldest Catholic friends were among the retreatants, and it was altogether a particularly happy moment in her life. Having paid her visit to Ryde, she was again at Roehampton in September, and had the pleasure of seeing Mr. Robertson, Mr. Palmer, Lord Lothian, and other friends of auld lang syne.

The brightness of 1873, and thenceforth that of nearly every successive year, was dimmed by the loss of some cherished friend or other. Mr. Robertson's death made the next gap, and was quickly followed by that of Mr. Hope Scott. To so affectionate a nature as Mrs. Leslie's, such losses were naturally very acutely felt, and as may be imagined, her departed friends were never forgotten. Their names, with the anniversaries of their death, were inscribed in a little book always at hand, and at each recurring date she had Mass said for the repose of their souls.

The next trouble was caused by Father Leslie's serious illness at Liverpool. When the news reached his mother, she was herself too ill to travel, and had to bear the double burden of anxiety, endured at a distance from the object of it. The damp, raw climate of Liverpool had occasioned a succession of violent chills, and the rupture of several small blood vessels in the throat. The hemorrhage was so severe, that grave fears were entertained for the patient's life. Then a change for the better took place, and on the day of Mrs. Leslie's arrival, when at last she was able to go to Liverpool, for the first time there was no hemorrhage. The Rector kindly allowed her to see her son, and to take him, as soon as he was strong enough to bear the journey, to Rhyl, where he rapidly regained health and strength.

Many delightful walks and talks they enjoyed together, and Mrs. Leslie felt well repaid for all the suffering and anxiety she had lately undergone. They went to Shrewsbury, and visited the Benedictine novitiate at Belmont, where they met the future Archbishop of Sydney. Mrs. Leslie always maintained that he was the handsomest man she had ever seen. At Gloucester, they were hospitably received by an old friend, and passed some pleasant days in this interesting Cathedral city. From thence, Father Leslie went on to the Jesuit Fathers at Bristol, his mother proceeding to London, Roehampton and Brighton, where he rejoined her for a few days. Mr. Falconer Atlee and his daughters were staying there, and the five formed a happy family party. When they dispersed, Mrs. Leslie returned to Edinburgh.

Active and energetic as she still was, signs began to appear of failing strength; 1874 opened with another slight illness, and again in April, the diary notes frequent attacks of giddiness, and of general indisposition, with touching prayers for patience. Her visit however, to England, took place as usual in July, and she made her annual retreat at the Training College, Wandsworth, where Madame Leslie was now Superioress. Her mother took great interest in this new foundation, and was present at the first Mass said in the old house on West Hill, which had souvenirs attached to it connected with her girlhood. She contributed many useful gifts towards the furnishing of the new convent, and among others a clock which is still a reliable timekeeper. Wandsworth had always been very near her heart, and in her anxiety to do something for the spread of Catholicity in the home of her early youth she half resolved to fix her abode there. Many friends wishing to keep her always with them urged her to do so, but for various

IN THE GROUNDS OF THE OLD HOUSE ON WEST HILL, WANDSWORTH, WHERE MRS. LESLIE'S CHILDHOOD HAD BEEN PASSED

(From Mrs. Leslie's Sketchbook.)

[To face page 382.

reasons it was thought better for her to continue to make her home in Edinburgh.

The next few years passed away almost uneventfully, except for the continued havoc caused by death in her large circle of relations and friends. A little increasing weakness might be noticed in her, a few downward steps bodily, but an ever-growing peace and child-like confidence in God's goodness and mercy. Her sister, Mrs. Maxwell, died in 1876, and three years later, her youngest sister Emily, Mrs. Dowson. The death of Mr. Sigismund Rücker, her trustee and adviser in past difficulties, had occurred in 1875, and was also a great sorrow; that of Lady Lothian in 1877 a still greater. She had gone to Rome, with some English pilgrims, to present an offering of money from the Catholics of England to the Pope, on the occasion of his episcopal Jubilee, and had been seized with inflammation of the lungs. The news of her death was first known in England by a telegram sent by the *Times* correspondent. Other telegrams and letters followed speedily, with the anxiously-awaited details. Father Wynne wrote from Bournemouth :

On Tuesday last, several letters were written from Rome, all giving accounts of Lady Lothian, and detailing all she was doing, mentioning that she had borne the journey better than any of her party, and was in extraordinary health and spirits. Lord Ralph had arrived, and Gilbert Talbot; the Kenyons were also with her, as well as her party of lady friends who had travelled with her from England. Last night Lord Henry had a telegram from Rome, followed by letters from Lord Lothian and Lady Alice, announcing that Lady Lothian had been seized with inflammation of the lungs, and leaving little hope of recovery. This morning I received a telegram dated *Sunday, 7.35 p.m., Rome*, from Mrs. Kenyon. *Break news to papa. Aunt Cecil has expired very peacefully this evening after receiving the last Sacraments.* I have neither time nor heart to make any comments, but you knew Lady Lothian well enough to be aware that if she had made the disposal of her end for herself it could not have been ordered more in accordance with her inclinations—at Rome, her last act to head a pilgrimage and lay her offerings at his feet on the Jubilee of the Holy Father, surrounded by her Catholic friends and relations, and fortified with the rites of the Church. I should apply to her the epitaph of the child of a friend of mine who died in Rome while I was there, " Venne a Roma per passare in Cielo."

When the obsequies had taken place, and the requisite formalities had been complied with, the remains of Lady Lothian were brought to England, and thence to Dalkeith, where they were buried under the sanctuary of St. David's Church, of which she was foundress. Mrs. Leslie was at the funeral, which took place on June 27, and on the 29th travelled to England with Lady Amabel Kerr. In their grief, Lady Lothian's children clung affectionately to her whom they remembered as one of their mother's dearest friends since their childhood. They had long called her their "Grannie," but now the word had a new meaning for them, and two of them at least came to her often for sympathy and advice. When Lord Ralph's marriage with Lady Anne Howard was decided, he brought her to Wandsworth, where Mrs. Leslie was then staying. On entering the room he kissed her affectionately, saying, "Mrs. Leslie, I have brought you a new grandchild. Anne, kiss your Grannie!"

Meanwhile the list of sorrowful anniversaries in the little book grew year by year. On April 5, 1879, Mr. William Palmer died, and left another painful blank. Whenever he had been in Scotland, he had passed hours in Mrs. Leslie's pretty sitting-room at St. Margaret's; and then there were the old delightful Roman days. Archbishop Porter, another valued friend, wrote to one of her daughters when he was in Rome about this time:

> Remember me very kindly to your mother. I never pass the Piazza Campitelli without thinking of Mr. Palmer, and somehow your mother is always associated in my mind with the memory of that holy man.

In June of this year, Mr. Falconer Atlee had a slight paralytic seizure, and his daughters were very naturally anxious about his state. It was always difficult for them to approach him on the subject of religion, on account of his extreme reserve, and Mrs. Leslie had a great desire to see him, and make another effort to win him for God.

She therefore determined to go to Dieppe, to which place he had been taken for change of air. She left Edinburgh on August 5, breaking her journey at York, and arriving the next day in London, where she was met by her son, who was to accompany her to Dieppe. It was her last, long journey. Having made a short retreat under Father Morris and seen a number of friends, she crossed over to Boulogne, and reached Dieppe on the 20th. There she remained for ten days. The undertaking was no trifling one at the age of seventy-nine, and her brother was deeply touched by so striking a proof of her affection, although the chief object of the visit was not then attained. Stopping for a few days at Wandsworth, on her return journey she wrote to one of her daughters:

> Your poor uncle was certainly better in some respects, but his life and state are always precarious, which I think he realizes with a gentle submission and patience. Pray much for him.

They never met again on earth, though Mr. Atlee had still ten more years to live, his sister outliving him by three. She was back in Edinburgh on September 17, and never left it again, except for two short visits to Perth, where the nuns of St. Margaret's have a branch house. After a few days' rest the ordinary rule of life was again taken up, and notwithstanding that she had already as usual, made the Spiritual Exercises while in the south, she followed the children's retreat at St. Margaret's, on the re-opening of the school after the holidays. No one could ever persuade her, on the score of possible fatigue, not to avail herself of every attainable means of sanctification. When urged to take a little extra rest in the morning, she would say cheerfully but with great decision, "At my age, the time must soon come when I shall be obliged to rest. How I should then reproach myself if I had ever missed Mass and Holy Communion through my own fault!"

As she was now unable any longer to extend the sphere of her usefulness to friends scattered about in so many distant places, Mrs. Leslie turned her attention more particularly to the needs of those nearer to her. She had been much struck by accounts which had reached her of the extreme poverty of the priests in the west of Scotland, who were often wanting in the barest necessaries of life. With her wonted energy, she set to work, and undertook in her eighty-first year to supply a number of them with warm under-clothing made with her own deft hands. These gifts were sent periodically for distribution to the Bishop of Argyll and the Isles.

The arrival of each day's post was an important moment in her well-filled day. One morning, a letter affected her deeply. A priest whom she had known intimately and esteemed highly in his days of fervour, had, owing chiefly to some misunderstanding, been suspended. In a fit of bitterness and discouragement on this account, he had lived for many years without practising his religion, though he had kept the faith. The letter was from this man, and it related that on the feast of the Nativity of our Lady, he had been at Farm Street Church, and a sermon, the subject of which was recourse to the Blessed Virgin and confidence in her intercession, struck him profoundly, not only on account of the words and the earnest tone of the preacher, but also because the voice recalled old associations of the good days long gone by. He had never before seen Father Leslie as a priest, and had not now recognized him, but the familiar voice had touched the right chord, and he resolved to return to the path of virtue. Having ascertained whose were the words which had moved him so strangely, he wrote to Mrs. Leslie to ask for her prayers, and to beg that she would see him, if he might venture to approach her, in spite of his unworthiness. In all the intervening years since they had met, she had never ceased to pray for him, and great was her joy in being able to welcome him back to repentance, and no less great the tact and delicacy with which she sought to strengthen his crushed and humbled heart. He persevered in his good resolutions, and died not long afterwards a fervent penitent.

Feeble as Mrs. Leslie's bodily health was now becoming, her mind was still vigorous, her sight and hearing unimpaired (she rarely used glasses except for reading very small print), and she could read, write, work and play the piano as well as ever, though not for so long a time at a stretch. Nevertheless she was careful to keep the end well in view, and she often spoke as if preparing for death at no distant period. Once, during her last visit to Wandsworth, her daughter found her room full of old letters, the contents of a trunk which must have been for thirty or forty years in charge of her trustee. "Dear child," said Mrs. Leslie humbly, "please burn all these letters. I used to keep them, I think from vanity."

The following letter to her niece, Miss Falconer Atlee, in answer to some queries about Darwin, is a proof of the clearness of her intellect and of her power of mind in her eighty-third year:

My Dearest Georgie,—My flannel work not being ready for me, I will endeavour in a few lines to reply to your last letter. First of all, however, I must express the hope that your father is fairly well in spite of persistent east wind.

The late Mr. Darwin was son of a Dr. Darwin, who wrote

a foolish poem called "Loves of the Plants." He was a professed atheist, and it is likely the son may have inherited some of his ideas from him. Mr. Darwin was, I believe, a plausible writer, and his theory of our derivation from apes was eagerly seized upon by sceptics. But there was always a most important link wanting, which neither tradition, history, science, nor experience has supplied. The *Tablet* newspaper of Sunday, I think, notices this; but in 1878 Willie wrote me the following: "If you want a fair exposure of the Darwin system, get *All the Articles of the Darwin Faith*—it is a pamphlet, price 6d., by the Rev. —. Morris, a Protestant clergyman—and by the same author, *The Double Dilemma of Darwinism*." Mivart has also written (if I remember rightly) upon Darwin and Huxley, but just now I could not lay my hand upon his criticism. If Mr. Darwin liked to believe he sprang from an ape, I cannot agree with his opinion, as I consider the Mosaical account of our creation both more noble and more reasonable. But it is not enough to have the eyes of human reason; we need the superior light of divine illumination—not, I may add, to unravel the ways of God with man, but heartily to accept the dealings of the Infinite, and bow before certain difficulties, which to me are far less than any human interpretations ever put upon them.

The Fathers of the Church called the devil the "ape of God," and I should imagine any progeny or scholars proceeding from him would be necessarily young monkeys, whose whole object would be to mock God's work in human beings, whether in their degraded form, their action, or by their clever instinct. Perhaps the person who wrote the following epitaph upon a schoolmaster in the churchyard of Curry, near Edinburgh, had some such thought in his mind:—

> Beneath these stanes lie Mickie's banes—
> O Satan should you tak' him,
> Appoint him tutor to your weans
> And clever de'ils he'll mak' them.

Let us be thankful that Almighty God breathed into us *living souls*, and earnestly strive to rise higher and higher, from such a beginning to a happy eternity with our Lord and Saviour Jesus Christ.

Willie is just now at Bath. When next I write, I will ask him to send you the tracts above-mentioned.

I am thankful to be fairly well, and at Mass and Holy Communion this morning.

With much love, believe me, more than ever,
Your loving Auntie,
ELEANOR LESLIE.

About this time, a pleasant renewal of intercourse took place between Mrs. Leslie and Lord Archibald Douglas, now a priest. On the occasion of the opening of a small Catholic church at Queensferry he was asked to preach, and accepted the invitation gladly, his interest in Queensferry dating from boyhood, when he lived not far from it. In those days, as there was neither priest nor church in the place, he used to give catechetical instruction to the children of Catholic parents on Sunday afternoons. For this reason he afterwards called Queensferry his first mission. On his return to Scotland he slept at the Hermitage at St. Margaret's, renewed his acquaintance with Mrs. Leslie and kept it up till her death.

In 1882 died Lord Henry Kerr and the Rev. Mr. O'Donnell, the "Padre" as he was affectionately termed by all connected with St. Margaret's. Mrs. Leslie's own health was rapidly declining, and on January 1, 1883, Holy Communion was administered to her in her room. For a whole month she did not leave her bed, and when again able to move into her sitting-room she required the support of a stick. It was procured for her by Mr. Reginald Horsley, whose conversion had been the subject of her intense solicitude. They had become fast friends, and, in spite of the disparity of their ages, enjoyed each other's society extremely, Mr. Horsley delighting in her keen intellect, fund of information and amusing anecdote. Her memory was so good, her knowledge of men and things of bygone time so accurate, that her reminiscences were always interesting. Just in the right place she would bring in an apt quotation, a witty allusion, and suit her conversation so admirably to her hearers that everyone was charmed. Mr. Horsley had been on the "Challenger" cruise, and had been introduced to the convent for the purpose of classifying a valuable collection of shells which it possessed. When his visits in pursuit of conchology were at an end, he continued to come for instruction in the Catholic religion; and after a time, to Mrs. Leslie's great joy, he was received into the Church. He then applied himself to medical studies, married and settled in Edinburgh, spending many a leisure hour in the society of her whom he regarded as a second mother.

September brought Father Leslie for his

annual visit, and after a happy fortnight the parting, now always a rather sorrowful event in the growing uncertainty whether each would be the last, was softened by the arrival of her brother's two daughters. This indeed was a farewell, but to Mrs. Leslie's nieces a storehouse of tender memories for years to come.

Then another beloved friend, the Dowager Lady Herries, was gathered to her rest. She had been a frequent visitor at St. Margaret's since the beginning of 1880, when she had passed the Lenten season there in a kind of semi-retreat, one of the reasons for her stay being easy access by rail to Dumfries, where she was founding a convent of Perpetual Adoration, in which prayers would be unceasingly offered for the conversion of Scotland and the welfare of her own children. Mrs. Leslie and Lady Herries were kindred spirits, and an endless source of edification to the nuns.*

In her growing infirmities Mrs. Leslie was naturally dependent on her daughter for all those little alleviations which her maid, devoted though she was, was incapable of giving. When the community retreat was about to begin, Lady Herries said to Mother Mary

* Soon after their first meeting Lady Herries wrote to her cousin, Miss Langdale : "You told me everything but what you ought about Mrs. Leslie. You said she was charming and delightful, but you did not say that she was a saint."

Sales: "My dear, you must make your retreat in peace. I'll look after your mother meantime." And this she did in the most careful, affectionate way. Nothing could exceed her admiration for Mrs. Leslie. One Saturday, Mother Mary Sales found her intently occupied in mending. On her expressing some surprise Lady Herries said: "My dear, you know I think your mother quite perfect, and I want to do everything just as she does. She always does her mending on Saturdays, and I mean to do the same."

Two extracts from letters, written by Mrs. Leslie in 1883, show how constantly her own death was before her eyes, and how earnestly she was preparing herself for it. Both letters were addressed to her Sacred Heart nun:

> The weather is very variable and trying, so that my old heart still beats feebly, though I have been able *(Deo gratias* a thousand times) to go to Mass three times this week. God is so good to me. I have no suffering, and everything for mind and body that I can desire. Pray, dear child, that I may make a good use of His mercy, and according to your dear prayer, that my last hour may be my best hour.

A little later she wrote:

> BELOVED CHILD,—I was intending to write to you for your birthday on Friday. Well, what can I say but to renew my fervent prayers that every fresh year may add to all those graces that may make your vocation more perfect, and thus make you more pleasing to the Sacred Heart of our blessed Saviour? Most gratefully do I thank Him for all that He has done for you, and for all that He has done for me. Let us praise Him

more and more for His goodness, think more constantly of it, love it more, and yet feel we can never praise Him enough. Your dear father's grave has now been enclosed in the little Catholic plot belonging to the Convent, in the Grange Cemetery. I have settled that it shall also be my resting-place when it will please our heavenly Father to call me hence. Willie and Mary are both pleased with this arrangement, and in the meantime, by their devoted prayers and care, are striving to keep me here a little longer.

Even had it not been for her holy vigilance, the gradual dropping away of her contemporaries, some of them younger than herself, would have kept their beloved mother's end constantly before her children's minds.

In the beginning of 1884 Lady Henry Kerr died, and for a time it seemed probable that Mrs. Leslie would not long survive her. A severe attack of the heart so prostrated her that the last Sacraments were administered, and she received the solemn rites with deep devotion, and that ever present gratitude which always made her piety so touching. But the measure of her days was not yet complete, and by degrees she was restored to much of her former health, though with strength greatly diminished. The following letter from Mother Henrietta Kerr, Lady Henry's daughter, who was herself slowly dying of consumption, was written on the occasion of her mother's death and Mrs. Leslie's illness :

CONVENT OF THE SACRED HEART, ROEHAMPTON.
March 6, 1884.

MY DEAR SISTER MARY SALES,—Since February 4, two pages of a letter to my dear Granny have been lying on my desk. When I got thus far, I was in hopes of having, in another couple of days, some souvenirs of my mother to offer her. But the Frenchman has kept me all this time waiting for photographs, and my remonstrances can elicit nothing beyond the courteous assurance "que dans quelques jours, il aura l'honneur," &c. Will you explain this to my dear Granny, with my best of loves, and do not let the thought lurk in her mind or yours, that I did not appreciate keenly the kind sympathy you sent me. I scarcely write any letters myself now; but my Granny knows that she is my only Granny in the world. I hear that she has had the Last Sacraments. I don't mean to be anxious, but send her my congratulations on sharing my spiritual luxuries. All the same, I would be very glad to have a postcard from you, with news of her occasionally. In spite of all one's arguments and reasonings with one's self, the words "Last Sacraments" in connection with those we care for so much, cannot but give one a pang. I think of her so often, and remind Almighty God that I know He will do whatever is best and most loving by her.

I send her and you two little leaflets, completed in spite of my enemy the Frenchman. I am sending one to Mother Chattie, who wrote me the kindest of letters. Pray for me, dear Sister Mary Sales, and believe me,

Yours affectionately in Christ Jesus
H. KERR, R.S.C.J.

After an illness of six weeks Mrs. Leslie noted in her diary a visit to the Blessed Sacrament, the first sign of her convalescence; and Mother Henrietta Kerr preceded to her rest, on December 1, 1884, the "dear Granny" whom she feared to lose.

A few more years remained, during which, although she seldom left the Convent, Mrs.

Leslie was surrounded by friends old and young, to whom the warmth of her welcome, and the unclouded brightness of her intellect were a never failing source of happiness and good. In a little note to Madame Leslie during this year, she says:

> Mary and I lately played Albert's favourite duet by Mozart, and we are going to have more music to-day.

In a longer letter to the same she wrote:

> I wonder and ask why do I live on? and sometimes feel afraid of God's patience and mercy, seeing how far I am from deserving it all. Dear Mary is fairly well, and has some nice children in the school. She has been reading to them Lady Herbert's account of Don Bosco from the *Month*. He is really a wonderful man. I wish we had him here, to make one of his admirable foundations for boys. As for the present educational system generally, I am still of the same opinion as the late Mr. Drummond of Albany, who said in Parliament, "You *teach* your children, but you do not *educate* them." And it is true, that their poor brains are crammed with much that is useless, whilst the heart and mind are untouched, and the will left to its dangerous self.

Resigned as Mrs. Leslie was to all the inconveniences and discomforts inseparable from old age, her natural energy never could accustom itself to her bodily infirmities, and in the course of 1885, one of her quick movements occasioned a bad fall, which again made her an invalid for some time, and from which she never entirely recovered. Her daily walks were henceforth limited to a few turns round the Convent garden, leaning on her daughter's arm, and on her trusty stick. But an unexpected pleasure was in store, in the form of a visit from Father Coleridge. The principal object of his coming to Edinburgh was to see and consult her with reference to a Life of Lady Lothian. The work had been already contemplated by Lady Georgiana Fullerton, and some part of it was already written. Mrs. Leslie had made over to her certain letters connected with Lady Lothian's conversion, had had several interviews with her concerning the Life, and had written to her some few times on the same subject, supplying Lady Georgiana with facts concerning her own history for the part that was inseparable from Lady Lothian's. But the talented writer had died before the book was half written, and Father Coleridge had been asked to continue it. Some difficulty as to dates having occurred, he visited Mrs. Leslie at St. Margaret's, and her faithfully kept diary proved an infallible guide. Another feature of his visit was a never-forgotten drive which they took together round Arthur's Seat, that he might get a notion of the environs of beautiful Edinburgh. When they parted, it was with the mutual wish that another meeting between them might be possible. But Father Coleridge fell into ill-health, the Life of Lady Lothian remained unfinished; and it was

MRS. LESLIE AT THE AGE OF EIGHTY-SIX.

From a Photograph by Dr. Horsley. [*To face Page* 299.

when too weak to endure the fatigue of ordinary visitors that he said to Father Leslie, "There are two people I should like to see again—Newman and your mother."

The only satisfactory portrait existing of Mrs. Leslie was a beautiful miniature by Robertson, painted in the bloom and heyday of her youth, shortly after her marriage, the reproduction of which forms the frontispiece to this volume. Her children and intimate friends had long desired to possess a faithful likeness of her charming old age, but she was extremely averse from having her photograph taken. She had yielded two or three times to their entreaties, but the result had never been entirely successful, and they had given up the hope of getting her to sit for her portrait again. Dr. Horsley was however, an excellent amateur photographer, and was one day taking views of the convent and garden when, after some persuasion, Mrs. Leslie consented to sit for him. The result was a very good likeness. She is represented sitting in her own chair, with a wicker table beside her, the gift of Lady Herries, with her favourite books, a photograph of her son, and some flowers arranged upon it.

June, 1886, was memorable in the annals of St. Margaret's by the celebration of the fiftieth anniversary of the foundation of the convent, the first to exist in Scotland since the Reformation. Mrs. Leslie entered warmly into the spirit of the celebration, and was able to be present at the High Mass and Te Deum.

About this time she wrote to Madame Leslie, then at Liége:

> I was very glad to receive your last interesting letter and to find that you had followed a retreat to your mind. My day is now over, both for retreats and sermons, and I sometimes wish for more oral instruction, as I think spoken words would make a deeper impression on my slothfulness than reading good books, although I should be most grateful for those I have, and for my old eyes being able to decipher their contents. The best retreats I ever had during the last thirty years were those of Père Rubillon, S J., at the Villa Lante, Rome, of Père Hubin, S.J., at Nantes, and that of Father Morris, S.J., at Roehampton, of which you furtively made such excellent notes.

In the same letter she alluded in terms of deep sympathy to the tragic death of the young Earl of Dalkeith and the sorrow it occasioned to his family, and continued:

> My beloved, when I hear of such sad events, though we know the mercy and wisdom hidden in them, I wonder at my exemption, and humbly think of those words of St Francis Xavier, "the greatest cross is to be without a cross." Pray, my dearest, that this may help me to do more for Him, who bore so cruel a one for me.

It will perhaps be remembered that when Mr. Falconer Atlee's wife and two daughters became Catholics in 1859, his eldest daughter, Julia, and her husband were extremely displeased and even antagonistic, but that Mrs. Leslie never would despair of her niece's conversion. Then Mr. Lauerbach, Julia's first husband, died, and some time afterwards his widow married the Comte de Coëtlogon, a good Catholic belonging to an old and well-known Breton family. She had suggested that the wedding should take place at the chapel of the British Embassy, but to this M. de Coëtlogon would not agree, her father and brother being entirely on his side. The ceremony was therefore a purely Catholic one. M. de Coëtlogon died suddenly in 1887, and in her deep sorrow Julia turned to religion for consolation. Eventually she abjured Protestantism and was received into the Church.*

In June of this year the whole empire celebrated the Queen's Golden Jubilee, and Mrs. Leslie, whose memory reached back eighty years and beyond, took a lively interest in the event. She had witnessed the Coronation procession, and could therefore enter the more enthusiastically into the general rejoicings. The address, presented by the nuns of Scotland, was illuminated at St. Margaret's, the greatest pleasure being taken in its preparation. As daylight faded on the memorable

* Two other nieces of Mrs. Leslie's became Catholics, her sister Emily's daughter, who married a good French Catholic, M. Perreur, and whose eldest son is a priest; and the only daughter of Mr. Leslie's sister Charlotte Geddes.

21st of June, the hills round Edinburgh were ablaze with bonfires, and when Arthur's seat was crowned with light, Mrs. Leslie's loyalty was as exuberant as any. Even at her advanced age she had much of the freshness of youth, and could the better sympathize with what was passing round her, remembering so vividly, not only all the chief events of the Queen's reign, but those also of the two preceding ones.

In August she again enjoyed keenly Father Leslie's visit, and at Christmas was able to be present at midnight Mass in the convent chapel.

The most notable event in 1888 was the visit of Monsignor (afterwards Cardinal) Persico, Papal Delegate to Ireland, who, when he went to Scotland, having old friends at St. Margaret's, took up his abode for a few days at the Hermitage. He was delighted with Mrs. Leslie, and spent some time in conversation with her. The following letter gives an account of his visit :

St. Margaret's Convent, Edinburgh,
June 2, 1888.

Beloved Child,—I was very glad to hear you had received your watch safely, and I hope your next will tell me it is going well. I am sure Julia will be pleased to hear from you, and accordingly I enclose her letter to me, which need not be returned. I must now tell you of the delightful visit we have had from Monsignor Persico. He wrote to ask if he and his servant could have rooms here, and being answered in the affirmative, they arrived at a quarter past five a.m. yesterday week. He said his Mass at six, and our Archbishop called for him at ten, took him out and lionized him all day. Monsignor gave us Benediction in the evening, and said he must be quiet and write letters next day—Saturday. He did so, dined with the Jesuits at 4, and again gave Benediction at 6-30. On Sunday he said the 8 o'clock Mass here and gave the Papal Blessing. About noon, he paid me a most charming visit, and really led me to open my whole heart to him (though not in confession), when he gave me some excellent and consoling advice. The last is for yourself alone, and I know will please your loving heart. He dined with Dr. Smith and came later, but retired early, intending to leave early on Monday, when he said all his office at 2 a.m., purposing to start at 5, and arranging to return here after his visit to Fort Augustus and his going with the monks to the Island of Iona, where he expected to meet all the Scotch bishops. Two of our nuns were under him in India and thus are old friends. But his manner was so kind and simple, everybody felt at home with him, and dear Mary was quite elevated.

Now I must ask you to pray for dear Mother Margaret Teresa, who is really ill and for some time past I have thought declining. I am thankful to be well, and Mary too, in health, but the foot not cured.

The rooms at the Hermitage were made most bright and suitable for Monsignor and his boy Donato, as he called him; and now here, the workmen have left and we look spick and span. God bless you; much love.

Ever your devoted mother,
ELEANOR LESLIE.

Unhappily, soon after the good report of her health in the above letter, the weakness of heart from which she had before suffered again caused serious alarm. Extreme unction was administered, and Father Leslie was sent for. Many visits of inquiry from anxious friends followed—from the Archbishop of Edinburgh, the Abbot of Fort Augustus, Mgr. Talbot, Lord Ralph and Lady Anne Kerr. Lady Alice

Gaisford brought her young sons to receive "Granny's blessing." Ceaseless prayers went up from the hearts that loved her that she might still be spared to them a little longer. These prayers were heard, and by slow degrees she recovered, and was able to resume something of the daily routine she had hitherto followed. But she had scarcely expected to live, and during this illness had written a letter to her children of which the following are extracts:

> MY BELOVED CHILDREN,—I have already written to you more than one letter, but my advanced age, and my increasing infirmities induce me to make some corrections, and in order to save you confusion, to state more clearly a few things that may occur after my death.
>
> I pray that the disposition of my will and personal effects may be satisfactory to all concerned. I have already parted with the greater number of my trinkets.* Louis de Champfleur's note enclosed will explain the conditions on which I gave advisedly the most valuable, my dear mother's diamond brooch, to his good little wife Marie. The remainder I have bequeathed as affection dictated, or according to promise. Such as are not named I beg you to appropriate as to you may appear most just or agreeable.
>
> I desire to be interred in your father's grave, and that everything connected with my funeral should be as plain and as unostentatious as is consistent with respectability.

After some directions concerning various arrangements she continues two days later:

---

* Among them was a thistle brooch which she gave for the Scotch banner, deposited by the Scotch pilgrims at Paray-le-Monial. She took great interest in the pilgrimage and the banner, which was made at St. Margaret's.

And now, my beloved children, having made notes of all I can recollect, what more have I to say? Much more indeed than I can express. First of all, gratitude to our heavenly Father for all His mercies, great and unceasing, for eighty-seven years, wholly undeserved and unsolicited—His mercies to me especially in *you*, my most dear and good children. I am aware, in your affection and charity, you have thought me much better than I am. But I implore you, from these very feelings, and still more for the love of our blessed Saviour, to have Masses offered frequently for my poor soul after death and never to cease praying for me. I pray Almighty God to bless you, as He alone can, for all your patience and dutifulness towards me. I beg your forgiveness for the many trials I have caused you. And once more commending you to the love of the Sacred Heart, to the prayers of His blessed Mother and all the Saints, I remain beloved ones, in life and in death,

Ever your loving, grateful mother,
ELEANOR LESLIE.

But the end was not just yet. Full and ripe as were the ears of corn standing waiting for the Master's sickle, the eyes of men were still to profit a little longer by so goodly a sight. Happily, the saints of God remain in exile, not only for their own profit and advantage, but also for the help and consolation of others. While Mrs. Leslie breathed she continued to do good: by her words, written and spoken, by her example, by her very presence in the world.

> For age is opportunity no less
> Than youth itself, though in another dress;
> And as the evening twilight fades away,
> The sky is filled with stars invisible by day.

CHAPTER XV.

WORK FINISHED.

When the Lord's work is done, and the toil and the labour completed
He hath appointed to me, I will gather into the stillness
Of my own heart awhile, and wait for His guidance.
                                                    LONGFELLOW.

THE last good work in which Mrs. Leslie took an active interest was the foundation, from St. Margaret's, of a convent at Berwick-on-Tweed. It promised to be a great means of good in that place, and she entered into every detail concerning the new house, and the welcome given to the Sisters in the old Border town. Her gift to the community was a complete equipment of vestments for the sacristy.

During the summer, Mr. Falconer Atlee died, and the following letter, written at the beginning of his more serious illness, is a testimony to his sister's wonderful mental capacity on the verge of ninety:

ST. MARGARET'S CONVENT,
March 16, 1889.

MY VERY DEAR FANNY,—Your report of your dear father received this morning is not good, and I shall be anxious for your next. As a young man he had always more of muscular than physical strength; and in old age, when the former fails, he will more sensibly feel the decline of the latter. Of course we never cease to pray for him, and shall do so more than ever. His early faith in simple Christianity, and belief in our blessed Lord as a *Saviour* has never been completely uprooted in him. although from the time that his clever friend, Theodore Dickins, poured into his mind his anti-Christian sentiments (as naturally more suitable to the immorality of his age), he has been constantly striving to convince himself of their truth. The following sentence which I recently met with in an article upon "Illusions," by Father Michael Maher, S.J., depicts, and to me most clearly explains, the real state of your poor father :

The wish to disbelieve, not the absence of rational evidence, is in truth the source of all infidelity. That this motive is frequently not clearly realized increases its force.

Tell me, dearest Fan, what you think of it. When your father came to Rome in 1858, when dear Albert was dying, he took a walk one day with Chattie, and having been much struck with Albert's perfect happiness and sweet composure since his conversion, he said to her : " I wonder if my opinions when I come to die will stand in good stead to me ! " Here at least was a *doubt*, and we must pray, with the help of St. Joseph, that now divine grace may confirm it, showing their fallacy. I will shortly write again. . . . .

The summer wore on, and the strength of the brother and sister declined perceptibly, so that it was a question which one would outlive the other. At the beginning of July Mrs. Leslie wrote to him :

VERY DEAR OLD BOY,—I must write a line, for with my whole soul I am with you night and day. A month ago the doctor found that my old heart had completely gone down. It has rallied somewhat, but I feel that my time, like yours, must be short. So I ask for you what I ask for myself, the grace that our *last* hour may be our *best* hour. Praying our heavenly Father to guide, protect and bless you,

I remain, as ever, your loving, grateful sister,

ELEANOR LESLIE.

This was the last communication that passed between them, and the object of so many fervent prayers, of such devoted attachment, died in peace on July 21. In the midst of her sorrow, Mrs. Leslie had the immense consolation of knowing that Mr. Atlee had been reconciled to the Church. Nevertheless, the death of her brother told upon her considerably, as did that of Father George Porter, Archbishop of Bombay. What remained to her henceforth of life was patient waiting for her own summons. It was as if she had been left on earth to watch over and save her brother's soul, and as if now her life's work was done. Her nephew Falconer, Mr. Atlee's eldest son, now remained the only member of that family out of the Church. He had been educated in infidelity, and had made an unhappy marriage which had ended in separation. His wife afterwards became a Catholic, and both his sons received a Catholic education. When he was made a C.M.G., Mrs. Leslie wrote to congratulate him, and expressed the wish that he might indeed be the companion of St. Michael and St. George to all eternity. Three days before his death, on the feast of St. Michael, he made his profession of faith, and died in the bosom of the Church.* But Mrs. Leslie had passed away before this happy consummation. Shortly after her brother's death she wrote to her nieces:

> Just a line, beloved children, to cheer your loving hearts and tell you I am better. My decline is so gentle, so rich in the tender mercies of our heavenly Father, a life of *Deo gratias* could not express it. Every want supplied, or rather anticipated, by my devoted Mary, and a freedom from all acute suffering. Oh help me to thank our good God and to respond more to His goodness.

On November 5 of this year occurs the last entry in the diary in her own handwriting. That of September 2—there are very few after this—chronicles the last but one of many partings from her son: "*My beloved one left to-day. May God bless him!*" They met once more and parted; after that she was beyond the sadness of farewells. On the 6th, her daughter's pen recorded: "Fell down."

She had risen as usual at half-past six, intending to go to Mass. Her faithful maid, Elsie, was laid up, and unable to be at her post, and Mrs. Leslie tried herself to light the gas in her room. Stretching higher than

---

* Yet another Atlee, a representative of the American branch of the family, had been received into the Church, about the time of Albert's conversion. This was Dr. Walter Franklin Atlee, who, finding that he had connections at the British Embassy in Paris, put himself in ccmmunication with them.

she was well able to reach, she overbalanced, and fell heavily on the floor. With a great effort she managed to creep back to bed, and when her daughter arrived half-an-hour later it was clear that something unusual had happened. All the morning she lay quietly, not appearing to suffer, but about noon she gave a great cry and said, "My dear, my back is gone." A telegram summoned the doctor, who pronounced that there was concussion of the spine, and great loss of nerve power. By degrees she recovered the use of her limbs, but was never again able to walk or even stand alone. The utter dependence on others, after such complete independence, was perhaps the greatest trial of the remainder of her life; but she was always resigned and unselfish, while her talk was as full of point and piquancy as ever. She interested herself at times in arranging the final disposition of various treasures. Hearing that Madame Leslie needed a paint-box, she sent her her own—one that had belonged to her master, the celebrated Samuel Prout, and which she had used at twelve years old—in perfectly good condition, still testifying to the habits of order and neatness which she had always cultivated.

Some little repugnance was expressed when it was suggested that her bed should be moved into her sitting-room as being more airy and convenient; but she soon made up her mind to this sacrifice also, and wrote afterwards:

I have, in accordance with all your wishes, turned my pretty sitting-room more completely into a bedroom; but I do not like it, and must try heartily to say with St. Philip Neri:

Vi ringrazio, o mio Dio,
Che non vanno le cose a modo mio.

Pray, dear child, that I may become more indifferent to all earthly things and little inconveniences, always remaining more closely united to you in the Heart of our dear Lord.

She was always cheerful, however much inconvenienced, and never allowed a murmur to escape her lips. She would scarcely ever permit any one to express sympathy with her in her sufferings, which were sometimes now very great. One day a friend found her suffering violently from neuralgia, and said, "How sorry I am that you have that dreadful pain!" But Mrs. Leslie answered brightly,

"My dear, it is a very *good* pain for me to have."

A petition having been sent to Rome that she might receive Holy Communion without fasting from midnight onwards, it was objected that such privileges were only granted to religious. The answer by Father Cardella was prompt: "But this lady for whom the privilege is asked is *more than a religious*," and the petition was granted.

Her humility was most touching, and showed itself in gratitude for the least service rendered to her, for every token of affection spoken or written. Once, in answer to some remark about God having taken away all her children, she said: "God took all my children away from me, and called them into religion because He knew that I could not make them good enough." In the course of 1891 she wrote to her son:

> Pray much for me, my beloved one. My time here must be short, and as yet I have scarcely begun. Helpless and useless, I think of God's immense goodness, and of that beautiful line: "They also serve who only stand and wait." God Almighty bless you. With Mary's love,
> More than ever your grateful, loving mother,
> ELEANOR LESLIE.

The year 1892 ushered in a time of general affliction throughout the country, owing to an outbreak of influenza, which made such havoc in Edinburgh that it was commonly spoken of as "the plague." St. Margaret's was severely tried. One lay Sister died, and nearly the whole community were prostrate. The faithful Elsie was one of the sufferers, and Mrs. Leslie was attacked with the same fell disease, complicated by bronchitis. A trained nurse was henceforth indispensable; and on February 17 she received Holy Viaticum and Extreme Unction. Father

WORK FINISHED.

Leslie came on the 22nd, and remained till March 3. It was thought that the end was near. He wrote to his youngest sister, then in Ireland:

When I arrived her voice and embrace were the same as ever. Her piety is very touching. When I was going to bring her Holy Viaticum yesterday evening, she asked like a child if it were preparation enough to say a prayer of St. Francis of Sales and the hymn of St. Francis Xavier "Deus ego amo Te." In the morning—she had been quiet for some time—she called me to say that she prayed for the Scropes every day. They had been so kind (in sending her grapes and flowers). Lord Ralph and Lady Anne were here yesterday. I think you know that Lady Alice had a very blessed end.

The Archbishop of Edinburgh called constantly to see all the many invalids at St. Margaret's, and said one day to Sister Mary Sales, "Your poor mother is very low to-day. I do not think she can last long." He died first, carried off in ten days by the terrible scourge then raging, to the grief of the whole Church of Scotland.

To the surprise of all Mrs. Leslie still lingered, but every day marked a decline. On March 22 she received Holy Communion for the last time; constant distressing sickness prevented her doing so afterwards. Still her mind retained much of its clearness. On April 1, she reminded her daughter that the Little Sisters of the Poor would call for their usual monthly alms; and she was anxious that

Father Whyte should say Mass on the 13th for the repose of the soul of her daughter Eleanor. Every conscious moment was spent in prayer; but there were long hours of stupor during the day, and the nights were restless. Those who have watched by the deathbed of a beloved mother will understand something of the anguish suffered by Mrs. Leslie's children at this time. Renunciation does not render hearts insensible to pain, but rather in raising them above earthly issues gives them a capacity for suffering unknown to weaklings. And Mrs. Leslie had been no ordinary mother. If her love for her children had been "excessive," it was at the same time generous and pure, untainted by selfishness, unspoilt by weakness, guiltless of all ambition, save the noble ambition of presenting them spotless before the throne of God. Such affection, though rare, calls forth the like in the objects of its tenderness, and is perhaps the only love that meets its full requital on earth.

Summoned by telegram, Father Leslie arrived on the morning of April 6. It had been scarcely expected that his mother would survive the night. Dr. Horsley had shared the vigil with Mother Mary Sales, and the devoted Elsie, till he should come, and once she whispered, "God bless all my children," naming them each by their name. But when her son entered the room, she was unconscious, and for the first time his beloved presence was unheeded. Once during the day, a glimmer of consciousness returned; she recognized him and called him by his name. Then came the Pope's Blessing, and afterwards, on April 8, feast of the Seven Dolours, the earthly end. With the dawn the change came. After a time of agitation her breathing became calm, then fainter and fainter. Father Leslie gave frequent blessings and absolutions, and at last the beautiful soul was with God.

The remains were clothed in a brown habit, with the well-worn beads in the white, once so capable hands, now folded and at rest for evermore. Friends brought flowers which she had loved so well; and the Little Sisters of the Poor came with their aged women to pray for their benefactress. When the coffin was closed, it was taken to the chapel and placed on a catafalque in the nuns' choir, and the office for the dead was recited.

Father Leslie said the Mass of requiem on the 12th, and officiated at the funeral service, which took place at 3 o'clock the same day, Father Whyte saying a few touching and appropriate words. A number of old men under the care of the Little Sisters of the Poor attended the funeral, as did also a deputation of the Brotherhood of St. Vincent of Paul.

At the close of the service, the coffin, preceded by the clergy, and followed by the Sisters and a large number of Mrs. Leslie's friends, was carried to the convent gate, and thence to the Grange Cemetery, where in accordance with her own wish she was interred in her husband's grave.

A recumbent cross of grey granite now marks the spot, and bears the inscription :

ARCHIBALD LESLIE, LAST OF BALNAGEITH,
DIED 26TH FEBRUARY, 1851.
ELEANOR FALCONER ATLEE, WIDOW OF ARCHIBALD LESLIE,
DIED 8TH APRIL, 1892.
JESUS MERCY! MARY HELP!

Innumerable were the letters and tokens of sympathy sent by friends, testifying in a remarkable way to the influence, widespread and powerful, of Mrs. Leslie's wonderful personality. Of these two extracts from letters may be taken as characteristic of the whole. Dr. Horsley wrote :

> I am so glad it happened that I was able to spend a little time at your dear mother's side during her last days; and the memory of her gentle pious life will be to me ever a holy and a dear one. So, too, the memory of her affection for me. My own regard for your mother was no weak love. To know her was a privilege beyond the estimating ; to remember her is rendered by love and affection a thing so natural, that it must become one of the dearest duties of my daily life.

The Dowager Duchess of Buccleuch could also speak for others:

> I always look upon her as *our mother*, who helped to bring us into the true Church. We are all her children—good Father Robertson, his aunt and children, dear Lady Lothian and her children, myself, and I do not know how many others. Pray accept and offer your good brother my most sincere and deep sympathy. Though you have enjoyed her so many years on earth, it does not lessen the pain of separation.

Perhaps the sympathy and understanding of what had befallen were no less eloquent in some who had never known Mrs. Leslie personally, or who had never even seen her. On the day after her death Elsie went out to do some necessary shopping. She returned much later than was expected, and when asked what had kept her, she said that she could not get along, for in every shop people wanted to know all about Mrs. Leslie. It was strange that so much interest should be felt among Protestants in the death of a Catholic lady whose life for many years had been so completely hidden, and whose charities had been mainly confined to those of her own religion. In some mysterious way the people about were conscious that a very holy woman had died.

THE END.

INDEX.

Abadie, Monsieur d', 147
Acton, Lady, 147
Addison, The Rev. Berkeley, 122
Aitken, The Rev. Robert, makes the acquaintance of the Leslies, his mental power and personal appearance, 56; his doctrine of conversion, converts Mrs. Leslie, 57; his past history, 58; services at Zion Chapel, 59; his preaching and manner of praying, 61; Mrs. Leslie persuades him to return to the Church of England, 62; appointed to a parish at Leeds, 63; his eloquence, 65; second marriage and subsequent poverty 69; methods after his return to the Church of England, 70; his unworldliness, 73; the extent of his influence on Mrs. Leslie, 85; Mr. Robertson's appreciation of him, 86; letter to Mrs. Leslie on her becoming a Catholic, 103; is recommended for the church at Coatbridge, 154; his disapproval of Mrs. Gerard's investigation of Catholic claims, 155
Alcock, Miss Jane, 2, *note*
Alexander The Rev. Mr., 106, 109
Archer, The Rev. Dr., 23
Atlee, Albert Falconer, 144, 145, 211, 221, 223
Atlee, Miss Eleanor Falconer, afterwards Mrs. Leslie. (*see* Leslie)
Atlee, Mrs. Falconer, 223, 225, 229, 262, 279
Atlee, Mr. Falconer, secretary to Lord Cowley, 144, 230, 235, 308
Atlee, Mr. John Falconer, senior, Mrs. Leslie's father, 1; is thrown early in life on his own resources, 2; is one of a deputation to Pitt on behalf of distillers, builds his distillery, 3; his love of Fordhook, 4; his marriage, 5; talent for music, 7; shrewdness in managing his family, 14; his generosity, 15; gives up the distillery and retires to Brighton, 75; his death, 143
Atlee, Mr. John Falconer, junior, eldest son of the above, 11; his aptitude for getting into boyish scrapes, early religious feelings, goes to Winchester, his friends there, the barring out, 12; a young dandy, 13; introduces boating at Cambridge, instance of his generosity, 15; thrashes a man who has duped him, makes the "grand tour" with an infidel tutor, 16; falls into infidelity, goes into business though he has no taste for it. introduces a steam engine into his father's distillery, his marriage, 17; settles in Paris, 18; takes a place in Scotland, 83; befriends his sister against the disapproval of her family, his liberality in religious questions, 143; goes to Rome, 217; his scepticism wavers, 218; his embargo on the reception of his wife and daughters into the Church, 229; his satisfaction at the event, 230, 232; sudden gleam of faith, and relapse into infidelity, 235; submission to the Church, and relapse, 259; slight paralytic stroke, 285; his reconciliation to the Church, and death, 308
Atlee, Dr. Walter Franklin, 309, *note*
Atlee, Mr. William, of Fordhook, 2, *note*
Atlee, The Misses Falconer, 229,

232, 262; letters to, 289, 306, 309
Balnageith, The Laird of (see Leslie)
Barat, The Vénérable Mère, 237, 249
Beaconsfield, Lord, 12
Becket, The Messrs., 34, 35, 38
Belcher, Admiral, 195
Berriedale, Viscount, 81
Besson, Le Rev. Père, 206
Bodenham, Madame de, 146
Bolton, Mrs., 147
Borgogelli, Contessa, 199, 204, 220
Borgogelli, Caterina, 200, 204
Borgogelli, Polissena, 200, 202, 204, 220
Bowen, Mr. George, of Coton Hall, 55
Bridges, Sir George, 74, 85, 91, 93, 135
Bridges, The Talbot... family, 5
Brown, Dr., Bishop of Shrewsbury, 217
Buccleuch, Dowager Duchess of, 167, 169, 170, 317
Buchanan, Mr. and Lady Janet, 46, 49, 89
Buckley, The Rev. Jeremiah, 157
Burgon, Dean, 115, 116
Burns, Mr., 42, 43, 44
Burton, Mrs. Hill, 129
Caithness, Earl of, 19
Caithness, Dowager Countess of, 19, 27, 79, 80, 88, 97, 129
Caithness, Countess of, "Lady Fanny," 81, 94, 98
Campbell, Lord of Clyde, 152
Campbell, Mr., 153
Cardella, The Rev. Padre, 216, 218, 222, 311
Castelbajac, Mademoiselle de, 146
Castelbajac, Monsieur de, 147
Caswall, Mr. and Mrs., 162-165
Champfleur, Madame de, 261
Clapperton, The Rev. Mr., 87, 94
Clarke, The Rev. Father, 137, 138
Clifford, Lord, 206
Cobb, The Rev. Father, Provincial, S.J., 135, 136
Coleridge, The Rev. H. J., 132, 178, 206, 298
Corry, The Rev. Father, 254

Cowley, Earl, 12, 13
Culbertson, Mr. and Mrs., 37, 38, 39
Culduthil, The Laird of, 33
Cullen, Cardinal, 184
Cumming, Miss, of Logie, 45
Cumming, Sir William Gordon, 19, 51, 52, 83
Cunningham, Miss, 248
Darwin, Charles, 289
Davidson, Duncan, Laird of Tulloch, and Mrs. Davidson, 33, 34
Dean, Mr. Fellow of All Souls', Oxford, 118, 119
Demaklis, Liberata Contessa, 177, 183
Denistoun, Mrs., 45
Douglas, Lord Archibald, 264, 291
Douglas, Lady Gertrude, 264
Douglas, Lord James, 264
Dowson, Mrs., 103, 225, 283
Duffus, Lord, 19
Dunbar, Major, 27, note
Eden, The Rev. Mr., Fellow of Oriel College, Oxford, 117
Ferron, Madame de, 190
Fessard, Le Rev. Père, 223
Ffoulkes, Mr., of Jesus College, Oxford, 118
Fitzgerald, Lady, 206, 227
Fraser, Captain, 33
Fullerton, Lady Georgiana, 298
Gargarin, Princess, 209
Gerard, Colonel, 152, 160
Gerard, Mrs., 152, 158, 162
Gerard, The Very Rev. John, S.J., account of the conversion of his family, 153-158
Gillis, Dr., Vicar Apostolic, 95, 96, 110, 111, 112, 114, 134, 138
Gladstone, Miss, 136, 206
Gleghorn, Miss, 39
Goesbriant, Mgr. de, 184
Gordon, Mr., 40, 41, 42, 44
Gordon, The Rev. John Joseph, 71, 72, 73, 86, 104
Gordon, Mr. Fraser, Writer to the Signet, 142, 265
Gordon, Mr. Michael, son of the above, 265, 266
Gordon, Colonel, 266
Gordon, Major, 266

INDEX.

Grant, Captain McDowell, of Arndilly, 69
Grant, Dr. Bishop of Southwark, 222
Guerry, l'Abbé, 149
Hardynge, Lady, 11
Harris, The Rev. Mr., 66, 74, 86, 91, 93, 135
Henderson, Miss, 92
Hermann, Rev. Perè, 147
Herries, Lady, 293
Honyman, Mr. George, 54, 74, 79
Honyman, Colonel Sir Ord, 53, 54, 74, 94, 113, 142
Hook, Dr., 63 154, 157
Horsley, Dr., 292, 299, 314, 316
Howard, Cardinal, 178, 183
Hughes, Dr., Archbishop of New York, 184, 186
Hutchinson, Mrs., 167
Huxley, Prof., 290
Innes, Mr. Cosmo, 128
Jones, Mrs. Henshaw, 113
Kenyons, The, 284
Kerr, Lady Alice, afterwards Gaisford, 173, 245, 265, 271, 274, 303, 313
Kerr, Lady Amabel, 284
Kerr, Lady Anne, 285, 303, 313
Kerr, Lady Cecil, 173, 226, 243, 249, 250, 271
Kerr, Lady Henry, 248, 253, 255, 295
Kerr, Lord Henry, 248, 253, 254, 255, 256, 284, 291
Kerr, Lord Ralph, 284, 285, 303, 313
Kerr, Lord Walter, 172
Kerr, Mother Henrietta, 295
Kersabiec de, family of, 263
Laing Mr., of Jedburgh, 170
Lauerbach, Madame, afterwards Madame de Coëtlogon, 231, 270, 300
Lennox, Lord Arthur Gordon, 7
Leslie, Mr. Archibald, aspires to Miss Falconer Atlee's hand, 18; his family and education, 19; tour in France, 20; character, personal appearance, marriage, 21; settles in London, 23; religious views, his graceful manner, 24; hospitality, political opinions, 25; unsuited to business, financial difficulties, honourable principles, his failing health, 26; visit to Scotland, 27, 46; his physical suffering on the journey, 47, 48; appreciation of Mr. Aitken, 56; disgust at the sensational services at Zion Chapel, 59; failure in business, 76; increased illness, 77; removes with his family to Scotland, 78; his attitude on his wife's conversion to Catholicism, 94, 101; his letter to her about their children, 102; perplexity with regard to their convictions, 104; assists at an interview between them and Mr. Suther, 106; withdraws his opposition to their becoming Catholics, 111; extracts from his diary, 123; his conversion, 124; his last illness and death, 126
Leslie, Charlotte, afterwards Geddes, sister of the above, 30; her daughter became a Catholic. See page 301, note
Leslie, Charlotte, Mrs. Leslie's youngest daughter, 64, 93, 96, 97, 104; reception into the Church, 112, 126, 132, 142, 145, 183, 198, 200, 209, 211, 218, 220, 223, 225, 228, 232, 237, 240; goes to the Noviceship at Conflans, 241, 243, 247, 249, 265, 270, 279, 282, 294, 297, 310, 313
Leslie, Eleanor, afterwards Mrs. Fraser Gordon, Mrs. Leslie's eldest daughter, 50, 51, 87, 88, 111, 121, 122; is received into the Church, 123, 130; her marriage, 142; her death, 265
Leslie, Eleanor, eldest daughter of Mr. John Falconer Atlee, 1; her talent for music inherited, 7; date of her birth, and some account of her childhood, 9; her education, has a bad fever, her sisters, 10; description of her person, friends, 11; her offers of marriage, 18; is married to Mr. Archibald Leslie, 21;. manner of life in London, 23; belongs to the Church of England, 24; her eldest child

INDEX.

born, 25; Journal in Scotland, 26-46; letter to her husband before the birth of her second child, 49; two other children born, removal to Wandsworth, goes with her family to Scotland, 51; their return to Wandsworth, devotion to her husband, 52; her business capacity, 53; friendship with Sir Ord Honyman, 54; visit to Shropshire, 55; makes the acquaintance of Mr. Aitken, 56; her "conversion," 57; the extent of Mr. Aitken's religious influence over her, and her advice to him, 62; Calvinistic narrowness, 63; High Church tendencies, 67; her love of order and authority, 69; recognizes the necessity of sacramental grace, 73; goes to Brighton with her daughters, 76; good sense and high principle, 77; an excellent "man of business," 78; winds up her husband's affairs and removes with him and their children to Scotland, 79; her advanced religious opinions, 85; nurses one of her daughters through an illness, 89; praying for the dead, 90; the last step, 93; reception into the Church, 95; sensitiveness to "Lady Fanny's" abuse, 98; rebukes Miss Maclaren, 101; justifies the step she has taken, 109; letter to Bishop Gillis, 112; confirmation, 113; helps her son in his study of Catholicism, 115; one of the happiest days of her life, 121; her account of her husband's conversion, 124; her spirit of sacrifice and aptitude for suffering, her "excessive" love of her children, 132; her grief in the loss of her son, 136; makes a retreat at Stonyhurst, 137; her progress in the devout life, 140; a further sacrifice, 142; meets her brothers and sisters at her father's deathbed, 143; visits her brother in Paris, 144; spends a winter at Pau, 146; her friends in Scotland, 150-172; first visit to Rome, 174-190; nurses Miss Taafe through an attack of measles, 180; a flood at Avignon, 191; visits relations in England and Scotland, and returns to Rome, 195; her defence of Dr. Newman at Florence, 196; goes to Spoleto, 199-205; to Albano, 205; her intimacy with Father Wynne and Father Coleridge, Miss Gladstone claims her good offices as nurse, 206; spends a summer at Castel Gandolfo, 208; nurses Mr. Palmer through a serious illness, 210; undertakes the care of her nephew Albert, 211; letter to him, 213; final departure from Rome, 222; meets her sister Emily at Dijon, proceeds to Paris and Ryde, 225; passes the summer in Scotland and visits Mr. and Mrs. Palmer at Mexbury, 227; spends the winter at Tours, 232; meets Madame de Pambour at La Roche Pusay, 234, desires to see her son, now a priest, 236; is prevented from going to England, 237; stays with the Wilberforces at St. Germain-en-Laye, 239; takes her youngest daughter to the Noviceship at Conflans, 241; her desolation, 244; letters on the subject of a daughter's vocation, 245; returns to England, and visits her son at St. Beuno's, 250; passes some time in Scotland, 252; is instrumental in the conversion of a somewhat remarkable man, 253; Baroness von Hügel's description of her at this time, 254; at Conflans, religious discussions with her brother, 262; is summoned to Glasgow, where her son is ill of typus fever, 266; severe accident at Nantes, 269; spends

INDEX. 323

the summer at Marmoutier, 270;
leaves France on account of the
war, 274; settles at St. Margaret's Convent, 275; her regular way of life, 276; visits her
son at Liverpool, and her daughter at Mount Anville, annual
retreat, 278; goes to Roehampton and Ryde, 279; nurses her son
through an illness, 280; declining health, retreat at Wandsworth, visits her brother at
Brighton, 282; after his illness
goes to him at Dieppe, retreat
at Roehampton, 286; some of
the objects of her charity, 287;
activity in spite of advancing
years; letter to Miss Falconer Atlee, 289; to her daughter Charlotte, receives the last
Sacraments, 294; letter to Charlotte, 297; a bad fall, visit from
Fr. Coleridge, 298; her portraits,
celebration of the 50th anniversary of St. Margaret's, 299;
letter to Madame Leslie, 300;
to all her children, 304; interested in foundation at Berwick,
letter to Miss Falconer Atlee, 306; to her brother, 307;
to her nieces, last entries in her
diary, 309; accident while dressing; last dispositions, 310; her
cheerfulness in bearing pain,
311; her humility, letter to her
son; attacked by influenza, she
receives extreme unction, Fr.
Leslie summoned, 312; last
charities, 313; Fr. Leslie again
sent for, her death, 314; buried
beside her husband, 316
Leslie, Ellen, Mr. Archibald Leslie's sister, 29
Leslie, the Rev. Eric William, 54,
74; goes to Woolwich, 76; is
placed with a surveyor at Oxford,
visits his uncle in Scotland, 83;
reads Catholic books, but accepts the branch theory, 116;
confession at Oxford, 117;
returns to Scotland and becomes a Catholic, 119; religious vocation, 133; retreat at
Hodder, 135; ordination, 236;
at Glasgow, 252; is sent occasionally to recruit at Carstairs
and Huntlyburn, is attacked
with typhus fever, 266; frequent
opportunities of seeing Mrs.
Leslie, 278 alls ill at Liverpool
and is nursed by her, 281; apostolic work, 288; is summoned
to his mother's death-bed and
assists at her last agony, 314;
says the Mass of requiem, 315
Leslie, Mary, Mr. Archibald Leslie's sister, 28, 30, 34
Leslie, Mary, afterwards Mother
Mary Sales, 93, 96, 97, 104; reception into the Church, 112
enters religion, 142, 167, 279,
295, 296, 303, 309, 310, 313, 314
Leslie, the Rev. William, Laird of
Balnageith, 19, 27, 28, 29, 30, 75
Leslie, the Rev. Father, S.J., of
Fetternear, founder of the Oxford mission, 116
Lothian, Marquis of, 279, 284
Lothian Cecil, Marchioness of, 87,
168, 170, 178, 243, 264, 271, 281
Lyte, Maxwell, Mrs., 148
Lythgoe, The Very Rev. ex-Provincial S.J., 136
Macdonell, Mr., 44
Macdonell, Colonel and Mrs., 166
Maclaren, Major, 99
Maclaren, Miss, 99, 101
Maclean of Col and Mrs. Maclean, 45
Mallac, Madame Louise, 260
Manning, Mr. and Mrs. Charles,
226
Marchi, The Rev. Padre, 182
Marriot, Charles, 116
Maxwell, Mrs., Mrs. Leslie's
eldest sister, 22, 87, 102, 225,
283
Maxwell, Miss, daughter of the
above, 279
McGregor, Lady Charlotte, 80, 84
McNabb, The Rev. Mr., 157
Menschikoff, Prince, 191, 193
Missy, Le Général de, 10
Monaghan, The Rev. James, 123
Monteith, Mr., of Carstairs, 122,
150, 156, 170, 253

INDEX.

Morris, The Rev. John, 280, 286
Newman, Cardinal, 72, 196, 299
Newsham, The Rev. Mr., priest on the Oxford mission, 116, 119
Nutt, The Misses, 65, 135
Oakley, Canon, 91
O'Donnell, The Rev. Mr., 124, 125, 126, 137, 277, 291
Olivaint, Le Rev. Père, 238, 277
O'Rourke, the Rev. Father Eugene, 155
Palmer, Mrs., afterwards Mrs. Falconer Atlee, Mrs. Leslie's mother, 5, 6, 75
Palmer, The Rev. Mr. and Mrs., 227
Palmer, Mr. William, 178, 179, 181-183, 206, 208-211, 212, 224, 227, 250, 267, 280, 285
Pambour, Comtesse de, Mrs. Leslie's sister, 76, 102, 132, 134, 143, 146, 234, 270
Parma, Duchess of, 166
Passaglia, Father, 179
Patterson, Dr., Bishop of Emmaus, 178, 267
Perreur, Madame, 299, *note*
Peter, Mrs., 184-189
Peters, Mr., 40-44
Phillips, Mr. Ambrose Lisle, 165
Plowden, Miss, 196
Pitt, William, Prime Minister, 3
Polding, Dr., Archbishop of Melbourne, 184
Ponlevoy, The Rev. Père de, 223, 230
Pope Pius IX., 184, 187, 197
Porter, The Most Rev. George, Archbishop of Bombay, 285, 308
Price, Mr., 45
Quakers, 7
Queensberry, Marchioness of, 262
Rew, The Rev. Mr., of St. John's College, Oxford, 117. 118
Robertson, The Rev. John Cunningham, 84, 86, 92, 111, 168, 248, 280
Roskell, Miss, 196
Rossi, Cavaliere, 182
Rubillon, Rev. Père, 234
Rücker, Mr. Sigismund, 283
Schrœter, Baron, 210
Scott, Mr. Hope, 152, 171, 280
Scott, Dr., Vicar apostolic, 171
Scropes, The, 313
Shain, Dr., Archbishop of Edinburgh, 113, *note*
Sinclair, Colonel the Hon. James, 18, 27, 33, 34, 81, 84, 87, 98
Sinclair, Miss, 32
Sinclair, Miss Catherine, the authoress, 81, 85
Sinclair, Miss Willy, 130
Small, Dr. 210
Smith, Dr., Archbishop of Edinburgh, 311
Strathallan, Lord, 36
Suther, The Rev. Mr., afterwards Bishop of Aberdeen, 97, 106, 107
Taafe, Miss F., 178, 180
Taafe, Miss M., 199
Talbot, Mgr. G., 178, 183, 197, 284, 303
Terrot, Bishop, 104, 106
Tickell, Mr., 91
Tomkinson, Mr., 5
Tramo, Dr., 218
Tritton, Miss, 100
Tritton, Mr. William, 45
Turner, the artist, 5
Vaughan, Dr., Archbishop of Sydney, 184
Walsh, Dr., Bishop of Halifax, 184
Waterton, The Rev. Father, 138
White, The Rev. Mr., 153, 154
Whyte, the Rev. Father, 314
Wilberforce, Mr., 239
Wood, Mrs., the authoress, 226
Wood, Captain, son of the above 226
Wynne, The Rev. W., 178, 179, 183, 206, 283

www.ingramcontent.com/pod-product-compliance
Lightning Source LLC
Chambersburg PA
CBHW031847220426
43663CB00006B/527